LIVING WHOLENESS

The Christian Wholeness Framework
for Professional Counsellors

Dr John Warlow
Adult, Child and Family Psychiatrist

Recommended prerequisite reading:

Cycles of Transformation: An Introduction to Counselling using the CWF
By Dr David Nikles and Susanne Nikles

Recommended viewing:

Christian Wholeness Counselling Competencies
for mental health practitioners and professional counsellors 2007:
'What is the CURE?'
By Dr John Warlow

CHRISTIAN WHOLENESS FRAMEWORK:
WHAT IS THE C.U.R.E.?

- **C**onnection: The essential ways to connect.
- **U**nderstanding:
  - » Locating where the person is at: using the checklist and the circles.
  - » Linking the issues: the present, the past and the future.
- **R**esponse: The tool bag and the map.
  - » Social, physical, cognitive, psychodynamic and spiritual tools.
- **E**ngaging other help:
  - » The role of the church, health services and others.
- **e**valuation: an important part of the process to keep on track.

...this is the CURE!

REFLECTIONS ON *LIVING WHOLENESS*

Dr Gary R. Collins
PhD
Psychologist & Author, Illinois, USA
Dr John Warlow is an insightful and perceptive thinker, a competent practitioner and a committed Christ follower. This book summarizes a lifetime of experienced-based reflection about the essence and practice of effective Christian counselling.

Dr Bradford M. Smith
PhD, Licensed Psychologist
President Care and Counsel International and Chair of the Lausanne Interest Group on Care and Counsel as Mission, USA
The Christian Wholeness Framework is the most comprehensive road map to the process of helping others I know of. It will be an invaluable resource to both the beginning counsellor whose need is to learn the basics and also the more experienced counsellor who is interested in seeing how it all fits together. Perhaps most importantly, it provides Christian counsellors worldwide with different cultural backgrounds and theoretical orientations, a common language for learning together how to follow Jesus in addressing the unprecedented suffering we see in the world today.

Dr Simon Yiu Chuen Lee
BSc BEd MDiv MTh MA DMin
Assoc. Fellow, Certified Counsellor and Consultant Supervisor, HKPCA,
Associate Director of Pastoral Program, DSCCC, Chinese University of Hong Kong (Formerly Professor, Alliance Bible Seminary, Hong Kong)
Living Wholeness is the best example of integration of theology and psychology that I have come across in my 30 years of ministry and counselling practices, having tried to put together my own model called 'Soul C.A.R.E.S'. Many Christians in counselling try to do integration, but some are simply lip-service, adding some use of Scriptures here and there to their professional practices, while others are providing good pastoral care but with very little use of psychological insights. Dr John Warlow's model spells 'CURE' and is totally biblical, psychologically sound, thoroughly systemic, holistic and comprehensive, methodical and practical. As a professional psychotherapist and marriage/family therapist, ordained pastor, seminary/university professor and author, I wholeheartedly recommend this

book to all who wants to practise counselling from a Christian and holistic approach.

Dr Carolyn Russell
MBBS FRACGP Masters in Social Science
General Practitioner and Counsellor, Australia
John Warlow is a 'mine' of information. In the years that I have known him, I have been showered with blessing, as I have been challenged and have struggled with understanding better my clients and patients, and ultimately myself, through 'mining' the vast untapped resources that he has stored away. General practitioners have some reserves about the practice of psychiatry and its relevance to our patients at times. However, John's framework for understanding people (the CWF) is now the predominant way that I assess all my patients, to achieve a more thorough understanding of them. It has allowed me to hone skills, to see persons not only as soma and to move closer to seeing transformation occur in my patients as the Spirit of God meets with them as with me, and breathes life into them also, whether they know Him or not. I am immensely and eternally grateful for John's presence in my life and my work.

Dr David Nikles
MBBS FRACGP DipObs
Medical Practitioner Counsellor Supervisor Trainer, East Asia
This long awaited book presents John's unique and profoundly insightful Christian Wholeness Framework. John's transforming application of scripture has been a gift for me personally; many of my clients now experience deep change, and it has been such a joy to use this framework for counselling training and supervision here in east Asia. Thank you John, from us working in the developing world, for this jewel which takes integrated Christian Counselling to a profoundly new level.

Susanne Nikles
BOccTh MCouns(Soc Sci)
Counsellor Supervisor Trainer, East Asia
John's unique framework integrates Christian Spirituality and Psychology in a way that is insightful, holistic and highly robust. His framework of Christian Wholeness will become the guide for Christian psychologists and counsellors in all aspects of practice, assessment, and interventions. The theology of this framework also encourages personal growth and ongoing transformation of the counsellor as well their client. We so value using this material personally as well as in many training contexts.

Peter Janetzki
*DipT GradDipSocSc MSocSc(Counselling) CCAQ(Clin) QCA(Clin) PACFA Reg.
21092*
*Counsellor/Educator, Adjunct Lecturer Christian Heritage College, Radio Host,
Australia*

A few years into my counselling career I was confronted with the reality that the modalities that I had been trained in were unable to facilitate change for some of those I worked with. My clinical supervisor at that time was skilled in the emerging modalities of Brief Therapies, yet I had a yearning for something deeper, more robust that would enable me to meet the challenge of working with the complexities of human experience that I meet daily in my office. In seeking a supervisor who could take me onto the next stage of my professional journey, I met Dr John Warlow who had recently established the Christian Wholeness Counselling Centre.

I was a young psychotherapist, full of enthusiasm, optimism and idealism, eager to learn and keen to cure the world. John joined and journeyed with me using the very principles contained within these pages, the five steps and the five shapes, to facilitate my professional growth from a beginning counsellor to a skilled specialist psychotherapist. I am still enthusiastic and eager to learn. However as I have developed professionally I am less idealistic and hold onto realistic optimism as well as being far more skilled particularly in understanding complex counselling cases.

What you will discover as I did is that the Christian Wholeness Framework (CWF) is not another counselling modality. It is as it is rightly named a 'framework', a framework that will enable any counsellor to develop a robust understanding of people; where they are at, where they have come from, and where they can go.

Unfortunately much of the counsellor training being offered today takes a modal approach, which sets up many beginning counsellors to manoeuvre their clients to where they want them or need them, so that their counselling approach works. I agree with Dr David Schnarch who refers to this as 'snare trap' therapy. (Two Day Sexual Crucible® Workshop Australia 2002). The CWF helps counsellors to avoid snare trap therapy by helping a therapist to understand people in a holistic way as well as enabling them to locate and utilise the skills of any modality in an integrated manner.

John is passionate about counsellors and psychotherapists seeing people as whole people, who are made in the image of God who can have the best quality of life this side of heaven irrespective of their personal beliefs.

His insights and understanding have had the most significant impact on my development as a counsellor. My capacity to connect, then understand, and more skilfully respond in all spheres of my work whether it be in the counselling room, presenting parent training, lecturing to student counsellors, or on my radio program are due to the Christian Wholeness Framework. I commend *Living Wholeness* to you.

Danny Ng
Founder of Family Connexion & Consultant Clinical Psychologist, Raffles Hospital, Singapore
There are good books and there are great books. *Living Wholeness* is a "must have" as it is a distinctive resource that provides Christian Counsellors a clear modern day GPS (Global Positioning Satellite). This enables practitioners a more integrated and holistic approach toward being a professionally competent and spiritually-enabled Christian Counsellor. Finally, a worthy bridge between the Biblical and Clinical dimensions of counselling.

Dr Jonathan Andrews
BSc MSc MPPsych (Clinical) DCP
Clinical Psychologist, Australia
Christian counsellors face a dilemma. How do we properly integrate current psychological tools with an ancient language of God's unfailing love for people who suffer? Though many have tried, this task has not been adequately addressed. Until now. This text represents a benchmark in the teaching of how to integrate these two realms. For all practitioners who take seriously the spiritual and the psychological, in their own lives and the lives of their clients, this book is a must. Don't hesitate: Make yourself a coffee, find a comfortable chair and get reading.

Dr Fay Woolfield
MBChB M Couns
Family Doctor with special interest in mental health and counselling, Australia
What am I missing? Why isn't this working? Where is God in all this? John Warlow challenges us to look at the 'big picture', find 'all the pieces of the jigsaw' and put God at the centre as we counsel. His wisdom, knowledge, experience and personal spirituality shine through his book. I have found the Christian Wholeness Framework to be comprehensive, sound, safe and helpful: worth the time it takes to grasp its complexity. I have found this overall approach immensely helpful in making the connections with my clients. It encourages me to look for the missing links and think of the wider connections.

Douglas A. Taylor
MSocSc(Couns) MCCAA(Clin) MQCA(Clin) PACFA Reg.
Manager / Counsellor, The Salvation Army Counselling Service, Australia
A basic premise of this book, writes author, Dr John Warlow is that the heart of the content of his book is based upon his personal journey, from being alone to being with others and becoming an integrated and whole person. Knowing John as a colleague and friend, I know Christian wholeness and integration is a passion central to his goal in helping others grow which is very evident in this text. In *Living Wholeness*, Dr Warlow draws from Scripture, clinical experience and psychological literature in his explanation of integration / wholeness counselling theory and practice which he developed. His use of case studies makes his CWF theory come alive and become as he says, a 'map that can assist you, with the approaches you already have, to achieve more holistic outcomes.' This innovative book is destined to be a milestone in the integration / wholeness theory. It is a masterful study for the serious student of psychology and theology who wants to help others in their life journey to wholeness.

Andy Pocock
Founder, livingreal.com.au, Australia
I have been privileged to learn and use the *Living Wholeness* principles over the past four years. The principles taught in this book, particularly the fundamental relationship tools of CURE and SAFETY, have influenced the way I interact with others both in my private and work life. The 5 Shapes have been key tools the Lord has used in my personal journey of healing and in my pursuit of wholeness. I have been so impacted by these truths that they are now the fundamental tools used in the Living REAL Ministry as we pursue the healing of men's hearts and help them fulfil their God-given destinies. I believe this Christ-centred framework is an incredible gift to believers throughout the world.

Neil Shuker
MCareerDevelopment GradDipEd BSc(Psych) AdvDipManagement
DipRelationshipCounselling, Australia
Living Wholeness is a capstone read for all who work as people helpers. Christian Wholeness provides a safe framework for you to apply to your art (attitudes, skills and knowledge) as a teacher, coach, counsellor or HR professional. I have worked in relationship and personal counselling, organisational development and career coaching for the last 20 years and I have known John during that time as a man of great integrity, insight and passion. In our journey together I have adopted John's model, confident that it provides me with a balanced approach to my interventions and

processes and allows me to recognise if my own 'stuff' gets in the way. To John: I look forward to the insights that we continue to gain from each other as we share each other's journey (through the Triangle, the Circles, the Square, the Pyramid and the Cross) and as we stand by (CURE!) each other throughout our personal and family trials and tribulations. Congratulations on this profound labour of love, fuelled by faith.

Gong Guang Hong
Chinese Counsellor Supervisor and Counselling Trainer
Having a structure that assists me understand the deep truths about healing and personal growth, so that people can experience this in reality is extremely important. Personally the CWF has helped me think through and create my own understanding of this process, so that I have been able in Christ to grow – from someone dealing with loneliness, low self confidence, and feeling somewhat out of control, to someone who knows I am loved, I can accept my self, and I generally feel in control of my life. Because of the application of the CWF I have been able to achieve this growth fairly quickly. For my clients, I am able to be with them, even in their darkest moments, because I know where they and I am, so I can guide the counselling process with confidence and thus see transformation occur. In supervision, again having a clear structure gives a guideline for the process and so the time is used most effectively, so growth within the supervisee is more rapid. The CWF means a lot to me – to me it is about understanding and being with the person (whether self, client, or supervisee) before God; and the deep truths found there is what the healing and transformational journey is all about.

Felix Holland
Coordinator of the Global Member Care Network, World Evangelical Alliance Mission Commission
During my many years as a leader in missions and member care, I have seen it over and over again: a one sided approach to growth, care and healing. You either have to pray, or read scripture, you need counselling or psychotherapy, coaching or mentoring, peer support or spiritual reflection, or you just need to stop being wounded and behave right.

Dr John Warlow has a particular anointing. When looking at our spirit, heart, mind, body and our external life, he sees connections and finds words and images to describe those. I am so excited to see his extremely good material now in print. It has moved innumerous people in the care profession around me to a new level of understanding and effectiveness. Be inspired and enjoy the Christian Wholeness Framework.

Deanna Pitchford
Clinical psychologist, Australia
This book takes a complex subject – the integration of Christian values with counselling principles – and presents it in a series of visual 'pictures' that are easy to remember. It gives the counsellor, at every level of expertise, a method of visualising the counselling process as well as a way of explaining complex concepts to clients. It also gives the counsellor a method of tracking progress and evaluating outcomes. Glad to see that you are writing again, John! This book would give a Christian psychologist the necessary framework to launch them on a very satisfying 'Integration' journey.

Linda Brice
Counsellor,and "Mandy" in the 200M video of the CWF. Now passed into glory!
...it's excellent, full of inspiration, with a clear Christian and Professional application, indispensable for the Christian practitioner.

ABOUT THE AUTHOR

Dr John Warlow MB ChB FRANZCP is a Christian adult, child and family psychiatrist. He lived in India with his parents, who were missionaries, before attending boarding school. Dr Warlow completed his education in the UK, New Zealand, and Australia. Currently he works in private practice in Brisbane, Australia.

He became involved with training lay and professional mental health workers in the late 1980s, including the directorship of training for child, adolescent, and family psychiatrists in Queensland, Australia for 10 years from 1995.

Dr Warlow has been developing, using and teaching the Christian Wholeness Framework throughout this period, and has wide-ranging experience with its various applications. He has counselled hundreds of people using the framework and this vigour is borne out of a passion to mobilise the church to care for people. He has been teaching the Christian Wholeness Framework to an international audience for a number of years, and is well regarded by the international Christian Counselling Community.

RESOURCES USED IN WRITING THIS BOOK

The counselling information outside of the CWF has come from numerous sources including textbooks, lectures, training programs and workshops.

While under construction since 1989, the first actual expression of this book was typed in 1999. The diagrams are from the DVD presentation in 2007, *Christian Wholeness Counselling Competencies for Mental Health Practitioners and Professional Counsellors 2007: 'What is the CURE?'*

Resources that have meant a lot to me are writing in relation to:

Theology: H. Marshall, L. Morris, G. Ladd, A. Stibbs

Psychiatry: The mainline texts and journals I have drawn from are Adult and Child Psychiatry from USA and UK, especially Kaplan and Saddock, Lewis and P. Barker. Diagnostic material has largely come from the Diagnostic and Statistical Manual (DSM version IV) (APA). Therapeutic material is based on mainline approaches to family therapy (especially *Basic Family Therapy*: P. Barker, Blackwell Scientific Publications), as well as Cognitive Behavioural Therapy and Psychodynamic Therapy.

Integration in counselling: Drs Garry Collins, David Benner, Larry Crabb

The 5 Shapes: A number of authors have drawn various shapes which may be similar to the 5 Shapes of the CWF (particularly Circles, Triangles and Squares). However, except for the Triangle, the contents of the 5 Shapes are specific to the CWF. The Triangle is an illustration of the link between God, oneself and another, arising from Old Testament times.

The 5 Steps: The 5 Steps are similar to the medical process of developing a doctor/patient relationship, assessing the problem, treating and referring, in the context of ongoing evaluation of change.

References are noted at the end of this book.

ACKNOWLEDGEMENTS

This text is based on my personal journey, from being alone to being with others and becoming an integrated and whole person. The counselling model I have developed has been informed by extensive work experience in clinical practice and academic development. It has been assisted by my many fellow travellers including:

Patients… you have taught me so much.

Colleagues in the Christian Wholeness Counselling Services… thanks for your fellow travelling along the way. I became a part of this because I knew I could not do it on my own. Thanks especially to Dr Carolyn Russell, Dr David Nikles, Susanne Nikles and Andy Pocock.

Many experiences have had an impact on my thinking including my missionary upbringing (India); boarding school; various churches (Open Brethren, Nazarene, Anglican, Baptist, Pentecostal); All Nations Christian College (UK); Medical training (UK); Psychiatry training (NZ and Australia); Christian Wholeness Counselling Services; Queensland Health, Royal Australian and New Zealand College of Psychiatrists (RANZCP); and in particular the 10 years as director of training of Child Psychiatry (thanks to my bosses, Prof. B. Nurcombe and Prof. G. Martin, and especially trainees); Private Practice (thanks Pat, Jono and the two Peters). Thank you so much Dr Gary Collins for your encouragement and being with me since the late 1980s.

Family... The CWF has become a mission and a passion over and above my work as a psychiatrist. I want to leave a (far from perfect) legacy for you, my five fantastic kids, of how God was able to have a greater part of my life. I so want Him to be central in each of your lives. I want you to have wonderful families, a great job, and I want you to pursue a God-centred vision and mission in a more successful way than I have. Jill… thanks for your patience in being with me and loving me!

Thanks to all of those who helped review this text, especially to Catherine Alexander and final editor Belinda Pollard for your attitude and skills with the editing. Thanks Fay Woolfield and Leonie Drew for your help.

God… You have given this to me. I am not the founder of it, I found it! Thank you. Take and use this for your body here on earth, the Church.

CONTENTS – OVERVIEW

CONTENTS

SECTION I:
INTRODUCTION

1: PURPOSE

WHY THIS BOOK?

Counselling has significant challenges in at times being abstract, confusing, and a lonely task. Counsellors can struggle with on the one hand wondering where they fit into the whole picture, while on the other hand, others view their own approach as the only way to go. Being a Christian and a counsellor can add further challenges to those who want to have a professional practice and yet remain true to their faith. This book attempts to address these issues and more, through providing a holistic framework which has been integrated with a clear Christian world view, tried over time, in a range of settings, cultures and counselling issues.

WHY CREATE ANOTHER APPROACH TO CHRISTIAN COUNSELLING?

The CWF is not so much another model, as a framework or structure that undergirds the models of counselling you may have already mastered. It is a map that can assist you, with the approaches you already have, to achieve more holistic outcomes. It is a tool bag, for all your therapeutic approaches. You will be able to recognise what tools you have and any that are absent and be encouraged to engage other help where needed. It also provides a common picture language through the 5 Shapes and the 5 Steps. Learning a new language or studying a map takes time. The illustrations are designed to reinforce the framework one layer at a time as you learn. This book will supplement and help you integrate what you already know into a holistic Christian framework.

WHAT SORT OF BOOK IS THIS?

It is a textbook that expounds a model of care and is best utilised as a workbook following the case study of Mandy. It is easy to read and provides practical ideas and a framework to understand counselling. It is a book which needs to be read in conjunction with standard texts on counselling.

WHO IS THIS BOOK FOR?

It is for counselling/mental health trainees and professionals who want to integrate their faith and practice into a Christian and holistic approach. It is for those who want to develop and excel in current approaches to counselling, yet want to be more than a counsellor who is a Christian (where the counselling is hardly influenced by faith). It is for someone who wants to integrate the Christian and the secular realm professionally and appropriately … and be a Christian counsellor.

It is specifically for those who ask themselves…

How can I become a counsellor who is:

- **Holistic:** How can I achieve a broader approach to therapy?
- **Safe:** How can I integrate spiritual issues safely, professionally and ethically?
- **Efficient:** How can I listen to the pin drop (the central issues) and not get distracted by the hay (the peripheral matters)?
- **Effective:** How does therapeutic healing and growth occur and what hinders me from facilitating this?

It is for those who are prepared to examine their concerns about their Christian counselling, and risk misunderstanding from the church which may see you as secular or unspiritual, or from your colleagues who may perceive you as extreme and fringe, dogmatic or exclusive. This book is for those who have concerns about spiritual matters related to ethical issues of consent and power imbalances, clarity of boundaries with patients and clients, and the interface between the role of the church and counselling. The CWF shares all of these concerns and addresses them.

The Christian Wholeness Framework is designed to help you:

By providing a framework
to place your existing skills and knowledge in,
and offer more integrated counselling
in relation to understanding and helping
from a holistic Christian approach.

WHAT ARE THE OUTCOMES OF THIS BOOK?

As a result of studying this material, you will have a greater understanding of the Christian Wholeness Framework as applied to professional counselling. It should be studied alongside your generic counselling education.

This text can assist your 'ASK' counselling competencies:

- **A**TTITUDES
  Attitudes are the heart of your counselling capacity. They are

developed in the context of supervised counselling practice and are standard in all types of counselling. Consequently, while clearly discussed, this text will not focus on the practical development of attitudes despite their critical importance. That occurs in supervised practice.

- **S**KILLS
  Skills will develop as you apply the knowledge of the framework to your practice and life. This is best done with others, particularly in the context of supervision.

- **K**NOWLEDGE
  The development of knowledge is the main outcome of this text.

My passion is for the Christian Wholeness Framework (CWF) to assist churches to care in a safer and more holistic way, with greater connection and understanding. My passion is that counsellors and those within the mental health field can provide more holistic services to their counsellees. My passion is for health professionals, the church and its ministries, as well as families and friends of those who suffer to have the understanding and tools through the CWF to provide greater support and networking to those who suffer and struggle. My passion for all of us, whether we struggle or succeed, is that we change to become more God-centred and more whole, more like Jesus.

The development of these three competencies is like developing the 'ASK' cube.

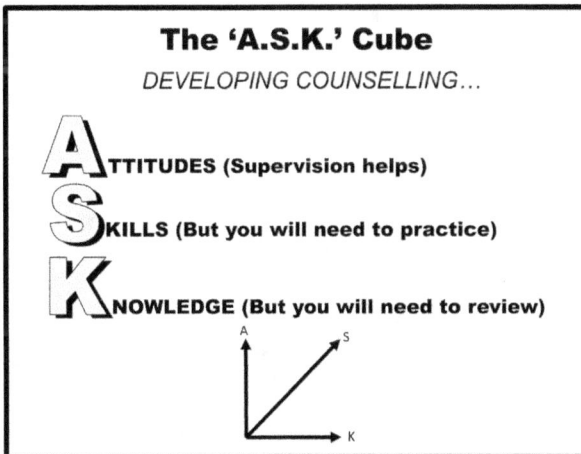

The 'A.S.K.' Cube
DEVELOPING COUNSELLING...

ATTITUDES (Supervision helps)

SKILLS (But you will need to practice)

KNOWLEDGE (But you will need to review)

This book is designed to help your development as a counsellor by assisting you to:

- integrate in a safe and professional way
- get to the core issues more quickly
- formulate a therapeutic plan more effectively
- integrate spiritual issues into therapy, in particular with Cognitive Behaviour Therapy (CBT) and psychodynamic approaches.

This book also examines questions such as: What makes a better counsellor? What are the essentials of healing? How does healing happen? How is a 'CURE' achieved? What hinders the 'CURE'ing process?

In reading the book, while you may want to use the Contents list like an index and go straight to a later section, be aware that each stage of the book is built on the previous one.

2: MEET MANDY

Mandy is a composite character designed to illustrate the Christian Wholeness Framework. You will be able to walk through the CWF alongside Mandy as she journeys progressively towards personal and Christian wholeness. The book is written for counsellors and you are invited to sit in the second chair of observation, beside the author, when Mandy and her family come in for therapy. The book has limited itself to one case scenario to enable a thorough analysis of the CWF through one person. There are many other cultures, ages, problems and their causes than are illustrated by Mandy. Males are also not a feature of this book. To progress further in the knowledge aspects of the CWF, it is hoped that further material illustrating the variety and complexity of these matters will become available to you (in books and on the web). However, through Mandy you will be able to see in intricate detail how the framework provides a comprehensive journey to wholeness through connection, understanding, response, engagement of other help and evaluation... **a CURE for Mandy.**

MANDY

A woman who introduces herself as Mandy comes to you for counselling. She is a 40 year old Caucasian woman who has been married for 20 years and has two teenage children. She works full time as a pharmacy assistant. Mandy tells you her pastor recommended counselling because he was concerned and thinks that you, being a Christian counsellor, might be able to help. Her sentences are slow and hesitant and she struggles to maintain eye contact. As she talks you begin to get a picture of her life. Some aspects of Mandy's life are good but there is a growing sense that things are not okay.

She feels that she is only just managing in her job and has become socially withdrawn except for two close friends. Mandy has not been getting on well with her husband and has decided to leave him. Over the past year she has met another man and is having an affair. Mandy has been finding it harder to 'feel and act like a mother' towards her children and is worried about the effect the separation will have on them. Mandy says she feels anxious all the time and 'everything is becoming too hard'. Recently she has started having thoughts of suicide. She says her Christian life is not very active but there is a strong underlying sense of faith in God and she has been spending more time reading the Bible lately. She feels the church hasn't been very helpful.

THE 5 CIRCLES

Mandy is described in terms of 5 Circles. Beginning externally and moving inwards, each circle details the aspects of her life.

The 5 Circles represent in diagrammatic form the 5 aspects of Mandy:

1. Spirit
2. Personality (soul or heart)
3. Mind
4. Physical
5. Social

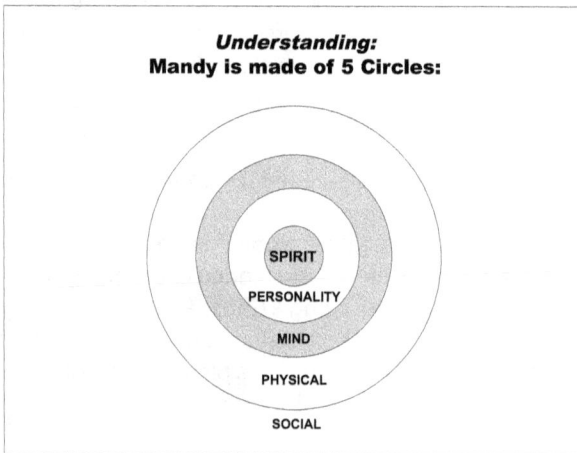

Understanding:
Mandy is made of 5 Circles:

SPIRIT
PERSONALITY
MIND
PHYSICAL
SOCIAL

These circles, illustrated as separate within the framework, are highly connected with each other and interlinked. Viewed three dimensionally they could be seen as:

• Disks… which rotate around each other.
• Spheres… one within the other.
• Colours… which flow and blur into each other.
• Systems… which are highly interrelated.

Why divide them if they are linked? When studying the physical anatomy of the body it is helpful to learn about the individual systems in order to understand the whole. So too when studying the psychological functional anatomy of the person, it is helpful to study the parts that make up the psychology of a person in order to see the whole person.

So let's look at Mandy's circles in detail.

Social

- **Work**: She is managing in the pharmacy but not performing as well as previously.
- **Friends**: She is withdrawing from social contact but still maintains a few long-term friendships.
- **Family**: There is little support from parents and siblings.
- **Intimate relationships:**
  - » Spouse: Mandy is separating from her husband after 20 years.
  - » Affair: She has been seeing another man for the past year and it has become sexual.
- **Counsellor**: She experienced a breach of confidentiality with a previous counsellor.

Physical

- **Health**: ('soma'/body) she has not been as well, generally eating less and the food she does eat is often poor quality or 'junk' food. Mandy has increased her alcohol consumption to three units of alcohol daily. Sleep and exercise levels have declined along with sexual activity with her husband.
- **Behaviourally**, Mandy is doing less with her time, including not keeping up with activities of daily living (ADL). Significantly, she is spending up to three hours a day reading her Bible and praying.
- **Communication**: In general Mandy's communication has diminished as she has become more socially withdrawn.

Mental

- **Mood**: She is increasingly sad, irritable, anxious and obsessive.
- **Volition**: Overall Mandy is experiencing less fun, pleasure and passion.
- **Perception**: There is the sense of an evil presence some nights when going to sleep.
- **Thoughts**: Mandy is more negative with some suicidal ideas and feeling a little bit 'got at' by others. She is also having some occasional blasphemous thoughts which are distressing to her.
- **Cognition**: Her memory and concentration have diminished even though she has a reasonably high IQ (intellect).

Personality

- **Self esteem**: This is deteriorating and she is becoming less caring of others.
- **Self identity**: She is becoming more confused as to who she is and where she is going. Associated with this is a sense of guilt.
- **Self control**: She is starting to feel 'out of control', blaming herself and despairing.
- **Self centredness**: She is becoming increasingly self-absorbed, whereas previously she was more altruistic.
- **Coping**: In order to cope, she is 'faking it to make it', withdrawing and becoming more of a perfectionist.
- **Sensitivity**: She is more sensitive than usual, taking things more personally.

Spiritual

- While her faith is still important to her, she feels that her relationship with God has faded, and that God is less real to her and less relevant. With her growing anxiousness and guilt, she feels compelled to read her Bible more frequently. Her feeling of spiritual unease is being aggravated by the distress of recurring blasphemous thoughts.

3: INTRODUCTION TO THE CHRISTIAN WHOLENESS FRAMEWORK

The Christian Wholeness Framework (CWF) is based on 5 Steps and 5 Shapes which are distilled from a biblical understanding of the nature of person and his/her relationship with God. It is integrated with an evidence based understanding of the psychological and physical functioning of the person. It is more a framework than a specific counselling model which allows workers to take into account the spiritual issues alongside physical/psychological issues.

The Christian Wholeness Framework (CWF) is a broad framework for counselling and coaching with the flexibility for integration into your own approach. The framework is transferable in the sense that it can address different types of issues for counsellees of different ages and cultures at different levels of experience. It also provides a common picture language for understanding the person and the family as well as for facilitating change. This language is based on 5 Steps and 5 Shapes.

What are the essential differences between the CWF and other counselling paradigms and what is essentially 'Christian' about the CWF?

The usefulness of the CWF, in the counselling context, is that it:

- reveals a 3D Jigsaw picture of the counsellee
- provides Safe Steps to journey on in each session with the counsellee
- provides a Map of direction in counselling, locating where therapy is at, and finding the next question/step to take
- provides a Tool Bag that can be filled with a broad range of counselling tools.

What we have found to be the specific value of the CWF is that it:

- can catalyse the rate of integrated growth and change in different settings, such as when two or three get together, as well as within small groups, churches, counselling/coaching ministries and professional mental health practices
- can be helpful across a range of different ages, genders and cultures

- can be applied to both counselling and coaching, providing a framework for a continuum of care, from those who are struggling through to those who are succeeding
- can be used by a continuum of providers, including lay people, small group leaders, and pastors, those in prayer/para-church ministry as well as professional mental health practitioners
- can provide a common and uniting language, a way of communicating understanding of helping people and their relationships. When used effectively, the CWF can provide a flexible and transferable way of communicating across:
  » Age, Gender, Culture
  » The Counselling – Coaching continuum
  » Providers: in terms of role/expertise, personality style
  » Theoretical models of counsellors.
- provides a flexible framework for Connecting, Understanding and Responding, so that any individual counsellor is released to operate in their own personality/style of working, rather than a restrictive 'cookbook' approach to change
- facilitates counsellors by providing a comprehensive framework for seeing and Understanding people in their present position, where they have come from and where they are possibly heading. This improves the accuracy, breadth and efficiency of Responding to another person and assists the counsellor in clarifying their own strengths and limitations, thereby reducing burnout and facilitating Engagement with others
- is Biblically based and integrated into spiritual, psychological, biological and social approaches to change
- can be used at church level to facilitate the presentation of the whole Gospel to the whole person in the context of the great commission of making disciples
- can help people to live out the great commandment, *to love God with all of their heart, soul, mind and strength, and their neighbour as themselves* (Mark 12:30, 31).

How does the CWF do this? It does all this through the 5 Steps and the 5 Shapes. Here is a brief preface to the framework.

THE 5 STEPS

There are five successive steps in the counselling process that build upon each other:

1. **C**onnect with the counsellee safely

6. **U**nderstand the counsellee

7. **R**espond with the counsellee to facilitate change

8. **E**ngage other help where appropriate... we cannot do it all ourselves

9. **e**valuate what has happened.

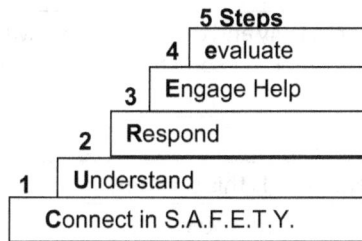

5 Steps

4	evaluate
3	Engage Help
2	Respond
1	Understand
	Connect in S.A.F.E.T.Y.

Each step is the ongoing foundation for the next. Unlike successive rungs of a ladder or one road consecutively leading on to another, each step continues to be dependent on the previous one. If you stand on the third rung from the bottom of a ladder, you no longer require the previous two rungs. Once you have travelled one road, you leave it behind for the second. However, when you stand on the second step the first step needs to remain in place. Unlike the third rung, the ability to stand on the third step is dependent on the ongoing presence of the two previous steps. The more advanced counsellor has to be able to stand on more steps at the same time with more complex problems.

Connecting

Connection is having the capacity to be truly with another person in an undefended relationship. For those starting out in counselling, this is the first and critical step. Connection and engagement with the counsellee is foundational and it is the beginning point of the relationship. The importance of connection must not be underestimated, however, there are those who so over-emphasise it that the other skills required for counselling are neglected or even seen to be a hindrance. Thus some people may say, 'All you need is connection,' and 'An unskilled counsellor can do as well as a skilled one.' Some may even go further and say, 'The counsellor should not even be an expert because that places them in a dominant role which can be controlling.' However, expertise and dominance are not the same and do not need to coexist in a counselling relationship.

In order to establish an effective and real connection, there are a number of critical factors and guidelines the counsellor should bear in mind. These factors are spelt out in the acrostic SAFETY, which is elaborated on in the chapter, 'Connection'.

Connect is explained by the acronym SAFETY

Size	It is easier to truly and deeply connect with smaller numbers (like one other person) than a small or larger group of others.
Attitude	Care
	Confidentiality (Is this private?)
	Consent (What do you want?)
Face	Being real together (not having to fake, flight, fight, freak, or flop)
Empathy	What is it like in your shoes, heart and head or through your eyes?
Time	It takes time to connect.
You	'You' questions ('How are you?' 'Where are you?'). Not 'You' advice!

These questions lead on to the next step of understanding:

Understanding the counsellee

This involves a steep learning curve for the counsellor and it is certainly the hardest step to master. The counsellor may want to fix problems and remove the pain and distress of the counsellee. Responding before an understanding is established may result in:

- getting stuck
- going in the wrong direction
- missing important issues, even to do with safety

- not being able to last the distance with the counsellee
- repeating mistakes.

Responding to the counsellee

This is where the 'therapy' occurs. Here, the counsellor needs to be clear regarding which skills they lack and which techniques they excel in. They do not need to have all the tools or answers to effect change.

Engaging other help

The counsellor who has one model for change is like the tradesman who uses only his hammer … and everything becomes a nail! Advanced counsellors, having a greater capacity for recognising their limitations, are more inclined to engage other help. Significantly, it is often the least experienced counsellor who thinks s/he has it all. Equally they are not as aware of their own limitations and so are less likely to engage help through referral or seek out supervision.

Evaluate

Evaluating and reviewing progress on the steps needs to be continuous and ongoing. This ensures feedback that ensures any necessary further changes.

Although the steps are separate and distinct they merge and overlap one other. When **Connection** happens change can begin. At this point the **Response** step has already started. Likewise, while **Understanding** is the major focus in the early stages of counselling, understanding, in itself, is therapeutic and results in a **Response**. The counsellor continues to grow in **Understanding**, even towards the end of the counselling relationship. Maintenance of **Connection** is essential for counselling to end and for disconnection to happen successfully.

THE 5 SHAPES

The Triangle illustrates connection with others and God

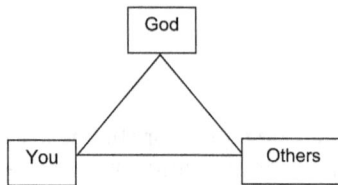

The Circles represent the structure of the whole person

The Circles speak of living increasingly from the Spirit. This being the centre of rotation of one's life and the source of one's being. Living spiritually, out through one's heart, mind and body into the life of family, friends, work, the church and the world.

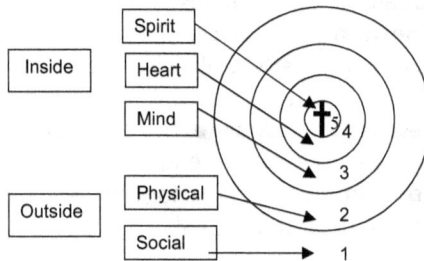

The Square shows change across two dimensions of a person's functioning/ experience/practice in life

Change from below the water level (suffering) to above the water level (success) and more importantly, from self-centredness on the left to God-centredness on the right. This allows freedom to be a living sacrifice. One can place oneself in any of the four quadrants. In any aspect of our lives we can be in any of the four quadrants.

	Self-centred	God-centred
Going well	Self-centred success	God-centred success
Not going well	Self-centred suffering	God-centred suffering

The Cross illustrates increasing consistency in being a Christian

Consistent Christianity is when a person truly lives from their spirit position below the crossbar. Here they can receive all the benefits of where they are placed and there are provisions for change. From there they can rise up above the crossbar on the right-hand side of the Square and practise in a God-centred way. The spirit is located in the central circle. On becoming a Christian, there are fundamental positional changes in this domain. The Cross illustrates where we are positioned in our spiritual life, in relation to God.

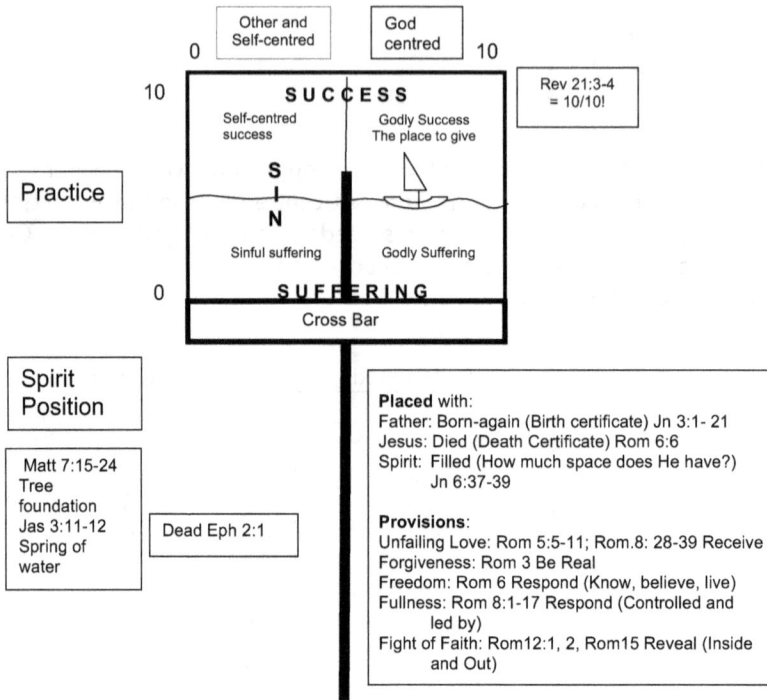

One's journey from self-centred to God-centred practice (left to right in the Square) is called the process of *sanctification*. However, in the practice of our life we often slip back into self-centred ways of functioning (moving in the Square from right to left). When this happens we can then fall at the foot of the Cross, receive our provisions, and return to where we are really placed, in our spirit position. From here, we can rise again; now back into the right-hand side column of the Square, into God-centred practice. This process is called *repentance*.

However, in order to be able to come to the foot of the Cross and receive these provisions, one needs to have come to this place and this position initially. When we are born physically into this world, our spirit position is dead. Our central circle is not alive. We have to make that move in our spirit position from being 'dead in sin' to being 'dead to sin.' In other words we have to be born-again. Then we can be grafted into a new tree and we are grafted into the vine. We can build our lives on the rock of our foundation, God. We can drink of living water and have that spring of water arise from within us out through the rest of our circles. This process of moving our spirit position is called *justification*. It occurs when we realise our spiritual poverty and come to God's unfailing provisions. *Justification*, ongoing *repentance*, and *sanctification* are the three aspects of a theology of change.

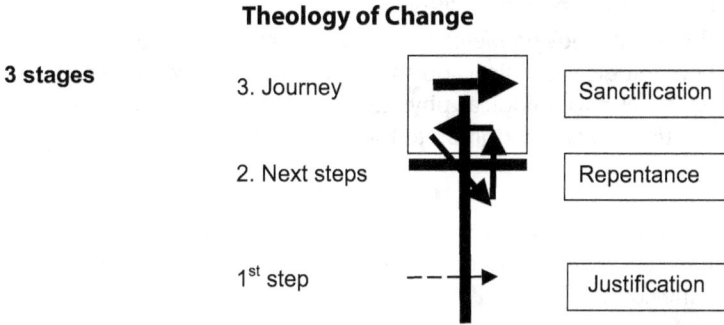

Theology of Change

3 stages			
	3. Journey		Sanctification
	2. Next steps		Repentance
	1st step		Justification

The Pyramid illustrates our support structure

Growth and change ideally occur in a support structure of connection with family and friends, the church, helping programs within the church (Parachurch/people helpers) and coaching/counselling professionals. God is at the top, linked with all.

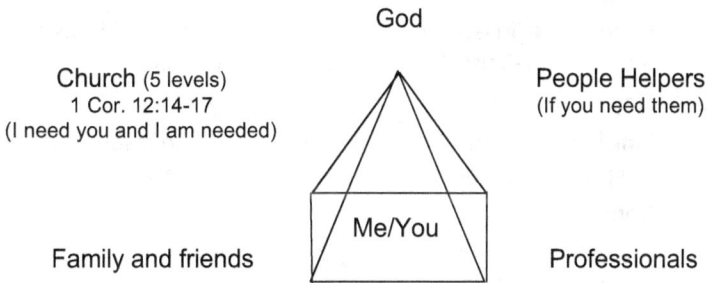

God

Church (5 levels)   People Helpers
1 Cor. 12:14-17   (If you need them)
(I need you and I am needed)

Me/You

Family and friends   Professionals

THE CWF VIEW OF HOW CHANGE HAPPENS

The Christian Wholeness Framework suggests and clarifies that better healing comes from:

Linking

- the counsellor with the counsellee, in the presence of God, with the problem placed in the middle
- the counsellee's *problems* and *positive strengths* (spiritual, psychological, physical and social) with the *positive* counselling *tools* (spiritual, psychological, physical and social) engaging the help of *positive people*, in addition to the counsellor.

'CURE'ing with the counsellee

This is a process of journeying with the counsellee over the five steps of the CWF. Indeed, the linking occurs on the 5 Steps, as the counsellor 'CURE's with the counsellee.

- Connecting:
    - » **Linking** the counsellee with the counsellor.
- Understanding:
    - » Locating all the relevant problems and positives (spiritual, psychological, physical and social) like with a jigsaw (assessment). Then **linking** all the jigsaw pieces to complete the jigsaw picture (formulation).
- Responding:
    - » **Linking** the jigsaw picture with the broad range of tools or positives (spiritual, psychological, physical and social).
- Engaging other help:
    - » **Linking** the counsellee with other people and resources through the process of referral and networking with other helpers.
- Evalution:
    - » Evaluating in an ongoing way, how the **linking** is progressing the process of healing.

The CWF also clarifies what is hindering the healing, or the 'CURE'ing process. Counselling becomes problematic when:

The Counsellor:

- does not **Engage** other help because they may not have an awareness of their own limitations, or be connected with other counsellors and helpers
- is unable to **Respond** with a broad range of positive therapeutic tools to link with the range of problems

- has not **Understood** a full 3D jigsaw picture of the problems and positives and is unable to link them with the positive tools for change
- has not fully located the problems and possibilities that make up the picture, so some parts of the puzzle are missing
- may not have **Connected** enough in SAFETY to get all the pieces of the jigsaw.

THE CHRISTIAN BASIS OF THE CWF

Theology

The text is based on mainline theology including a biblical theology of change, focusing on the importance of an underlying, *positional* change in your spirit, or *justification*, which occurs when you become a Christian. This change in position allows for a change in *practice* over time in terms of moving from self-centredness ('I' in the middle where God needs to be) toward God-centredness. This is a process of change from sin towards *sanctification* and is ongoing throughout our lives. Through the process of *repentance* you are born-again into a new family, the *church* and become a part of the *body of Christ*, (the most common metaphor for the church in the Bible).

In addition, we have:

- a significant past which is relevant even though we have become Christians. While fundamental changes have occurred within the central circle of our being, the impact of the past and the influence of the other circles are not completely removed
- the capacity for goodness, despite the fact that our sinful nature/self-centredness is totally depraved. This is because we are made in His image
- emotions which need to be recognised but which must not be central to our lives
- a mind which needs to be renewed
- a social life (the horizontal aspect of our relating) which is important in addition to our spiritual life (the vertical aspect of our relating)

- an ability to use God-given common (secular) knowledge, and the sciences (e.g. social, medical, psychological) as well as remaining primarily Bible based.

Scripture

The theological underpinning of this text is based on many scriptures. Christian Wholeness is best illustrated by the greatest commandment:

Love the Lord your God
with all your heart,
all your soul, all your mind
and all your strength
and love your neighbour as yourself.
(Mark 12: 30, 31)

Note this is not a 'proof text' for Christian wholeness, but rather a verse which describes what living in Christian wholeness means.

Terms used

God is described in the Bible as the *Triune Person* who can be both *with* us and *in* us.

Spirituality is the vertical dimension of our faith, that part within us that relates with God. Here, spirituality is defined in the biblical context, which is *different* from a more postmodern approach to spirituality which is defined according to one's own definition of 'truth'.

For Christians, there may be times our spirituality seems to have little relevance to our lives. We appear no different to the non-Christians around us. We may have a correct understanding of God and the Bible, yet our underlying personal theology and core beliefs about God may be different. They may be shaped by the 'truths' (or 'lies') of our experiences, rather than a theology based on the Bible.

Religion is different from spirituality. It represents social formalities and rituals, church traditions and structures (the horizontal aspect) of spirituality. While religion may be lacking in spirituality in terms of relationship with God, all denominations (including the more expressive/free branches of the church) develop their own formalities and much of this may be helpful.

Spirit is the part within us that connects us with God. It is the place where God's presence dwells and it changes when one becomes a Christian regardless of a lack of change in other parts of our lives. This is different from what is often loosely defined as 'spirit' which can mean anything from an airline marketing strategy (Qantas the 'Spirit of Australia') to levels of motivation, energy and wellbeing (when someone says 'That's the spirit' or 'He has lost his spirit in life.') It is also differs from terms such as meaning, purpose and direction, which are more related to an integral part of the personality.

Counsellor describes a trainee or professional (someone who receives income from counselling) who, equipped with knowledge and skills, provides emotional, psychological and mental health/wellbeing assistance to someone in need.

Counselling is the generic term for talk or experiential intervention. It includes other terms such as management and therapy.

Counsellee is the term for the person receiving these services. They can also be called patient and client.

Christian counselling is the active, appropriate and ethical integration of Christian understanding and responses into the counselling process. This is distinct from counselling which is Christian, defined as such in view of its using a generic Christian ethical code, involving ethical attitudes (such as care, boundaries, consent and commitment). I wonder if the majority of Christians, who are practising counselling, are counsellors who are Christians as opposed to Christian counsellors. Clarify for yourself where you stand regarding this. The CWF provides an example of integrated Christian Counselling.

WHERE DID THE CWF COME FROM? MEET JOHN

The CWF developed in the context of my own personal life as well as my professional practice. The emergence of the CWF from these settings has made it a framework which can indeed apply to oneself as a person and also as a professional.

One way to illustrate the steps and the shapes is to explain how I use the CWF in my own life. The CWF has grown out of my own journeying and from my own struggles. It developed out of a need to have a broad *picture* of the foundational premise for life. In other words, I needed a framework to live by. What was life about? Where was I going? In the complexity and confusion of life, the CWF gives me the big picture of the principles of life.

In a post-modern world saturated with information, and an emphasis on indulgence in as many experiences as possible, what should my *priorities* be? The framework provides me with a sense of order and clarity. I have a greater confidence in what to say 'yes' to and so what to say 'no' to.

By applying the CWF I can discern more accurately where I am at, where I need to get to, and how to *plan* for change. The framework provides me with a map so I can be more honest about where I am in life's journey. From there I can better plan in which direction I need to progress.

In thinking about the CWF, I wanted an approach that I could hold in my hands, and carry with me, whether I was succeeding or suffering, going on with God or failing Him. I was not looking for a rigid or detailed cookbook approach that could not be adapted to different situations or be generalised into the complexities and variety of life. Encouragingly, though I do often fail Him, the CWF provides me with foundational biblical principles and challenges me regarding my priorities. It assists me to track my own development and provides direction for the future.

My life started out somewhat alone. I was not a whole person and I felt confused and lost. I began to passionately pursue wholeness and the vision for wholeness arose from these needs. I wanted the framework to be Christian because the Christian aspect is so important to me. It needed to be theologically based and God-centred to create an emphasis on 'Christian Wholeness.'

The Christian Wholeness Framework has been developed during my life journey. Others have joined me along the way and assisted as I have mentioned.

How and why I use the CWF in my personal life

This section has been placed here to help earth the framework by introducing myself and Mandy. We are both 'case' examples, we are both on the same road, but just at different points. You have briefly met Mandy. Meet John.

THE CWF AND THE BIG PICTURE

The CWF allows me to see the big picture, especially of myself. I am a wide angle person, someone who needs to see the whole picture of what is happening in me. I picture myself as a three-dimensional entity consisting of 5 Shapes. The 5 Shapes in themselves are two-dimensional yet they have a third dimension (time) and lie on the timeline of my life. I can see trends such as where my shapes have come from and where they are going.

The Triangle
* It shows the *big picture* of my connections with God, myself and others.

The Circles
* They are helpful in a number of ways. They are like…
  » A jigsaw picture: I need an outline or a template so I can see where the jigsaw pieces of my life fit, so I can place them together. The jigsaw pieces are made up of the parts of my own life which I can place on the template of the sectors of the circles. The whole picture helps me see the puzzle and make sense of where I am at in the various parts of my life. Whether I am falling and failing or succeeding the jigsaw picture shows me where I can go to from there.
  » A tree: Like the growth rings across a section of tree, the Circles enable me to see the reasons why I have grown in a particular way and in which direction my branches are currently growing. I am particularly aware of where my fruit or my behaviour and words have come from.
  » Boundary lines: The Circles provide a set of boundary lines that clarify what is mine (and if it is mine how deeply it is affecting me) and what is not mine. For example, if I have difficulty sleeping because my mind is busy, I find it helpful to let go the things that are external to me, such as the particular events or people I am thinking about, and locate and release to the Father the aspects that may have entered into my heart. Also the boundary lines allow me to 'externalise,' or put outside of myself, problems which I may have in any of my circles. As a result I am more able to master and address these issues in a more objective and less personalised way.

The Square
- Challenges me by showing a picture of the parts of my life that are above and below the water level (functional and dysfunctional) and the parts that are self-centred compared to God-centred in my journey of sanctification.

The Cross
- Is there to remind me about my decision to become a Christian (justification). The Cross challenges me about how much I access and use my spirit position (who I am in God as a result of my rebirth, and the place for repentance).

The Pyramid
- Illustrates what supports I have or am lacking in terms of family and friends, church, ministry and professional input.

THE CWF AND PRIORITIES

In a world of information overload, I need to know what is important and what I can discard. Life is short and there is no dress rehearsal. To make the most of my life, I need to prioritise. I need to know which aspect is more important than any other. I need to identify where to put an emphasis and what to ignore. In the context of busy-ness and the complexity of my life, setting my priorities has been a life-long challenge, which I am still working on. When the young, rich and powerful man came to Jesus, the conversation centred on what was most important in life. Jesus' response was for us to choose to live in the triangle, *loving God and others as ourselves*, with all our circles (*heart, soul, mind and strength*) (Mark 12: 30, 31).

The CWF gives me a sense of priority and whether I have the right balance or not, I am gradually moving towards the right emphases in my life. As time has gone on, the CWF has challenged me about whether I have my priorities somewhat back to front. Learning to effectively prioritise has been a gradual process. Many of my earlier attempts to rearrange my timetable have felt like rearranging furniture on the Titanic. In other words, these attempts did not seem to have changed my course. At times there were still icebergs dead ahead! Reassuringly, life is not always that desperate and changes are being made. Yet on a personal level with a busy job, a large family and a passion for developing and passing on the Christian Wholeness Framework, I have found prioritising difficult.

How do the shapes and steps of the CWF help me identify priorities, and distinguish what is more important than what?

The Triangle

The Triangle reminds me of the importance of connecting with myself and what is happening in me as I connect with God and with others. While it is important for me to have personal space, the Triangle points out that I cannot do life on my own. The best horizontal (social) connections I can have are those which include the vertical one (with God).

The Circles

The Circles help me see where to place the most importance in my life. They show me what is central and what or who is influencing me the most. Like a wheel, my life has a centre of rotation. I am becoming more aware of my axis, and how often I am off balance, and not living from my centre, which is my spirit position. The Circles teach me that my 'being' (the inside circles) is more important than my 'doing' (the outside circles). It is important nonetheless, to have an outward expression in action, of my inner being. In the New Testament, James asks if the inside is not expressed outwardly, how real is the inside anyway?

Through the Circles I realise the best way to prioritise my life is to live from the inside out. My spirit influences my heart and personality, which changes my mind, which affects what I say and do. Likewise, the Circles help me prioritise what is important in my own professional development and also the development of others (e.g. in selection processes). In this context, I particularly focus on three things, Attitudes, Skills and Knowledge (ASK). The attitudes of the inside heart circle are more important than knowledge in the next circle out, and the mind leads to development of skills of the outer physical circle. The most important form of change is becoming and staying a Christian. Although a theology of change is paramount for me, it has to be expressed outwards through all the circles with a psychology of change that is associated with a biology and a sociology of change. The significant changes that occur deep within us when we are saved must have an impact on the outer circles of our lives and find expression through them. This in turn reinforces the central change.

The Square

The Square tells me there are two dimensions of change and growth, not one. While it is important to develop and to succeed, the Square reminds me that it is more important to be like Jesus, and live a God-centred life. This process is called 'sanctification'. The Square helps me recognise that when I am going well I can become proud and self-centred and forget God. I can place the sectors of my circles on the map of the Square, challenging myself about where they are located. As I look at the big picture of myself, I can be more honest about where I am. Am I falling and suffering below the water level, or succeeding above it?

The Square helps me to be more honest when I fail and sin, when I am living in the left-hand column where 'I' or others are at my centre, instead of God. If I am in the top right-hand quadrant, I am free to go and give to others, in whichever quadrant they may be. If I am below the water level in either of the lower quadrants, I can receive from others and from God. The Square shows me how congruently I am living my life in practise with who I really am in my position in God as shown by the Cross.

The Cross

The Cross sits underneath the Square and it is the key to change. It tells me that the most important, underlying and central change, is my decision to become a Christian (being 'justified'). How do I change? When I fail and fall as a Christian, I can keep coming back to the foot of the Cross (repentance), and find again who I am, where my centre is, and what I have already received. At the foot of the Cross, I find again who I really am in God, and allow the Spirit of God within me to influence me. I can now live according to the Spirit rather than according to my selfishness. How do I do this? It is at the foot of the Cross that I receive His provisions of unfailing love for my shame in my empty love sector, Forgiveness for my guilt in my truth sector, and Freedom for my despair in the control sector of my heart. I also receive the Fullness of His presence to pervade the sectors of my heart.

In kneeling at the foot of the Cross I receive my spirit position. I can stand up again and reveal this position and His presence more effectively in practice. I can get up again, reappearing in the right-hand side of the Square, to live for a period of time (often much too short), in a more God-centred way. I can get up again and fight the fight of faith. I can rebuild my house, and now on the rock as opposed to building it on the sand. I can drink of living water and let that spring of water flood my outer circles. I can remain and abide in the vine and produce fruit of the Spirit. Where there is hate and aloneness, love can come in the love sector. Doubt and confusion can be replaced by faith in my truth sector. Where there was despair in my control sector now can come hope... love faith and hope.

As my heart circles change, there is a move in practice from the left-hand side to the right-hand side of the Square (sanctification). My mind circle can also be transformed. In the mood sector of my mind, feelings of love, joy and peace can arise, replacing or at least influencing any anger, sadness and stress. My passion, imagination and ideas can be influenced and conformed to His presence. Because of the changes in my mind, my physical circle can become more of a living sacrifice in terms of my actions and words being conformed to the image of Jesus.

These ongoing acts of repentance, with which I am becoming increasingly familiar, are becoming an accepted and regular part of my life. As I repent further, I can slowly move through the process of sanctification, trending from the left to the right-hand side of the Square. As I move in this direction, I am also more likely to rise to a higher level in the Square. I am so grateful that the Cross, representing my spirit position remains unchanged in my central circle, despite what may be occurring in the more superficial circles.

The Pyramid

The Pyramid reminds me I cannot travel the journey alone. I am placed in three different pyramids. The first is my own Pyramid where I am surrounded by family, friends, church and people helpers and professionals whom I am prepared to pay to assist. These people are all there for me. This has been a radical insight for me, as I had previously focused mainly on the second Pyramid in which I play part. In the second Pyramid I am a part of others' Pyramids. I am family and a friend to my family and friends; I also serve the church, people helpers and other professionals. There is a third Pyramid, where I am in the professional corner for my patients, their families and friends, their churches and people helpers, and also the other counselling professionals involved in their lives.

THE CWF AND PLANS

I am a man on the move! In the context of the big picture and being more aware of my priorities, I need to be clear about where I am at and where I am going. I need a map to help me plan where to go. The CWF gives me that map. I am someone who needs to know where I am at and where I am going, without wasting any time getting lost. I find it hard when I am lost, not just in the car, but also in life. Time is precious and just as I need clear priorities, I need a map... I cannot afford to get lost!

Importantly, although I am a man on a mission, and in somewhat of a rush, having a map does not mean I have to drive like a lunatic. The map will highlight places I can stop and refuel, and there will even be places where I can take a moment to celebrate where I have come from. I need to know where the main highways are. On other occasions I need the more detailed map of the suburban roads where I may need to linger. I also need to clearly know the difference. The map gives me this information. The 5 Shapes and 5 Steps are a bit like a road map, telling me where I am, where I should be and how I can get there.

The Triangle

The Triangle tells me I cannot navigate by this map on my own. It helps me to plan to be in connection. It maps out who I am connected to, and identifies whether I am journeying alone, with God, with others, or all three. It reminds me to connect with myself, God, and others. It reminds me to search for the people I can be with while at the same time being in connection with God.

The Circles

The Circles map out where I can go when I fall. They give me a plan of healing and resolution. They help me to collect my distressed *mind* (feelings, pictures, thoughts and memories) and lead me to gather the shame, aloneness, guilt, confusion, despair and disappointment of my *heart*. Then I can bring it all into the central circle of my life where the presence of God dwells. My *spirit*, the central circle, is already and always there, beneath the rubble waiting to be accessed when I fall or fail. From here, I can go out again and have my heart refreshed, my mind renewed, and my body restored. From here I can go and find companionship with another, and even better, connect with that person and God at the same time (this is the basis of the concept of 'trialogue').

The Square

The Square with its four quadrants helps me to see the map of the journey of my life in practice. This map helps me intentionally plan where to go. It is a journey towards the top right-hand quadrant, a God-centred, positive and successful place. This map reminds me that I have not arrived at the top right-hand corner, where heaven is. It also makes me aware of how often I drive into the left-hand side of the Square, self-centred success (above the water level) or suffering (below the water level). The Square maps out for me 'no entry' signs to the most dangerous place to be, the top left-hand quadrant. Here I am doing well on my own, and not giving what I have, to those struggling beneath the water. The square helps me respect those who spend time in the bottom right-hand quadrant, suffering but focused on God. Many of the great hymns of old were written as a result of difficult times spent in this quadrant. They express such vivid connection with God. I wish that more modern Christian songs were written here.

The Square is also a map that shows me there is an evil and not so good place (bottom left quadrant), where there is destruction, death and devastation.

The Cross

The Cross provides me with a plan for change. With the crossbar sitting beneath the Square I have a place to go when I fall or fail. This place is even beneath the bottom of the Square, under the rubble and the chaos of life. Whereas the Squares are there to map out my practice, this part of the map locates my spirit position. Here I can fall at the foot of the Cross, and receive again what I have already been given when I first became a Christian.

In this part of the map am reminded that I have His:

- Provisions: Unfailing love, Forgiveness, Freedom and Fullness. Armed with these, I can get up and Fight the fight of faith.
- Placement within the Trinity:
    » I am born-again into a new family with my *Father*. I have a birth certificate.
    » I have died and risen with *Christ*. I have a death certificate.
    » I am filled with the *Spirit*.
- Presence: An abiding, communing, and indwelling presence.
- Purpose for my life:
    » Intimacy with Him.
    » Imitation of Christ.
    » Interaction ... that all things are from and to Him.

The Pyramid

The Pyramid helps me plan my support structure by mapping out the source of my own support. My family and friends occupy one corner. The church claims another, and the ministry arm of the church fills the third corner as a place where I can give and receive. At times I may need to access professional assistance in whatever area I need. This is available in the fourth corner.

How and why I use the CWF in my social life

The **5 Steps** are underlying principles for my relationship with others. They give me an order of priority in relationships with family, friends in the church and at my place of work with clients and colleagues/staff. In my interactions with others, the 5 Steps help me to focus on the importance of firstly establishing a **Connection**, and then an **Understanding**, prior to trying to **Respond**, by fixing or solving issues, for another person.

The longer I journey through life, the more I find myself needing to walk these 5 Steps of Connection and Understanding before I Respond, then **Engage other help** and while I am doing this, **evaluate** how things are going. In some ways, as I have progressed forward in life, I have often found myself going backwards down the steps! Over time, my focus has moved back from the Response step of trying to fix problems, to spending a lot of time and effort on the Understanding step. Significantly I have become more aware of the importance of **Connection**, as the foundation of all of these steps. I use these steps in relation to my family, with friends, at church, and at work.

I have found my growth in Connection, to be considerably helped by the SAFETY acrostic. I use this as a filter when wondering whether or not to start connecting with someone. The ongoing monitoring and maintenance of connection is also assisted by this. Relationships go much better if they are built on a safe foundation. SAFETY is my method and measurement of connection.

- **S**ize: Smaller is safer. With family, friends and church, the connection I enjoy increases the smaller the size of the group. With my family of origin as well as my family, I try and find those one-on-one times to get closer, heart to heart. In church I have deeper fellowship when with one other than in my small group or the larger congregation.

- **A**ttitudes: The emphasis is on caring, respectful relationships that enhance the choices of others.

- **F**acing and **F**un: In the context of a busy life, fun becomes a scarce commodity. Gradually I'm learning to laugh more! Facing issues that arise in my marriage, or with my children and friends, does so much more for connection in the long term than when I fake it, withdraw or just don't talk.

- **E**mpathy: Trying to get into the other person's shoes, heart or mind can be a real challenge, particularly in the context of business or family life, yet it is critical to establishing a safe connection.

- **T**ime: Making time to be together has been an immense challenge and it is something I'm still working on. Quality of relationship does depend on spending at least some quantity of time together building the relationship.

• **'You'** Questions: 'How are you?' 'Where are you at?' I'm attracted to a person who can ask these questions.

How and why I use the CWF in the Church

The 5 Steps
In walking these 5 Steps, I find myself focusing not so much on the big congregation (which is still important), but the small group where there is a greater ability to 'CURE' with others. I find myself going even smaller, to meeting with twos or threes where even safer connection can occur. My definition of church includes all three of these levels of connection from twos and threes to small groups through to the big congregation.

As I search Scripture, I notice the prevailing metaphor for the church is the body of Christ. This concept describes connection at various levels of organisation. The church is the body of Christ. The more I have seen this, the harder it has become to define church as being primarily based on the Sunday/weekend service.

The Triangle
My experience of living in the Triangle (trialoguing) has particularly developed with my connections with David and Suzanne Nikles and Andy Pocock. In 2006, I met David and Suzanne. They were looking for a framework for Christian counselling in a Cross-cultural setting. They adopted the CWF in their work, and personally came to see the value of 'trialoguing' or fellowshipping in 'twos and threes'. In the context of safe sharing in the presence of God, change occurs.

I met Andy in 2007 in my churching in 'twos and threes'. We started talking about the CWF with the 5 Steps and the 5 Shapes. Subsequently, Andy has taken the CWF, and in his own way, in conjunction with the work of John Eldridge (the 'Wild at Heart' man) and others, developed twos and threes, as well as small groups. Andy calls his small group a pod, a safe environment, where I can ask and be asked, 'How are you?' and 'Where are you at?' Initially each individual shares how they are and where they are at in terms of the 5 Shapes. The rest simply Connect and Understand. Then each person shares how they may Respond to their own issues or an issue which the facilitator focuses on from the first round of sharing, again with others only connecting and understanding. Then, the group breaks into twos and threes to trialogue, sharing and praying, praying and sharing. This is a model which is being developed to serve the church. Members of the pod are encouraged to go back and continue in twos and threes with others.

In the big weekend church, trialogue is operating at a larger, corporate level. The challenge for church leaders in this setting is to be able to engage in this trialogue, as opposed to the service being a monologue event (one person/music system). A service that is driven from the front without a connection with the congregation has less opportunity for more intimate trialogue.

The Circles

The Circles provide a depth gauge of the level of conversation. The deepest levels of conversation originate from the inner circles. The more central the circle, the safer the conversation needs to be and the more the SAFETY acrostic must apply.

The Square

For me, church is the place where I can receive and also give, depending on where I am in the Square. The church is the body of Christ and the body is connected in such a way that any one part cannot say to another 'I don't need you,' nor can any part of the body say 'I'm not needed' (1 Corinthians 12). If I am suffering (below the water level) I have a need to receive. If I am succeeding above the water level, I need to give. How different this can be from the Sunday stage-centred church, where there is the danger of being in the top left-hand quadrant. There we can come and warm the seat each week without giving or receiving and without connecting or understanding. Such churches run the risk of emphasising becoming a Christian for one's own selfish benefits, not accepting or caring for God-centred people suffering in the bottom right-hand quadrant.

The Cross

The church is a place where I can come and be with others at the foot of the Cross. Although the Cross is very personal and at the centre of one's own individual life, we can all come together at the foot of the Cross, receiving who we are in God, in the context of trialogue in particular, and also in the other expressions of the church.

The Pyramid

Although the formal church is in one corner of the Pyramid, I see the whole of the base of the Pyramid as being made up of Christians, of the body of Christ. Thus all of the corners of the Pyramid from the local church to people helpers in church ministry to health professionals are in fact, the whole church.

How and why I use the CWF with family and friends

The CWF specifically applies to me as an individual and it can also be applied to family and friends, particularly in relation to the big picture, priorities and plans. The CWF helps me to see where my family and friendships are in terms of connection in trialogue, the depth of our connections (using the Circles as a depth gauge) and where the relationships fit on the Square in terms of centredness and function. The Cross challenges me to have relationships which can now be undefended. There is no need for defence in the context of being together, where there is unfailing love, Forgiveness and Freedom. While I need my own Pyramid, my family and my marriage also need a Pyramid around them.

The 5 Steps
The steps have become important in relating with friends and family. I now try to spend more time on connection and understanding and less time on the response step. When my five children were younger they needed lots of parental responses. As a parent, I attempted to respond in love, with an understanding of where they were at individually. As the children grew into teenagers, I became aware of how my parental discipline fell into a crumbling heap if I had not maintained an underlying connection with my child.

The Triangle
The Triangle prompts me to live a proactive life of servant leadership i.e. God first, through me (and this means I am second... but I am crucified with Christ), and then on to others. This helps me to be less reactive, and also to be more willing to receive from others when they give to me. The Triangle in my marriage reminds me of the strength of a three stranded chord, which is much harder to break than one or two strands. The Triangle provides me with an opportunity to be more proactive in living from God, rather than reactive in my relationship with my wife.

Trialoguing at deeper levels occurs most with family and friends. Here, we can be together, sharing our mind circles and being undefended in our heart-to-heart communication. I have a couple of mates with whom I have exercised over the years. This is one place I can come out of myself and share with others in the presence of God, i.e. we 'trialogue', or 'church' in twos and threes. At the end of our workout together in the gym, we usually relax in the sauna. This is an opportunity to bring the issues we have shared into the presence of God. In relation to marriage, my wife and I have come to value the Third Person (or should I say first!) in our relationship as someone we can both be 'heart to heart' with in trialogue.

The Circles

In my marriage relationship, the Circles help us see more clearly where we are at as a couple. In particular, I can see how the heart sectors of our relationship are in terms of love, respect, releasing each other to grow, and looking at the ways we are coping with various aspects of life.

The Square

I am learning to build my wife up and assist her in her journey towards the top right-hand quadrant of the Square, to a place of God-centredness and positive living. I want us both to inhabit this place together. My plan is to be constantly moving our marriage in that direction. Using the Square, I now have a map to locate where on the journey my wife is, where I am and where our marriage is heading.

The Cross

I am so aware of my inadequacies, particularly as a husband, but also as a father. At these times, the foot of the Cross is becoming my familiar place of comfort and reassurance, where I receive the provision of God's unfailing love for my shame, His forgiveness for my guilt, and His freedom for my despair. It is a place where I can come, together with my wife and close friends.

The Pyramid

My wife and I are grateful for the families with whom we share positive relationships. We value couples whose company we can both enjoy. We value our church community. There is always room to receive ministry within our marriage as we encounter difficulties, and professional coaching/counselling has been helpful too.

How and why I use the CWF in my professional life

I needed a map in my professional life as well! During 1988, I was studying (and struggling) for my fellowship exam as a psychiatrist. Psychiatry was somewhat abstract for me. I recognised I needed a way to think about the structure of the person and also the process of change. It was at this time that I started developing a map to guide my thinking and understanding of counselling, particularly coming up to my major exams. After a number of attempts to design this, starting off with a spreadsheet format, the Circles began to emerge. Those *circles*, now over 20 years old, are still largely the same! They seem to have lasted the distance.

In addition to my need for a map, I needed a way to understand integration. I had just moved from Christchurch, New Zealand, to Melbourne in Australia to commence child and adolescent psychiatry training. As I approached my professional career, I focused heavily on integration and the *Square* started to develop. This was when I met Dr Gary Collins, who for me became a mentor, encourager and fellow traveller on the journey of integration. The Square was placed on to the Cross bar around 2005, which is quite recent, in relation to the development of the shapes. Prior to that, I often placed the shape of a Cross in the middle of the Square as opposed to underneath it.

As I supervised others, I began to notice a recurring issue that was also a challenge to me. I realised that counsellors often run into problems because of incomplete understanding of the counsellee and the process of change. I recall an abdominal operation I assisted with, during my medical training. One evening the on call surgeon opened up the patient's belly, found such a mess and simply closed up their abdomen. I was always unsure whether the surgeon had a full understanding of what he was going into in the first place. It occurred to me that counselling is like that at times. I was beginning to see the value of the *understanding step*. Around 1996, I attended some workshops in New Zealand by Michael White (of Narrative Therapy fame). The trend in counselling was to de-emphasise the 'medical model' in practice (probably for many reasons), which included the bypassing of the 'assessment' of a person. This again challenged me to evaluate the importance of the understanding step to the whole process of counselling.

For me within my professional practice, the framework has made it so much easier to know where I am at and where I am going in my counselling. In *supervision*, it has assisted me to have a clearer understanding of where my supervisees are at, thus enabling me to challenge them with questions to explore where they need to go. In *training*, the Pyramid provides a way of identifying levels of trainees along the professional side of the Pyramid, from beginning counsellor, counsellor and advanced counsellor through to the specialist level. The Circles and their sectors can provide headings or slots for a curriculum, including theory (theology, psychology, biology and sociology), problems and also therapy (e.g. interventions based on the various circles as outlined on the response step). The steps highlight processes of counselling for those who are training. In my passion for *networking*, it has been useful to have a language to first understand and then communicate with other parts of the Pyramid. The application of the framework in my *clinical practice* is what this book is all about.

So, the CWF has provided me with the big picture, priorities and plans. It will always be very much a work in progress. I'm grateful for the framework and those who have travelled with me along the way helping me to learn more about it. I pray that you also find the framework useful in your personal and social life and are able to pass it on to others as you journey on in your life.

SECTION II:
CONNECT

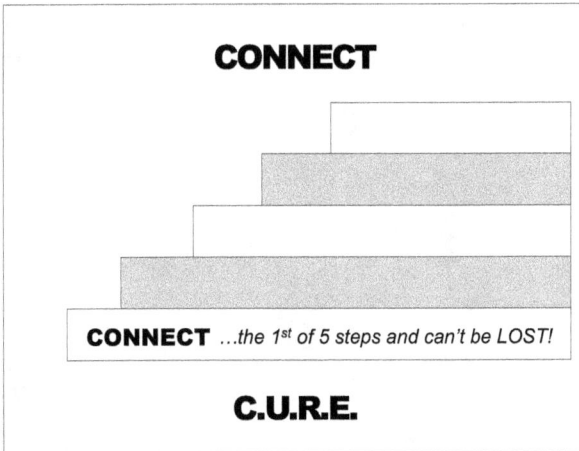

CONNECT

CONNECT ...the 1st of 5 steps and can't be LOST!

C.U.R.E.

4: CONNECTION

The capacity to stay on this step is expected at all levels of learning.

THE ESSENTIAL WAY TO CONNECT IN SAFETY

Connection warrants a section of its own. Although the section is short, the process of connection is the longest step, lasting right through to the end of counselling. It also has to be the strongest of all the steps, as the others stand on top of it. In consequence, connection is the foundation of any counselling and it needs to be present from the beginning to the end of each session as well as through the whole of the counselling process.

Connection is defined by the acrostic 'SAFETY' which embodies the concept of the '**invitational posture.**' While mentioned before, it is further emphasised here.

Size of connection: It is easier to promote safety with a smaller number of people. A more advanced counsellor can retain a sense of safety with more people, for example in marital and family counselling.

Attitudinal behaviours, including:

- Care
- Confidentiality, clarity of roles and boundaries, with respect
- Consent, accountability and responsibility
- Consistent commitment and motivation.

These attitudes are essential in providing the safe '**invitational posture**'. Here the counsellor can be an expert without being dominant. This is one of the safest ways of ensuring the counsellee is not taken beyond where they are able to cope. The invitational posture represents where the counsellor is situated in relation to the counsellee:

- one step beside (with)
- one step behind (not pulling, pushing or kicking in a particular direction)

- can see ahead. i.e. is aware of the map and the options yet…
- does not go ahead (unless there are issues of physical safety involved).

Face issues: It is critical that the counsellor has developed the capacity to address their own issues openly (rather than in a defended way) and to help others to do the same. Therapy is not the place for negative coping mechanisms (Fight, Flight, Fake, Freak or Flop!). It is a safe place for the counsellee to Face issues and let go of them (Forgive), enabling them to be Free to live in the present and move on into the future.

Empathy: The capacity to get inside another's heart, brain, eyes, ears and shoes. Those operating at advanced levels of training will demonstrate the capacity to empathise at deeper and more complex levels in more challenging cases.

Time: The ability to travel with another person reliably over a period of time. Connection takes time and requires availability over an appropriate duration. In a group setting, if attendees tend to come and go, there will be less capacity to connect, as there is less consistent time spent together. The capacity to retain connection, understanding and to respond over a longer period of time, in more challenging cases, is a feature of those operating at advanced levels. Both too little or too much time can be problematic.

'You' questions. The capacity to think and ask appropriate questions:

- **Entry Questions**: Open-ended, non-leading questions like 'How are you?' 'Where are you at in the 5 Shapes?'
  - » Triangle: Either on your own, dialoguing with one other person or with God, or sharing and praying with that person and God
  - » Circles: In terms of where your centre of rotation is located (defined as being in the most dominant circles and sectors)
  - » Square: 'Which quadrant are you living in regarding this issue?'
  - » Cross: 'What difference is being a Christian making to your life?' 'To what extent is the presence of God within you making a difference in your life?' 'To what extent are you experiencing God's provisions of unfailing love, Forgiveness and Freedom?' 'To what extent is your practice above the crossbar in the Square, consistent with your spirit position beneath the crossbar?'
  - » Pyramid: 'Who else are you engaging help from?'
- **Centralising Questions:** 'What is that like for you?' 'What does that mean for you?' 'Where does that leave you?' These questions facilitate one to go deeper into the circles.

- **Linking Questions**: 'Does this link with any other experiences/ situations/people (including the therapist) in the past/present?' 'Where do you think this could lead/leave you in the future?'
- **Response questions:** Based on the connection and understanding steps in the context of the 5 Shapes.
  - » Triangle:
    What could happen if...
    ...we could bring this to God together?
    ...you could find someone to share and pray about this together?
  - » Circles:
    What could happen if...
    ...you lived your life from your central circle, instead around this issue, that seems have so much dominance in your life?
  - » Square:
    What could happen if...
    ...you were living more in the top right-hand corner?'
  - » Cross:
    What could happen if...
    ...we could come to the foot of the Cross together and receive His unfailing love, forgiveness and freedom in relation to this issue?
  - » Pyramid:
    What could happen if...
    ...we could engage other help such as from the church, from a particular ministry, or a professional relevant to this issue?

Connection facilitates safe integration. It is essential as a professional Christian counsellor to connect in an ethical way. There are two extremes of therapist in relation to integration:

- Avoidant therapist: Mandy says, 'My therapist doesn't want to include my spirituality.'
- Zealot therapist: Mandy says, 'My therapist pushes his/her spiritual stuff onto me.'

The Safe Therapist operates somewhere between the avoidant and the zealot by connecting in SAFETY.

The final part of the SAFETY acrostic is the 'You' questions, which allow one to move on to the Understanding step and then the Response step. The entry, centring, linking and responding questions are vital capacities to learn.

You can use safe questions which retain connection to explore spiritual issues. This can be done through introductory/screening questions regarding where the counsellee is at spiritually. You can ask 'You' questions about reality, relevance and sense of relationship in regard to issues of faith, the church and God, including the present and the past and the aspects that may have been helpful or a hindrance.

SKILL DEVELOPMENT FOR CONNECTION

Developing safe connection skills is best done in the context of supervised practice, where the supervisor has the opportunity to observe counselling by video, one way mirror facilities or sitting in on a session with a client. Also there are numerous books on micro skills of connection available. The more advanced you are as a counsellor, the greater will be your capacity to retain connections with a greater number of people and problems. If the sense of SAFETY starts to deteriorate or crumble during a therapy session, disconnection either by the counsellor or the counsellee is the likely, classic reason. Implementation of the rest of this book will stand or fall, dependent on the strength of this step.

SECTION III:
UNDERSTAND–LOCATE

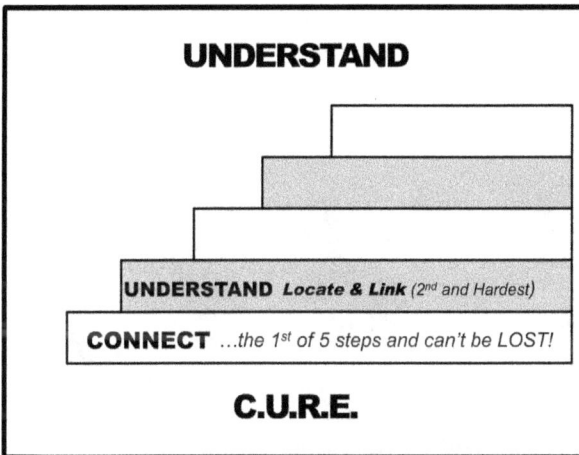

UNDERSTAND

UNDERSTAND *Locate & Link* (2nd and Hardest)

CONNECT ...the 1st of 5 steps and can't be LOST!

C.U.R.E.

5: UNDERSTAND–LOCATE

For training purposes, the capacity to stay on this step is expected at Beginning Counsellor level of learning.

Understanding the counsellee, is probably the most neglected step in counselling and training. There is often ample emphasis on micro skills and connection. Having mastered these, counsellors often shortcut the assessment and understanding step, wanting to get to the therapy and response stage. Second to the connection between counsellor and counsellee disappearing from underneath one's feet, the next area where most counselling problems occur is where there is an insufficient understanding of the counsellee, their problems and their possibilities. The understanding step is insufficient to hold the response step.

The commonest problem on the understanding step is simply not having enough information. It is as if some of the jigsaw pieces are missing. A lot of supervision time can be spent just trying to locate these pieces. The Understand–Locate step addresses this. Even if a counsellor has located all the relevant pieces of information, they can remain disconnected, and not make sense. The jigsaw pieces have not been linked to define the picture. The Understand–Link step addresses this. Once a counsellor has mastered these two aspects of understanding, s/he can not only maximise their time in supervision, but can also be best equipped to move on to the next step, Therapy.

The amount of understanding required is relative to the complexity of the issues at hand. While understanding commences from the first connection, until the last goodbye, a significant proportion of it occupies an early stage of counselling.

The contents of this section

Using the checklist and the Circles to locate the counsellee in the:

- social, physical and mind circles
- personality circles
- central circles of the spirit:
  - » Spiritual *provisions*, the *purposes* and *position* of the spirit and God's *presence*
- past circles

The issues raised in this section

In order to be a better therapist, it is critical to:

- have as much of the essential information as possible
- be able to make sense of it
- be able to use it to help the counsellee to change.

It is important to re-emphasise, most mistakes appear to occur from losing connection with the counsellee and then not having a sufficient understanding of what is happening for the counsellee and their issues.

The outcomes obtainable from this section

At the end of this section, you should be able to respond to the following questions:

- Understanding: The important information required
  - » What is a helpful checklist?
- Locating the issues (jigsaw pieces) on the Circles:
  - » In which four areas of functioning can the Circles be placed?
  - » What are the three 'brushes' that colour the Circles?
- The social circle:
  - » What are the components of this?
- The physical circle:
  - » What are the four sectors made of?
- The mind circle:
  - » What are the five sectors made of?
- The personality circle:
  - » What are the six sectors of personality?
  - » How are the six sectors connected to core beliefs?
  - » What are some strengths of the CWF approach to understanding personality?
  - » How does the CWF link with other models of personality?
  - » In what ways do all the circles contribute to personality?
  - » How are the six sectors ordered in relation to the developmental lifespan?
  - » In what way does the 'centredness' sector provide a second dimension for change?

- The central circle of the spirit:
    - » What is the 'spirit' circle?
    - » What are the spiritual *provisions* one can have?
    - » What is the *purpose* of the spirit?
    - » Where can one be *positioned* in the spirit?
    - » What are the two aspects of God's *presence* in relation to the spiritual? (Answer: with and in)
- Which are the relevant past circles to locate?

You will be able to find out what information you are missing through locating:

Where Mandy is at NOW
You will be able to locate many of the *Jigsaw* pieces, or the details of how Mandy is, as she gives them to you. Then you can define and ask for the pieces of the jigsaw (information) she does not volunteer. You will then be able to identify what is above and below the *water level* i.e. what is going well and where she may be struggling.

Where Mandy has come from in the PAST
You will be able to graph the relevant issues in terms of the amount or volume of problems and positives over time. Then you will be more able to link the connections between what might be termed her *roots* from her past, to where she is at now and where she is heading in the future, or her *shoots*.

USING THE CHECKLIST AND THE CIRCLES

To determine: What information am I missing? To get all relevant jigsaw pieces to gain a clear picture of Mandy use:

- A checklist, and/or
- The shapes, especially the Circles.

SAMPLE CHECKLIST

This is an example of a standard checklist to ensure you are not missing essential material.

Contact

- Referral: 'Why?' 'Who?'
  - » 'Why have you come?' (What were the precipitants?)
  - » 'Who recommended that you come?'
  - » 'Why have you come to see me?' (As opposed to anyone else)
- Demographics: age, culture, gender, location of accommodation and who they are living with, job/school.
- Observation: (otherwise known as Mental State Examination MSE). Especially observation of social aspects (i.e. what is happening in the interaction between you and the counsellee), physical, mind and heart circles.

Current issues

- 'What are the problems that are concerning you?'
- Use the screening questions below to exclude other concerns in the present.

Past issues

Locate these by linking the present with any past similar problems relating to the following areas:

- External: stress/trauma/events
- Social: work/school, legal, loss and separation
- Medical: hospitalisation, head injuries, thyroid problems
- Physical: substance abuse/alcohol
- Mental: educational/psychiatric/psychological/counselling
- Spiritual: experiences, relationship with God and the church
- Developmental
- Family

And/or use the Circles and the Square to locate where Mandy is at. So...

This is what I do!

I use the Circles with virtually every patient I see. Normally I have two pieces of paper, one A3 portrait rather than landscape, where I draw the set of circles for the present. I then have a separate sheet of A4 paper with a set of circles for the past. In my consultations and supervisions I normally place the one A4 piece of paper in a landscape position. On the left of the paper, there is a small set of circles of the past. Over the rest of the page, there is one set of circles for the present. These circles provide me with:

- a pair of spectacles to see the patient/client clearly
- a jigsaw puzzle template so I can collect all the relevant pieces of the jigsaw and complete the jigsaw picture.

I receive the pieces of the jigsaw puzzle as the patient provides them, in the order they choose. Often they commence with information for the outer circles. I prefer to start with the present and with the most relevant issues if possible. Here are some examples of what I do.

For counsellees I am seeing, the present circles are laid out on two A4 pieces stuck together, as in the example below.

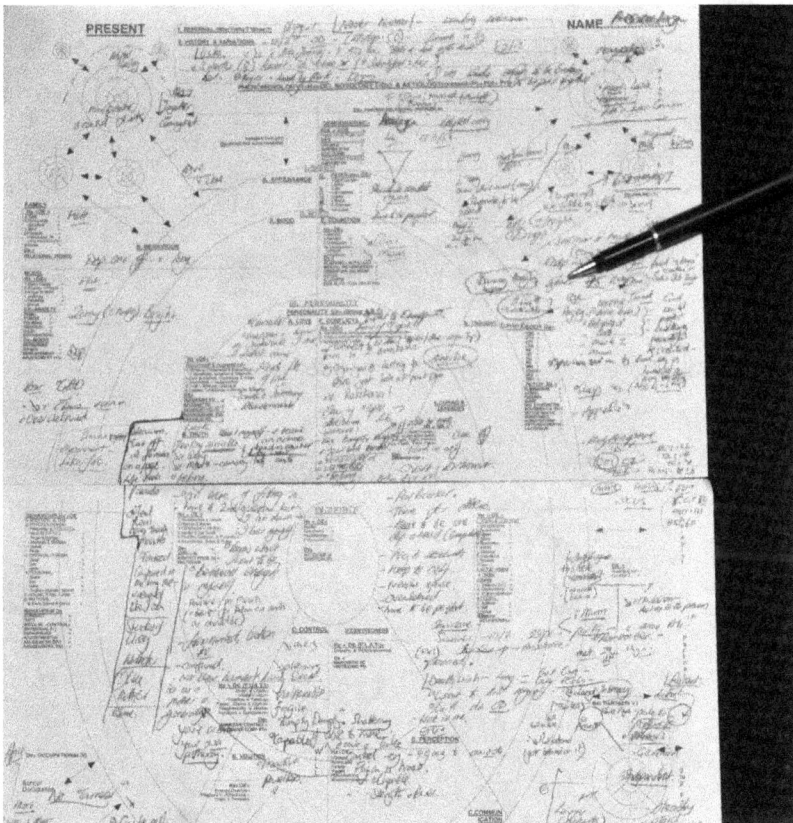

For supervision, I tend to use a single A4 sheet in a landscape position, as in the example below.

On the following page is a copy of a template I have also used.

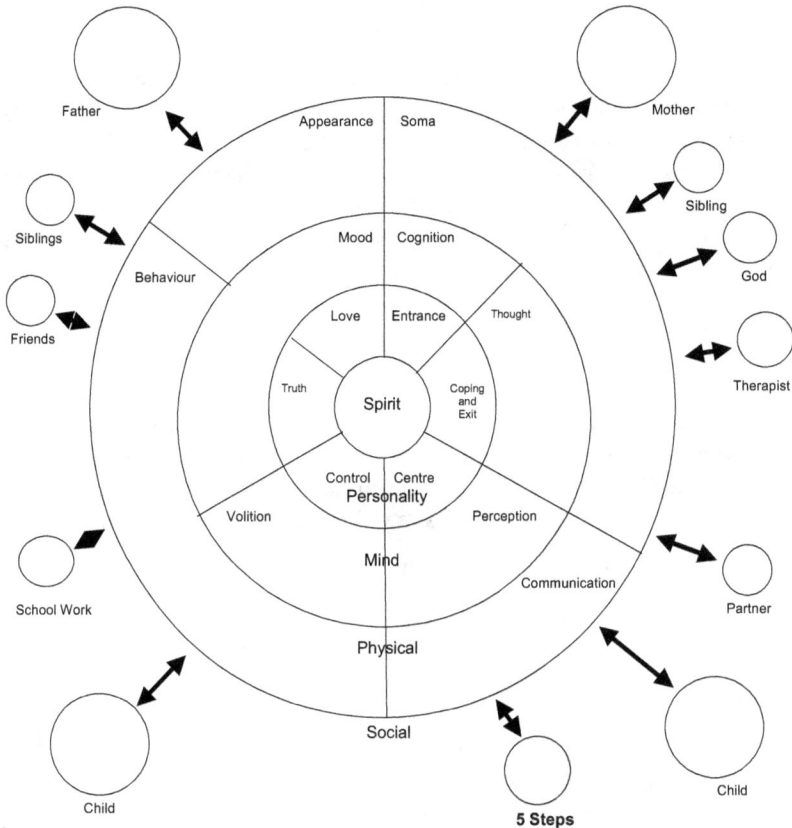

The Circles and the sectors

The sectors: The Circles are subdivided into a number of sectors. These sectors contain various elements relating to the particular circle of the person. The sectors are structured like a jigsaw puzzle and sequenced in a similar order to:

- Personality Development
- The Mental State Examination (MSE)
    - » The MSE is based on the various components of the person which one can observe in an interview. It is widely available, particularly in psychiatry textbooks. Interestingly, it was after the order of the CWF sectors was developed that it was recognised

that the sequence of the sectors correlated with the various components and headings of the MSE.

The sectors within the Circles are like jigsaw pieces. The sectors also interact with each other both within the same circle and with sectors of other circles. Each sector can influence other circles/sectors and each sector is also affected by input from other circles/sectors. Each circle expresses itself/exits in a centrifugal (moving outward) direction, through one of the four sectors of the physical circle. Knowing the sectors of the circle ensures you don't miss out information from the counsellee.

The Square and the quadrants of the Square

As mentioned at the beginning of the book, **Mandy is made up of five circles: spirit, personality, mind, physical and social.** Each of these circles can be located in any of the four cells or *quadrants*. These four quadrants illustrate where any of our circles may be functioning in practice at any particular time.

	Self-centred	God-centred
Going well	Self-centred Success	God-centred success
Not going well	Self-centred suffering	God-centred suffering

The Square
Categorical boxes are outlined for ease. In reality, both sides of the Square are dimensions of change on a continuum (e.g. from 0–10). Thus on the

vertical axis one can be functioning from 0–10, from not going well to superior functioning. Indeed, sanctification is a journey from self-centredness to God-centredness. On the horizontal axis, one may have degrees of self-centredness or God-centredness.

In addition to the quadrants are:

The rows

- On the top row of the Square, things are going well. There are strengths, gifts, healthy functioning and life satisfaction/actualisation.
- On the bottom row there are struggles, needs and suffering.
- The line between the two rows is known as the *waterline*. When a person is above the waterline they are functioning/flying and when they are below they are struggling/sinking.

The columns

- The left-hand column is sinful living, where sin is defined as 'I' (or other people or anything else) placed in the middle of one's life, where God should be. (A helpful hint to remember this is noting that 'I' is the middle letter of the word, 'sIn'.)
- In the right-hand column is Godly living.

The corners

- The top right-hand corner of the Square represents heaven where we receive *new bodies* (Rom. 8:23-25). Heaven is where the presence of God dwells and there is *no more suffering* (Rev. 21:2-4). This is a place which is good and right. This is a place where people can truly live – forever!
- The bottom left-hand corner of the Square represents hell. This place is an evil place of destruction representing all that is bad and wrong. (Interestingly 'evil' spelt back to front is 'live'.) Hell is a place God never initially designed or intended.

Christianity is not an insurance against suffering. Suffering is very much a part of a biblical life. We are called to expect and to use trials for growth (Rom. 5:3-5). Indeed, trials and suffering can be used for our good in that *we become more like Christ* (Rom. 8:28, 29).

Therefore any part of our life may be placed in any of these four quadrants including our:

- Social life: Our relationships, work and church life.

- Physical life: Our time, health, behaviour and communication. *Offer your bodies as a living sacrifice* (Rom. 12:1).

- Mind: Our feelings and intuition, passions and interests, our imaginations and visions for our lives, our thoughts and ideas, our intellect. Right sided living surrenders all of these to God. *Be transformed by the renewing of your minds* (Rom. 12:2).

- Personality/heart: Having God-centred self-esteem, self-identity and self-control.

- Spirit: Even expressions of spiritual life can be self-centred like the Pharisees.

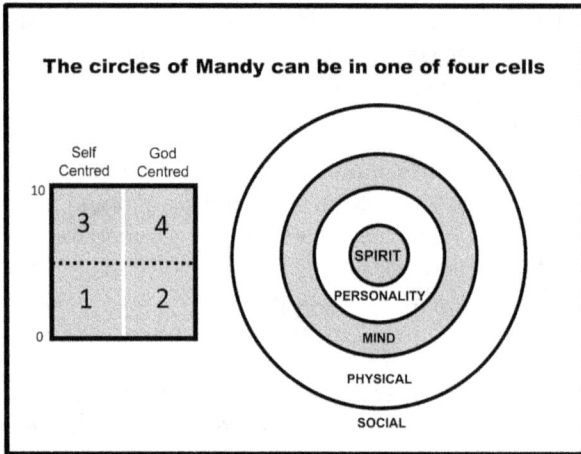

The circles of Mandy can be in one of four cells

God wants all of our circles, i.e. the whole of us to be holy. *May the God of peace sanctify you* (place you in the right-hand column) *wholly*, i.e. through and through. *May your whole spirit, soul and body be kept blameless.* (1 Thess: 5, 23) It is important to look at all the circles, not just the ones that lie under the water level (the dotted line of the Square), but also the circles above. Identifying their strengths can assist the counsellee to look at and face their struggles.

UNDERSTAND–LOCATE WHERE THE PERSON IS AT IN THE CIRCLES

The reason for starting in the outer circles is that it is often the location of the initial conversation. The social circle relates to anyone outside oneself, including God. Although He is within us, He is also external to us. He is the God who is with and the God who is in. He is the God who is 'within.'

A reminder of the questions in the social, physical, mind, personality circles:

- The social circle: What are the components of this circle?
- The physical circle: What are the four sectors made of?
- The mind circle: What are the five sectors made of?
- The personality circle: Refer to the section on understanding the personality.
- The spirit circle: Refer to the section on understanding the spirit.

The Three Brushes that colour the Circles

Over all of the circles are painted three different colours of the three main demographic variables; age, gender and culture. these colours do not change the structure of the circles. The colours are deeper/stronger as they spread outwards from the centre. Thus the influence of these three variables is most apparent in the social and physical circles,but becomes less strong in the more central circles. Thus a young Asian boy outwardly is very different from a senior Caucasian female. However, both have similar heart needs and can have the same spirit position.

The Social Circle

As with all circles, the social circle can be located in any of the four quadrants. We succeed or suffer in our social lives in a God-centred or self-centred way. In order to have a comprehensive view of the picture, it is important to know what parts make up the social circle.

Of all the circles, the parts of the social circle are arranged and ordered most loosely. The main positions are defined with firstly God being in the top right-hand area, to coincide with where the person is placed in relation to God in the shape of the triangle. Secondly, the family of origin, one's spouse and children are placed to coincide with the layout of a genogram. You may want to change the order of these to suit your liking or culture. You may want to place the components to fit more in line with the base of the Pyramid.

Within the social circle, counsellees will talk about the following:

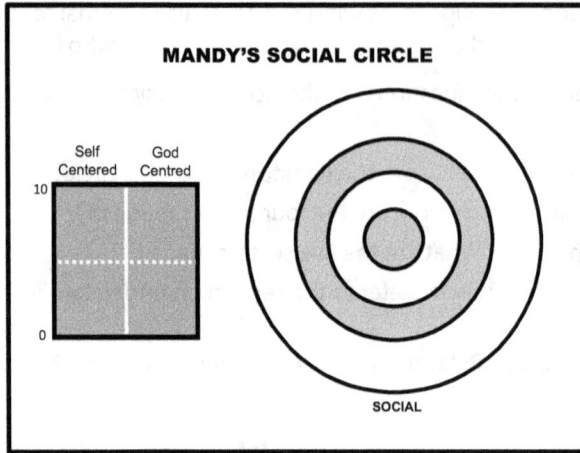

MANDY'S SOCIAL CIRCLE

Self Centered   God Centred

10

0

SOCIAL

- **Family**: Including spouse and children.
  - » Mandy is having an affair. This means she has severe marital problems.
- **Family of origin**: Including siblings and parents.
  - » Mandy's family of origin is distant and she has little support from them. Ideally her extended family would have an appropriate degree of closeness (not enmeshment) for support and would be empowering and releasing of her.
- **Friends**: Including peers.
  - » Mandy has withdrawn from most of her friends/acquaintances except for a couple of close friends. Her friendships need to be a place for closeness and respect that release rather than restrict her.
- **Church**:
  - » Mandy feels disconnected from church, as though she does not belong. She feels restricted within herself by her church experience. She feels she must fake it in front of other church attendees, in order to be acceptable.
- **Work**: (school for children/younger people)
  - » Although work is going satisfactorily, Mandy recognises she is not performing as well as previously. Obviously, work and school include other functions in addition to the social aspects like intellectual capacity, which is located within the mind circle.
- **Counsellor**:

» Mandy has recently experienced a confidentiality breach from a counsellor.

- **God**:
  » Mandy has experienced a distancing not just in her horizontal social life with others, but also in her vertical life with God. She has also become legalistic in her relationship with God.

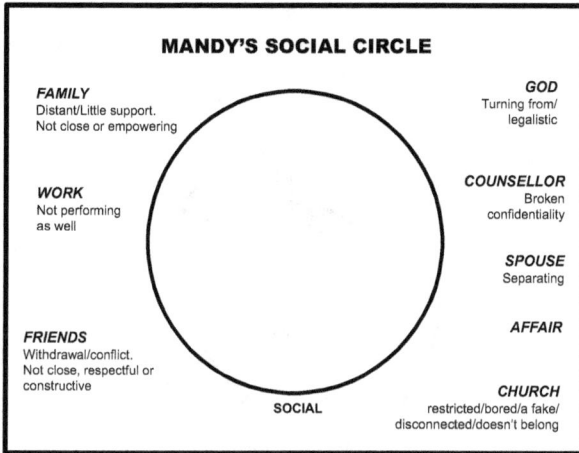

MANDY'S SOCIAL CIRCLE

FAMILY
Distant/Little support.
Not close or empowering

GOD
Turning from/
legalistic

WORK
Not performing
as well

COUNSELLOR
Broken
confidentiality

SPOUSE
Separating

FRIENDS
Withdrawal/conflict.
Not close, respectful or
constructive

AFFAIR

SOCIAL

CHURCH
restricted/bored/a fake/
disconnected/doesn't belong

The Physical Circle

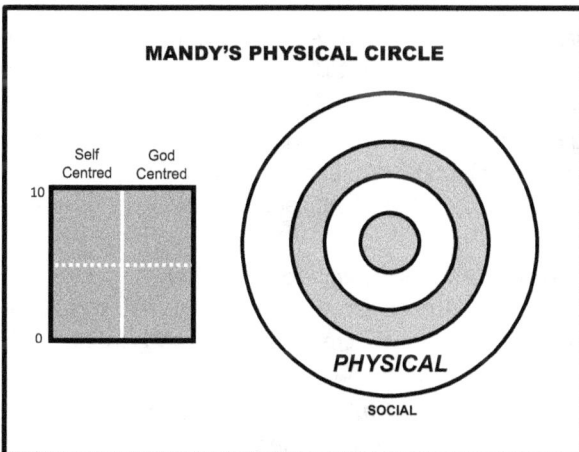

MANDY'S PHYSICAL CIRCLE

Self
Centred

God
Centred

10

0

PHYSICAL

SOCIAL

As with any circle, the physical circle can be in any of the four quadrants. In this way our physical life can be succeeding or suffering in a God-centred or self-centred way. Also, anything occurring in the inside circles, whether good or bad, has only four exits of expression, the four physical sectors. Because the sectors of the physical circle are the only exits, it makes the evidence found here to be more significant, and are thus also windows into the internal circles.

Mandy's inner functioning is expressed through the sectors of her physical circle.

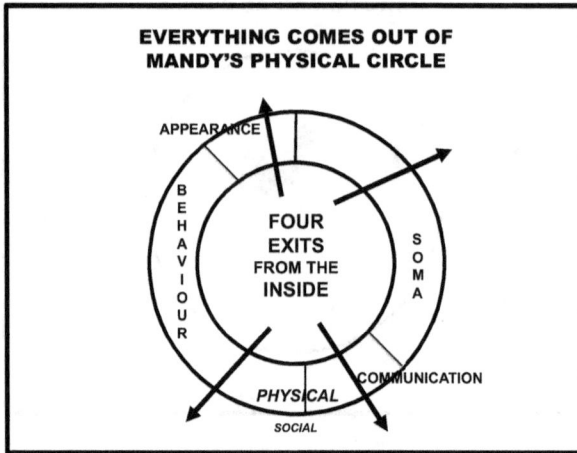

EVERYTHING COMES OUT OF
MANDY'S PHYSICAL CIRCLE

APPEARANCE

BEHAVIOUR

FOUR
EXITS
FROM THE
INSIDE

SOMA

COMMUNICATION

PHYSICAL

SOCIAL

These are the four sectors within the physical circle in an anticlockwise direction.

1. **Appearance:** Mandy is not dressing as well as she could, or keeping her appearance as she used to.

2. **Behaviour**: Behaviour relates specifically to activities and actions including doing tasks/activities of daily living and use of time (including leisure activities). Mandy is less active and is not as focused on completing tasks of daily living. All sectors and circles have a behavioural expression including:

   » **Spiritual behaviours**: Including spiritual disciplines, such as the use of Scripture, prayer and worship. Mandy's Bible reading and prayer time has increased, significantly influenced by her worsening anxieties.

   » **Attitudinal behaviours** (from the personality circle in particular): Mandy's behaviours are less caring and less respectful. She is doing less, as she becomes more desperate. She is less outward looking and copes by faking and withdrawing. There is also more conflictual behaviour with those around her.

» **Behaviours of the mind**: Moods of depression, irritability and anxiety are expressed in her behaviour and actions. Her diminished energy is expressed as boredom. Poor concentration and memory results in problematic behaviour like flitting from one activity to another and not focusing on anything in particular.

» **Physical behaviours** (in other sectors than behaviour): Communication is expressed through behaviour in things like silence or non-verbal communication. Her bodily systems (soma) are expressed through behaviour by things like having less sexual activity, sleep or exercise and eating more junk food.

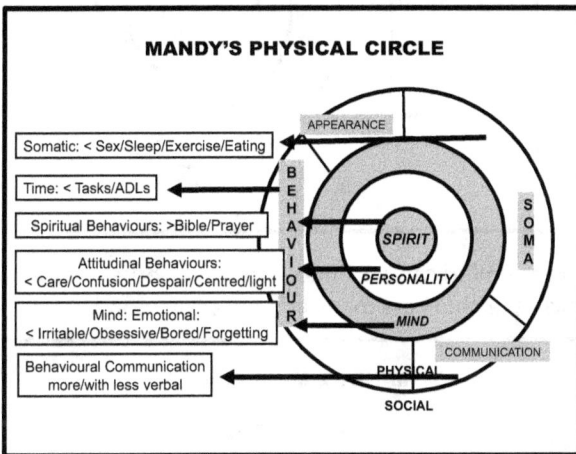

MANDY'S PHYSICAL CIRCLE

APPEARANCE

Somatic: < Sex/Sleep/Exercise/Eating

Time: < Tasks/ADLs

Spiritual Behaviours: >Bible/Prayer

Attitudinal Behaviours:
< Care/Confusion/Despair/Centred/light

Mind: Emotional:
< Irritable/Obsessive/Bored/Forgetting

Behavioural Communication
more/with less verbal

BEHAVIOUR

SPIRIT

PERSONALITY

MIND

SOMA

COMMUNICATION

PHYSICAL

SOCIAL

Legend: < is worse or less of > is better or more of

3. **Communication**: The communication sector refers to verbal (oral and written) communication received (especially through eyes and ears) and transmitted through the mouth. For communication to be effective it needs to be clear, consistent, considerate, constructive and cooperative. Mandy's ability to communicate, i.e. listen and express herself effectively has diminished.

4. **Soma**: This refers to the systems of the body. In counselling the major systems involved are the brain, the endocrine system and sexual function. The soma also includes aspects of physical wellbeing including diet, drugs/alcohol and exercise.

The Mind Circle

As with any circle, the mind circle can be in any of the four quadrants. In this way our mind realm can be succeeding or suffering in a God-centred or self-centred way.

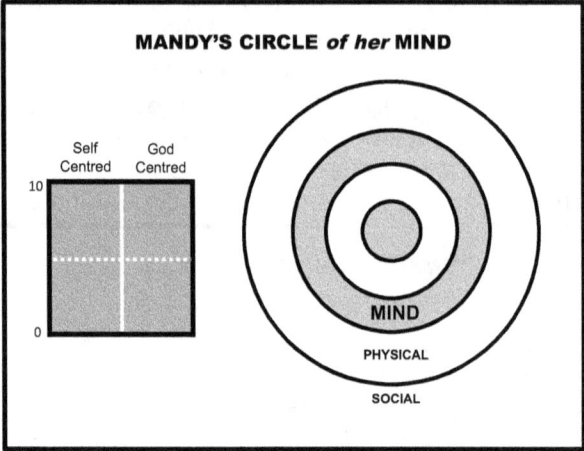

Any sector in the mind can be influenced by any other sector in any other circle. For example, there are many influences on mood.

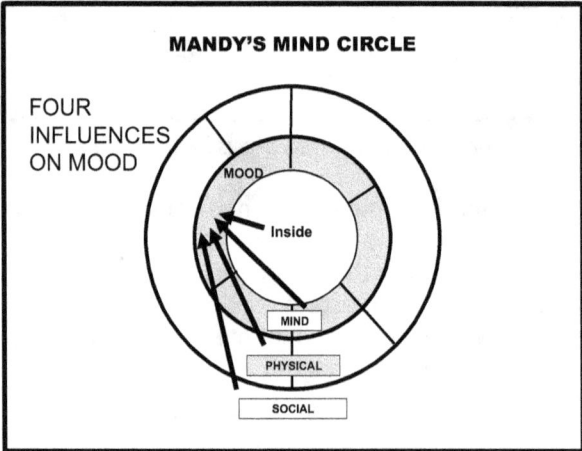

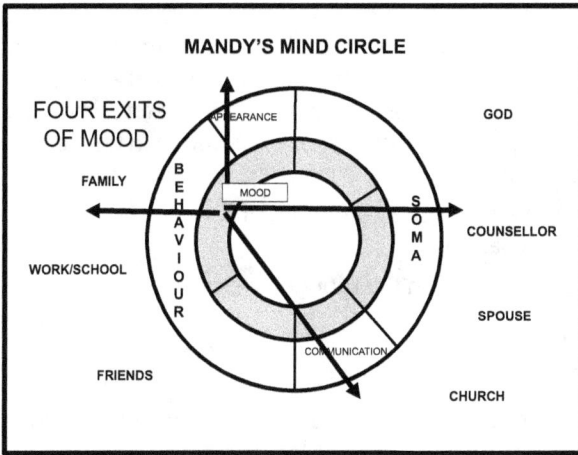

MANDY'S MIND CIRCLE

Any sector in the mind circle (e.g. the mood sector) can exit through any of the physical sectors. We will look at the **five sectors** within the mind circle in an anticlockwise direction. The order of the five sectors is the same as the order of the standard Mental State Examination.

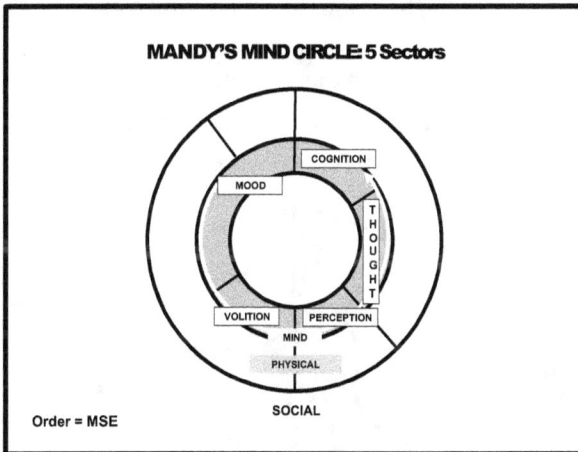

Most of these sectors are affected in a negative way with Mandy.

1. Mood

All aspects are worse with Mandy.

> » The three negative moods include anger/frustration, sadness, anxiety/worry.

» The three positive moods include the emotion of love (although love located in the heart circle is deeper than the feeling love in the mood circle), joy/happiness (not mania) and peace. Interestingly, the first three fruits of the Spirit are *love, joy and peace* (Gal. 5:22). Love, faith and hope are referred to in the personality at a deeper level than in the mind.

» Erotic feelings are a composite of somatic changes as well as mood changes.

» Mood mixed with the thought sector results in *intuition*.

2. Volition

All aspects are lowered with Mandy.

» Volition is like the petrol tank of the person and includes energy, passion and pleasure.

» It is part of the will. If someone is depressed their volition will be low and this can affect their will. The other part of will is in the personality under the control sector. The sectors of volition and control combine to form the segment of the will.

» Includes passion for things like tasks, sexual energy/libido and life in general.

» Volition mixed with the thought sector results in *interest*.

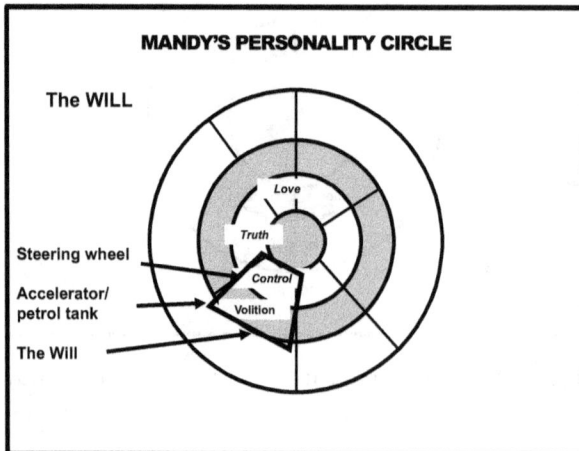

MANDY'S PERSONALITY CIRCLE

The WILL

Love

Truth

Steering wheel

Control

Accelerator/ petrol tank

Volition

The Will

3. Perception

» Involves the five senses of hearing, seeing, touching, tasting and smell.

> » Abnormal sensory experiences include hallucinations and mis-perceptions. Mandy is most likely having hypnagognic hallucinations as she is going to sleep, but demonic influence may be a possibility.
>
> » Perception is the place of vision for life (or anything), for coaching purposes.
>
> » Perception mixed with the thought sector results in *imagination*.

4. Thinking

> » Thoughts, plans, ideas and beliefs. Beliefs are stronger than ideas. Abnormal, unreal beliefs are called delusions, an example is delusions of persecution.
>
> » Distorted thinking includes catastrophic thinking. This is where something is all good or all bad, for example with eating disorders if one biscuit is eaten, the whole packet might as well be consumed. (See the mind tool bag for other types of distorted thoughts, including distant, personalised, defended and mood based thinking.)
>
> » Suicidal and self harm ideas. Mandy has negative *ideas*.

5. Cognition

> » The cognitive sector of the mind is connected to the biological brain.
>
> » Memory, attention/concentration, intelligence and orientation. Orientation is more affected in situations such as delirium. Mandy's memory and concentration are reduced.
>
> » Cognition mixed with the thought sector results in *inventions*.

The Personality Circle

The personality is referred to in other contexts (e.g. in lay situations) as the heart or the soul and even the spirit.

Questions for this section:

- What are the six sectors of personality?
- How are the six sectors connected to core beliefs?
- What are the five strengths of the CWF of personality?
- How does the CWF link with other models?
- In what ways do all the circles contribute to personality?

- How are the six sectors ordered in relation to the developmental lifespan?
- In what way does the 'centredness' sector provide a second dimension for change?

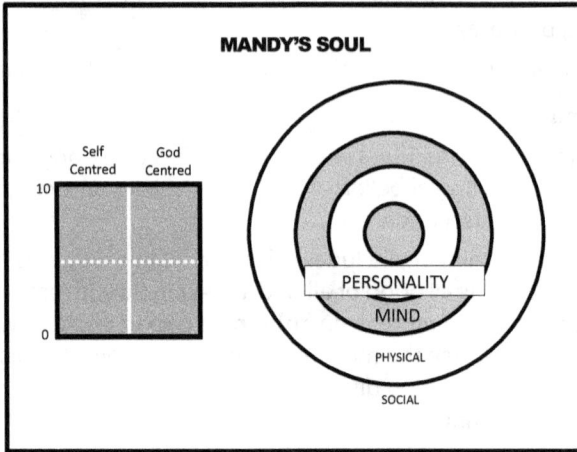

As with any circle, the personality circle can be in any of the four quadrants. In this way our heart/personality can be succeeding or suffering in a God-centred or self-centred way.

The personality circle has six sectors, summarised in an anticlockwise direction. Notice how love, faith and hope fit into the first three sectors. Christians often get the 'four selfs' confused, particularly when referring to self-denial. Let's look at the personality of Jesus.

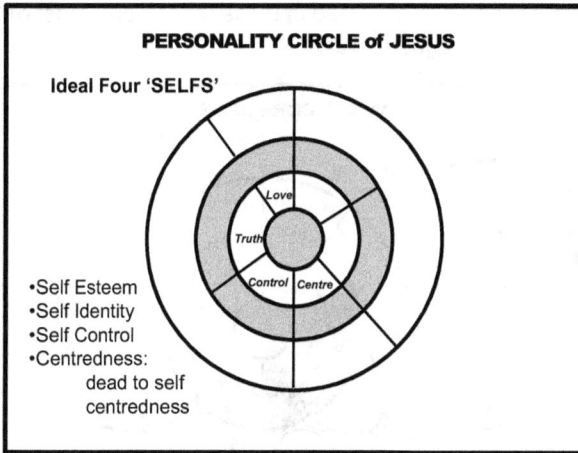

PERSONALITY CIRCLE of JESUS

Ideal Four 'SELFS'

•Self Esteem
•Self Identity
•Self Control
•Centredness:
 dead to self
 centredness

Jesus had high self esteem, self identity and self control yet was very much God-centred and dead to self or selfishness. Notice how the core beliefs are attached to various sectors and how the first three of the 5 Steps are placed in the various sectors, as detailed below.

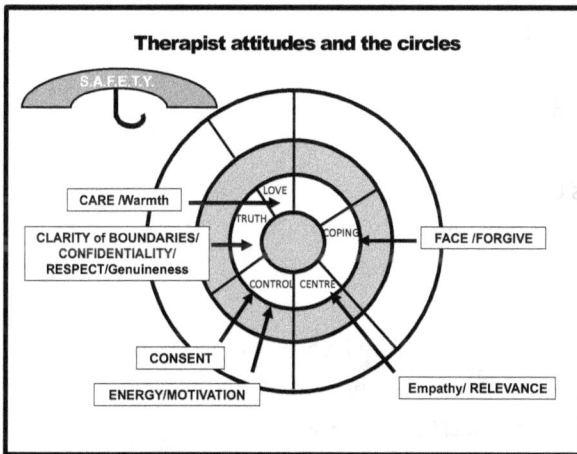

Therapist attitudes and the circles

Heart safety or an internal sense of security is largely seen as an umbrella over the whole person. Interpersonal safety at its core needs a basis of connection and love, which is associated with the love sector. Therapist attitudes, therapy and church culture can also be categorised in these sectors.

Mandy's core beliefs can be located in these sectors and most of these sectors are affected in a negative way.

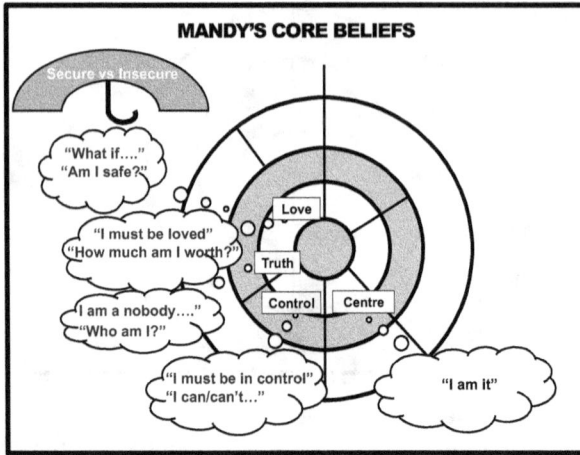

MANDY'S CORE BELIEFS

Most of these sectors are affected in a negative way with Mandy. The sectors of Core Beliefs and their contents:

1. Love sector includes:

- Self-esteem
- Worth/value
- Care
- Trust vs betrayal
- Intimacy vs isolation
- Attachment
- **Love**
- Core beliefs: How much am I worth? I must be loved...
- 5 Steps: The first step of connection is located here
- Therapist attitudes: Care and warmth
- Church culture: Relationship is central to church values.

2. Truth sector includes:

- Self-identity
- Respect: Involves seeing the reality, truth and existence of the other person
- Boundaries: Clear vs unclear/confused. Represents the truth of where self begins and ends.

- Role clarity/confusion: What is my role and what is yours?
- Purpose/sense of direction: Where am I going in life?
- Genuine and real
- Morals: A sense of right and wrong (now blurred in a post-modern world)
- **Faith**: Involves seeing the reality, truth and existence of God (doubt/ questioning is located more in the mind sector, while unbelief is here)
- Core beliefs: Who am I? I am a ...
- 5 Steps: The second step of understanding is located here
- Therapist attitudes: Confidentiality, clarity of boundaries, genuineness and respect
- Church culture: Reality is encouraged.

3. **Control sector** includes:
- The will: The steering wheel of the will is linked with volition; the petrol tank of the will is the mood sector. Control and volition sectors combine to form the segment of the will
- Choice
- Capacity to respond
- Confidence
- Courage
- Responsibility and blame
- Impulsiveness vs compulsiveness
- **Hope**
- Core beliefs: I must be in control. I can/I can't...
- 5 Steps: The third step of responding is located here
- Therapist attitudes: Consent
- Church culture: Leadership that is releasing rather than restricting.

4. **Centred sector** includes:
- Empathy
- Narcissism: self-centredness
- Altruism: other-centredness
- Sanctification: God-centredness
- Sinful nature/sin: 'I' (or others) in the middle where God should be
- Sacrifice, servanthood, stewardship, submission, surrender

- Core beliefs: The world revolves around me!
- Therapist attitudes: Empathy and a sense of relevance
- Church culture: God-centred relevance.

5. Coping and the exit of the heart/personality includes:

- Constructive: Facing, forgiving, having fun and living the fight of faith
- Destructive: Fight, flight, freak, flop, fake
- Living the great commandment; obeying the great commission; communication, commitment and capacity for change
- Church culture: Openness in an undefended, safe atmosphere.

This sector was originally defined as the 'coping' sector. It is the sector of the 'defences' in psychodynamic language. More recently, there is an increased awareness of this sector being also the exit of the heart. The expression can be constructive or destructive.

6. Conflict and the entrance to the heart/personality includes:

- Conflict: The place where stress/trauma enters the heart
- Entrance to the heart of messages from self (aspects of the mind including thoughts and beliefs as well as memories), from others and from God.
- Sensitivity spectrum to the entrance of the heart: Some of us are like an egg without a shell, taking things personally and being easily hurt. Conversely, some of us are like soccer balls, kicked around by the knocks of life yet seemingly unaffected.

This sector was originally defined as the conflict sector, particularly focusing on the core aspects of issues that caused conflict. There is now an increased awareness that this sector is the entrance of the heart. It is the door of the heart and contains the most sensitive issues. (Often these issues refer to the main sectors of the heart, including shame and rejection vs love in the love sector, guilt and confusion vs forgiveness, clarity and faith in the truth sector, and despair vs hope in the control sector.)

The exit and entrance sector are combined as a segment and they influence each other. Accordingly the more defended one is in the exit of the heart, the more closed off one will be in the entrance of the heart. The combined coping and entrance sectors are a bit like a hotel revolving door, allowing people and influences to enter and exit. For example someone hurt in childhood may be closed off to bad things. However, that also closes off the entrance of good experiences. They remain fixated and unable to progress from the original hurt. This causes ongoing and compounding grief and loss.

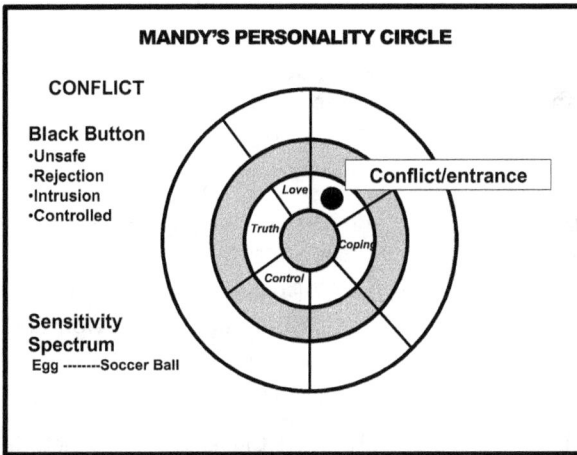

MANDY'S PERSONALITY CIRCLE

CONFLICT

Black Button
•Unsafe
•Rejection
•Intrusion
•Controlled

Conflict/entrance

Love

Truth

Coping

Control

Sensitivity
Spectrum
Egg --------Soccer Ball

Mandy is not coping well with conflict.

WHAT IS THE CWF VIEW OF PERSONALITY?

Having the right understanding of personality is critical for assessment purposes. Also a significant amount of in-depth therapy is based on having a robust framework of the heart of the person. Personality can be viewed from a number of approaches or perspectives.

Dimensions
Dimensional and Categorical: The CWF encourages an approach which defines personality issues on a scale or line as a continuum as opposed to 'either/or' categorisation. In this way the framework views people with varying degrees of fullness/emptiness, function/dysfunction, progress/delay expressed in a combination and variety of sectors.

Variables
Multiple vs Unitary: The CWF promotes understanding the combination of multiple factors to define the whole. The use of sectors within the Circles provides multiple variables which can give a unique picture or finger print. The CWF regards people through a number of defined personality variables/sectors.

Usefulness

- Practical and Theoretical: Both are encouraged by the CWF. The CWF seeks to be thematically rigorous and integrates with mainline theories of personality.
- Assessment and Therapy: An understanding of personality and its consistent and useful application to assessment and therapy is central to the CWF.

Application

- Gender, age and culture: The framework is flexible across gender, age range and diversity of cultural expression.
- Individuals and systems: The CWF view of personality applies to individuals as well as systems like marriage, family, work and social groups.

Style

- Visual Pictures and Words: The CWF Circles provide a pictorial language where words can be used with shapes and pictures to explain personality.

HOW DOES THE CWF APPROACH TO PERSONALITY FIT WITH OTHER MODELS?

The following models of personality are described relating the parameters and variables to the CWF Circles and sectors.

Diagnostic Statistical Manual (DSM IV)

Personality is defined as an enduring pattern of inner experience and behaviour, in terms of:

- Relationships (social sector)
- Affect (mood sector)
- Ways of perceiving (perception/thought sector)
- Control of the impulses (control sector).

From a CWF perspective, this is a broad and loosely defined definition. By adding things like personality variables that include issues to do with worth, identity and significance the CWF builds on existing ideas and models.

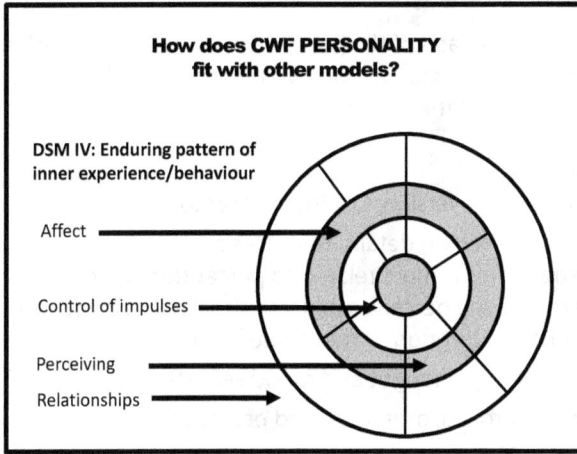

How does CWF PERSONALITY fit with other models?

DSM IV: Enduring pattern of inner experience/behaviour

Affect

Control of impulses

Perceiving

Relationships

Cloninger's approach to personality

- Harm avoidance (related to the serotonin system): Coping sector.
- Novelty seeking (related to the dopamine system): Coping sector.
- Reward dependence (related to the adrenaline system): Control sector.
- Persistence: Control/coping sector.

Five Factor Model

- Kindness/agreeableness: Love sector (Can also be used in a defensive way and therefore is included in the coping sector).
- Responsibility/conscientiousness: Control sector.
- Neuroticism: Coping sector (anxiety is also included and is located in the mood sector).
- Extroversion: Coping sector.
- Openness to experience: Conflict sector/entrance.

Other models, including their variables and corresponding CWF sectors, are as follows.

Thomas and Chess

Rhythmicity, mood, task orientation: Control, mood and cognitive sectors.

Erikson

The developmental basis of the person: This model is closely linked to the CWF. The extent of this connection was recognised only after the development and ordering of the sectors.

Myers-Briggs

- Extraversion-Introversion: Coping/exit sector.
- Sensing: Determining details, tangibles and intuition or big picture and abstract. This is more related to perception sector, determining whether someone perceives in details (through a microscope) or in the big picture (through a wide angle lens).
- Thinking-Feeling: Thought and mood sectors.
- Judging: Controlled, organised and perceiving vs spontaneous, casual: Control sector

La Haye

- Melancholic: mood sector
- Sanguine: coping sector
- Choleric: control sector
- Phlegmatic: control sector

A.A. Milne

Winnie the Pooh: For interest think about how Pooh, Eeyore, Tigger and Piglet vary in terms of personality!

COMBINING THE CWF AND OTHER MODELS

From the CWF and theories of personality, the personality circle is contributed to and influenced by:

The 3 Brushes

1. Gender.
2. Culture.
3. Age.

Although personality has enduring patterns, there is a developmental aspect to personality and its expression, particularly in childhood where the personality is still elastic (psychology uses the word, 'plastic') and impressionable. However, the basic structure remains the same.

Physical circle

Personality has a biological basis to it which is generally referred to as 'temperament' (Thomas and Chess).

Mind circle

- Mood: Melancholic or the feeling/intuitive/right brain aspects of personality.
- Volition: Energy and affect or mood intensity.
- Perception: The big picture person vs the person focused on details.
- Thought: Thinking/cognitive/left brain personality.
- Cognition: Intellect has a lot to do with personality.

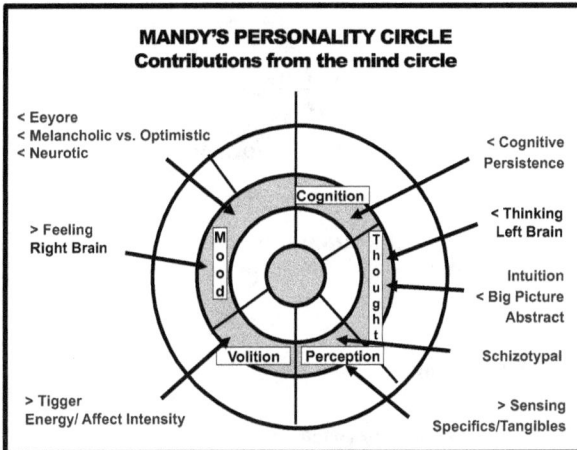

MANDY'S PERSONALITY CIRCLE
Contributions from the mind circle

< Eeyore
< Melancholic vs. Optimistic
< Neurotic

< Cognitive
Persistence

> Feeling
Right Brain

< Thinking
Left Brain

Cognition

Intuition
< Big Picture
Abstract

Mood

Thought

Schizotypal

Volition   Perception

> Tigger
Energy/ Affect Intensity

> Sensing
Specifics/Tangibles

Legend: < is decreased or less > is increased or more
In Mandy's Mind Circle, > energy refers to Tigger not Mandy.
Eeyore and Mandy have similarly decreased mood levels!

Personality development

After developing the personality sectors, a link between the type and order of the personality sectors and Erikson's stages of development became evident:

Age	Stage	CWF sectors
0-1.5	Trust vs mistrust	Love
1.5-3	Autonomy vs Shame and Doubt*	Control vs Love and Truth
3-5	Initiative vs guilt	Truth
5-13	Industry vs Inferiority	Control vs Truth
13-21	Identity vs Identity Confusion	Truth
21-40	Intimacy vs isolation	Love
40-60	Generativity vs Stagnation	Control
60+	Integrity vs Despair	Truth

*Erikson's 1.5-3 stage is more of a composite of
the sectors control vs love and truth.*

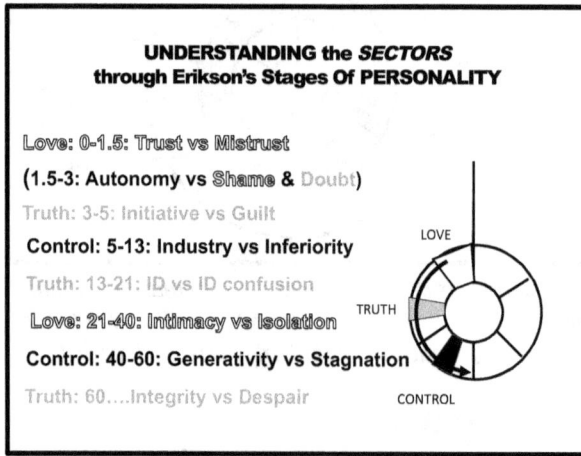

**UNDERSTANDING the *SECTORS*
through Erikson's Stages Of PERSONALITY**

Love: 0-1.5: Trust vs Mistrust

(1.5-3: Autonomy vs Shame & Doubt)

Truth: 3-5: Initiative vs Guilt

Control: 5-13: Industry vs Inferiority

Truth: 13-21: ID vs ID confusion

Love: 21-40: Intimacy vs Isolation

Control: 40-60: Generativity vs Stagnation

Truth: 60....Integrity vs Despair

LOVE

TRUTH

CONTROL

Self-centred sector and personality

The self-centred sector is highly relevant to both mental health and spirituality. It involves issues of narcissism, empathy and altruism as well as matters of sin and sanctification. Centredness provides a *second dimension* of change. Central to the CWF is the idea of considering change from two perspectives: psychological as well as spiritual. Change includes alteration in functioning as in the DSM: Global Assessment of Functioning (GAF) continuum from 0 to 100 or for example an alteration in life satisfaction/

actualisation. In addition, change is also rated in terms of a continuum of centredness, from self-centredness (and indeed other centredness) to God-centredness. Essentially, one can also have a Global Assessment of Centredness (GAC) dimension of change from left to right. Any of the circles/sectors can be assessed according to these two dimensions of change. This is illustrated in the context of the Square shape.

Two Dimensions of Change

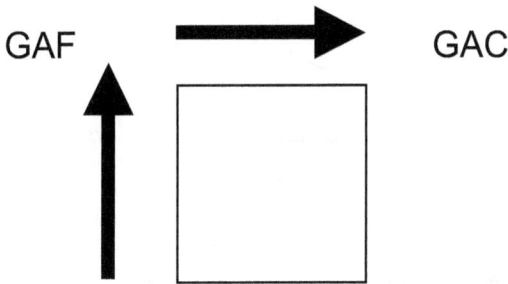

The Spirit Circle

Questions for this section:

- What is the spirit?
- What are the spiritual *provisions* Mandy can have?
- What is the *purpose* of the spirit?
- Where can one be *positioned* in the spirit?
- What are the two characteristics of God's *presence* in relation to spiritual aspects? (Answer: with and in)

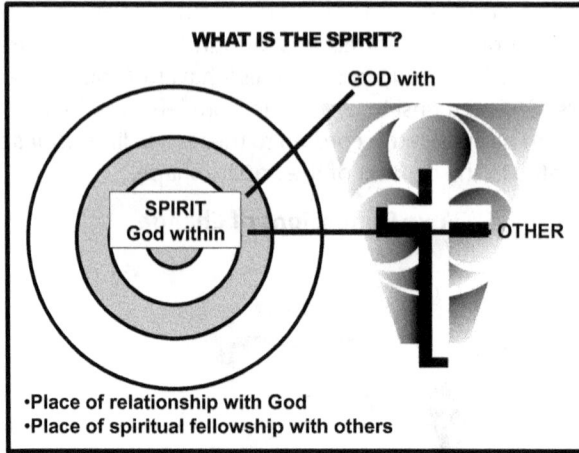

The spirit is the place of relationship with God and the source of the out-flow of that relationship through one's life to others. It is the place of ind-welling of the Holy Spirit. With non-Christians, there can be the indwelling of evil spirits resulting in 'possession.' There is a general opinion that those who are 'born-again' cannot be totally possessed but they can come under demonic influence, otherwise known as 'demonisation.'

The spirit is the centre of our being and the source of our lives. In the Hebrew language it is the 'ruah' and in the Greek it is the 'pneuma.' Both words speak about breath/life. The Bible does not define the spirit in text-book fashion. Instead it provides a range of meanings for this part of the person.

The spirit position: Someone who has become a Christian has had a change in the position of their spirit. They have been born-again into a new family and are transferred into a new kingdom. Metaphorically, they are now grafted into the vine, with a new foundation and can now drink from the source of living water. All of these changes are considered to be past tense in that they occurred when the person became a Christian. In theological language these changes are 'positional' and 'indicative.' *The Spirit of God is living in us* (Rom. 8:9-11). Yet significantly, many of us do not live a life that is congruent with this. For those who have not been born-again or transferred into God's kingdom, their spirit is *dead to God* (Eph. 2:1). The spirit is the place where the shape of the Cross resides.

The spirit practice: The particular expressions of the spirit include spir-itual disciplines like prayer, sacraments, song, Scripture, spiritual warfare and spiritual gifts. These can be found in any of the four quadrants. For example top left-hand quadrant expressions of the spirit are like the Pharisees in the gospels.

The influence of the spirit on the personality/heart

For Mandy, the spirit circle has been having less influence on her. This is because she has forgotten what her spirit position is and has less faith in the reality of what happened to her when she became a Christian. It is easier for her to believe her experience in life, past and present, influenced by things like depression, instead of her positional status in Christ.

Mandy can change. It needs to come from within, as she allows what she already has in the spirit position in her central circle to enter her heart/personality. Change comes through the entrance (conflict) sector and moves into other sectors as she begins to receive God's gifts.

These purposes, provisions and position in God which she receives are illustrated by the circles below.

1. **Mandy's Love sector** can receive:
   - » Provisions of God's unfailing love for shame and aloneness.
   - » Purposes of intimacy with God.
   - » Placement in a justified position with God (Rom. 5: 1, 2).

2. **Mandy's Truth sector** can receive:
   - » Provisions of God's forgiveness for guilt.
   - » Purposes of imitating Christ.
   - » Placement of a new identity with the Father, as a *child of God* (Rom. 8: 15-17) and identification with Christ to the point of being, *united with Him,* in His death, resurrection and ascension (Rom. 6: 5, Eph. 2: 6)

3. **Mandy's Control sector** can receive:
   - » Provisions of freedom to respond to Him.

4. **Mandy's Centred sector** receives:
   - » Placement in a sanctified position set apart for Him and crucified to the old life.

5. **Mandy's Coping/ exit sector** is able to:
   - » Express/reveal the presence of God through all her outer circles.
   - » Live the great commandment and do the great commission.
   - » *Transform her mind* (Rom. 12: 2).

» Change behaviour i.e. *offer her body as a living sacrifice* (Rom. 12: 1).

6. Mandy's Entrance (Conflict) sector is able to:

» Be responsive to the presence of God within, above other influences like self, others, the present or the past.

God's Spirit perfuses into her heart resulting in further changes.

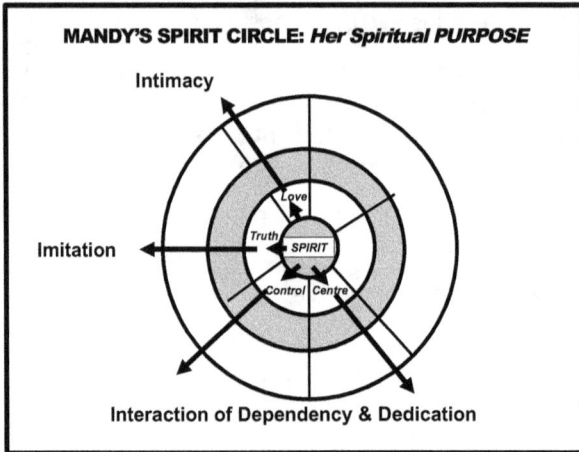

MANDY'S SPIRIT CIRCLE: *Her Spiritual PURPOSE*

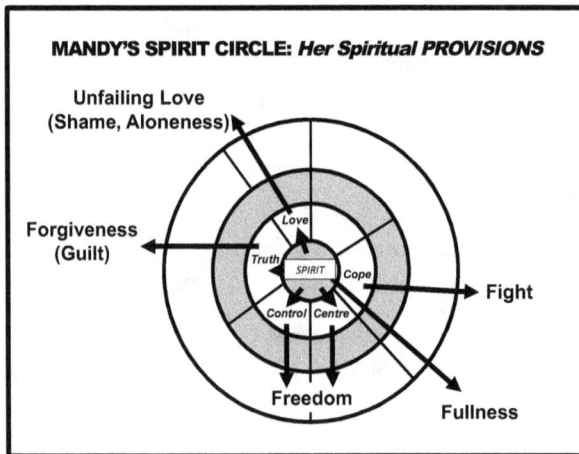

MANDY'S SPIRIT CIRCLE: *Her Spiritual PROVISIONS*

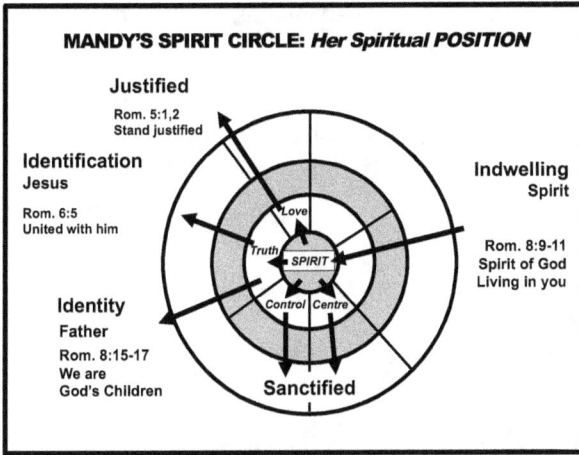

MANDY'S SPIRIT CIRCLE: *Her Spiritual POSITION*

Justified
Rom. 5:1,2
Stand justified

Identification
Jesus
Rom. 6:5
United with him

Indwelling
Spirit
Rom. 8:9-11
Spirit of God
Living in you

Identity
Father
Rom. 8:15-17
We are
God's Children

Sanctified

Love
Truth
SPIRIT
Control Centre

The Past Circles

Understanding Mandy's circles from the past will provide information to understand her circles in the present. As one looks in the past, it is important to look at the circles which have been above as well as below the water level of the Square. For skill development, it's useful to have a big set of circles for the present and another smaller set of circles representing the past alongside.

When looking at the past circles:

- Ask the counsellee about similarities or differences between the past and the present.
- Try to graph extremes of positives and negatives (perhaps using a 0-10 score), noting beginnings and endings.
  - » 'When did this begin?'
  - » 'What was the worst it got to and when was that?'
  - » 'What was the best you've ever been and when?'
  - » 'How have you been in the last couple of weeks?'

Once the patient/client has provided their jigsaw pieces from the past, use a checklist of the Circles to ensure important information is not missed:

- External: Stress/trauma/events
- Social: Work/school, legal, loss and separation

- Medical: Hospitalisations, head injuries, thyroid problems
- Physical: Substance abuse/alcohol
- Mental: Educational/psychiatric/psychological/counselling
- Spiritual: Experiences, relationship with God and the church
- Developmental
- Family

CHECKLIST FOR MANDY'S PAST CIRCLES

SOCIAL

Mandy's past summarised:

- **Family**: Mandy grew up in a dysfunctional family.
  - » Love sector: There was a lack of love.
  - » Truth sector: A role reversal where she had to look after her parents. In addition, she was used in the marital dynamics of one parent against the other (triangulation).
  - » Control Sector: A sense of being blamed.
- **Friends**: Largely a loner with no intimate relationships during teenage years.
- **Church**: Felt used by Church, partly related to being obsessively helpful.
- **School**: Experienced a number of moves and was somewhat obsessive in her work.
- **God**: A long standing, strong faith in God.
- **Events**: One episode of sexual abuse.

Remember to look at the strengths as well as the sufferings and struggles in her social life.

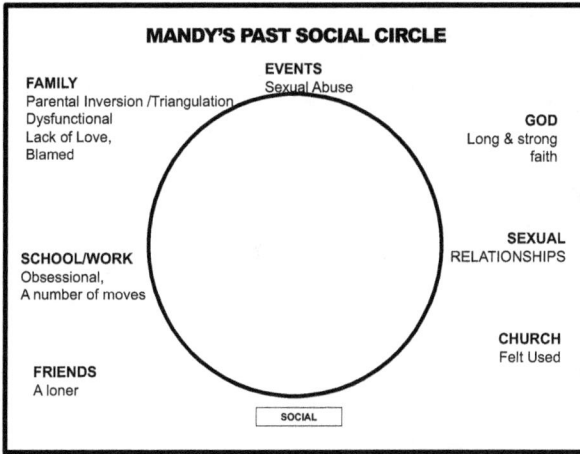

MANDY'S PAST SOCIAL CIRCLE

EVENTS
Sexual Abuse

FAMILY
Parental Inversion /Triangulation
Dysfunctional
Lack of Love,
Blamed

GOD
Long & strong
faith

SEXUAL
RELATIONSHIPS

SCHOOL/WORK
Obsessional,
A number of moves

CHURCH
Felt Used

FRIENDS
A loner

SOCIAL

PHYSICAL

Mandy has been physically well in the past. However check for:

- **Somatic**: past medical issues especially looking at the
  » Central Nervous System: neonatal influences, birth process, developmental milestones, head injuries and fits.
  » Psychosomatic related systems: eating/sleeping problems.
- **Substances**:
  » Alcohol and drugs.
  » Medications. (Antidepressants and Antipsychotics)
  » Food and eating issues
- **Illnesses**: including hospitalisation and visits to doctors other than for the usual mild/common problems.

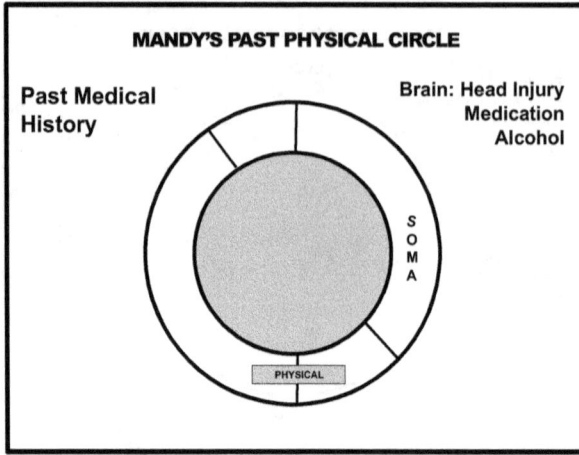

MANDY'S PAST PHYSICAL CIRCLE

MIND

Mandy has experienced depression, anxiety and suicidal tendencies in the past.

Also check for:

- **Problems/sufferings**: Seeing a psychiatrist, psychologist or counsellor and their view and management of the problem.
- **Positives/strengths**: When they have been free of various problems and when they have functioned above the water level in the past.

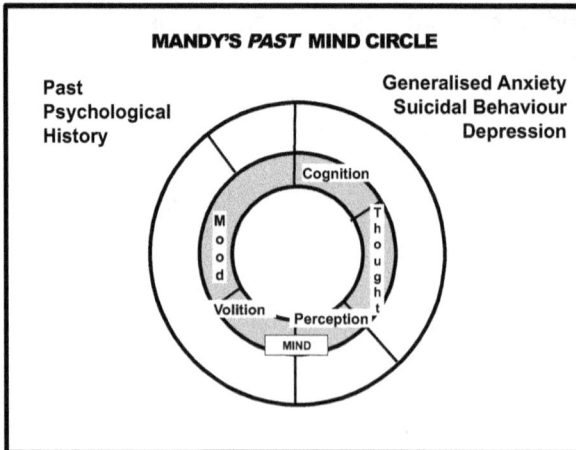

MANDY'S *PAST* MIND CIRCLE

PERSONALITY

Mandy has experienced problems in her heart sectors:

- **Love:** Reduced self-esteem. Secure vs Insecure attachment.
- **Truth:** A sense of confusion.
- **Control:** Being more controlling/choleric, compulsive and conscientious.
- **Centredness:** More altruistic.
- **Coping:** Internalising hurts, avoiding harm, closed and defended, tending to fake i.e. pretend/perform and be perfect for others.

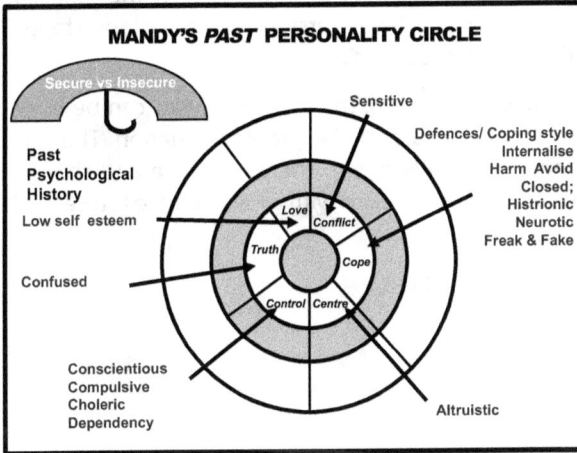

MANDY'S *PAST* PERSONALITY CIRCLE

SPIRIT

Mandy has had a longstanding and strong faith. In the past she has experienced a relationship with God which is:

- **Real**.
- **Releasing**, freeing and helpful.
- **Relevant** to her everyday living.

Having information from the past will enable you to make sense of Mandy: Why she is the way she is, where she is at, and where she is going.

It will provide:

- A link between the roots (past), the present, and the shoots (future).
- A graph of her progress through life.

- A measurement of the depth, length and breadth of the rut she is in.

It will also enable you, as the therapist, to move on to the next section of understanding/linking.

SUMMARY OF UNDERSTAND–LOCATE

This has been a long chapter! The Understand–Locate step is hard. Getting all the jigsaw pieces of all the circles and sectors is fundamental to any professional counsellor. Locating the pieces allows the counsellor to move on to the second stage of the understanding step, Understand–Link. It will be hard to link with pieces missing.

Once they have been located, the missing pieces can be linked together to make the jigsaw picture of the present situation. The jigsaw picture can make sense once linked with the past. Hope and change can come when the jigsaw picture is linked with an alternative future, and a different story.

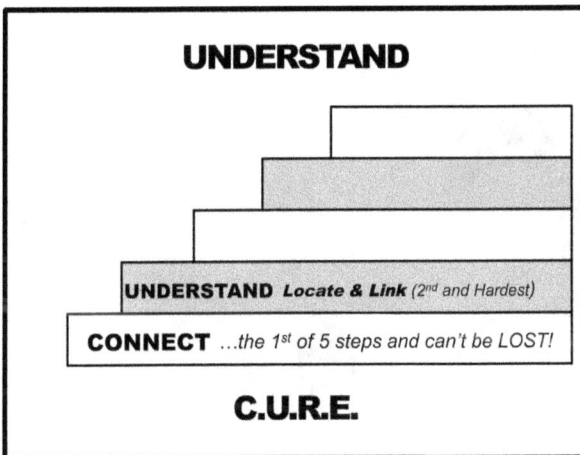

SECTION IV:
UNDERSTAND–LINK

UNDERSTAND

UNDERSTAND *Locate & Link* (2nd and Hardest)

CONNECT ...the 1st of 5 steps and can't be LOST!

C.U.R.E.

6: UNDERSTAND–LINK (FORMULATE)

For training purposes, the capacity to stay on this step
is expected at Counsellor Level of learning.

Understanding. As mentioned, while the commonest problem on the understanding step is simply not having enough information, even if a counsellor has located all the relevant pieces of information, the jigsaw picture can remain disconnected, and not make sense. The jigsaw pieces have not been linked to define the picture. The Understand–Link step addresses this. The process of linking is called formulating. The end product is a formulation, and consists of three main parts or paragraphs, relating to the present, the past and the future.

Firstly the current and whole picture of the counsellee and his/her problems are seen from the Understand–Link step. Titles to the problems (more than the person) of the picture are called diagnoses. The CWF facilitates diagnosing the pattern recognition resulting from linking problems in different sectors. Secondly, the Understand–Link step helps to make sense out of how the current picture came to be, by understanding the links between the present and the past. This provides an aetiological formulation. Thirdly, the understanding of the present and the past, can be linked to an understanding of the future, in terms of a prognostic formulation and management plan.

Having these three paragraphs of information, maximizes communication and efficiency in supervision, as well as summarises information with others in the counsellee's Pyramid. The formulation can be most helpful in consolidating one's own understanding of counsellees, and helping them to make sense of and to understand themselves and their issues. This in itself is therapeutic. It also allows for a firm foundation for the response step.

The scenario

Mandy's current jigsaw pieces have been located. The shapes of the past, especially the Circles, have been found. Future directions can now be considered. It is important to make sure that as a therapist you are on the same page as Mandy, so that there can be an ongoing connection with Mandy as you move on from the understanding step to the response step. In order to do this a number of helpful questions and comments need to be raised with Mandy to Cross check the Understand–Locate/Link step with her.

- What pieces of the jigsaw am I missing?
- Where am I at on the dartboard in terms of accuracy?
- To what extent have I got the main issues right and identified other issues which are relevant?
- Have I missed any other matters (which should be on the dartboard) and have I excluded the issues which are not part of the picture?
- 'I wonder if the rut from the past has been fairly deep and in some ways goes back even to your mum and dad's time?'
- 'Without help, I wonder if the road is leading to...?'
- 'With help, I think that you could be looking at a different road/ direction, such as...'
- 'In view of the type of issues and the depth of the rut, I think change could take (x) number of sessions/months/years...'
- 'Ways of speeding up the change could include...'

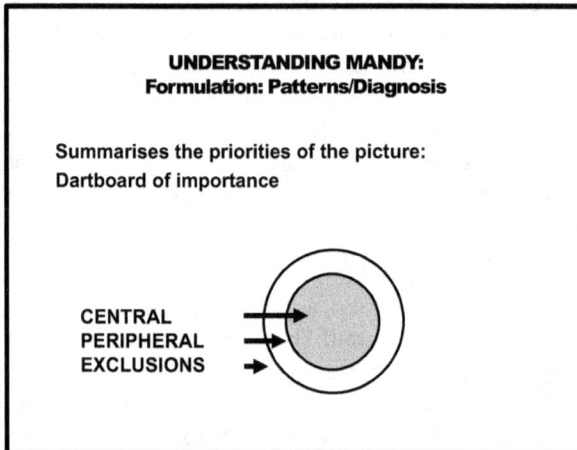

The questions addressed in this section

In this section on linking, a number of issues will be raised relating to diagnosis, aetiology (prognosis), and management plan. These include linking the following:

1. Link the present jigsaw pieces to make the present jigsaw picture (diagnosis).
- What are the uses and abuses of classification?

- What are the possible problems/diagnoses in the areas of the following circles?
  - » Social: family and marriage.
  - » Physical.
  - » Psychological/mind.
  - » Personality/heart.
  - » Spiritual.
2. Link the past with the present (aetiology).
- What are the general causative factors arising from the five Circles?
- What are the linear and circular causative patterns?
3. Link the present with the future (management plan).
- What are five aspects of feedback to a counsellee?
- Goals: How can these be defined using the Circles, the Square and the Triangle?
  - » What plans can be located in the various circles?

The issues

Linking is a critical aspect of the **understanding** step and prepares you for the move to the response step. It includes linking the present issues with the past and the future. This linking results in a three-dimensional (cross sectional and chronological) picture of the Circles with their problems and possibilities. These can then be linked with the tools to enable change on the response step. In linking the problems with the interventions, there is a greater linking and connection between the counsellee and the counsellor.

Ultimately it is this linking which will provide the healing, especially if there is a linking of the counsellee and the problems with the presence of God.

Therapy is hindered in the absence of these linkages:

- The present jigsaw pieces (phenomena/symptoms) with the present jigsaw picture (diagnosis).
- The present with the past roots and ruts (aetiology).
- The past roots and ruts with the future shoots and routes (prognosis).
- The problems with the possibilities (management plan).

In therapy, problems can occur even at the basic stage, if the counsellor fails to link together the problems in the present to make sense of them. A significant amount of supervision is often spent helping the supervisee bring the present problems together, as jigsaw pieces to make the jigsaw puzzle, of the present picture. Once the jigsaw puzzle is constructed, it can then be linked with the past. This will clarify the problems and explain how they have come to be where they are, at this time and in this way. From linking present and past, a link can then be established between the present issues and the future (prognosis). In other words, the problems can now be linked to positive therapeutic interventions to interrupt the natural course of events to create positive and different outcomes.

The contents of this section

1. **Diagnoses and metaphors**: Linking the present jigsaw pieces to make the picture, using the CWF to identify issues in the:

- Social circle
- Physical circle
- Mind circle
- Personality circle
- Spirit circle

2. **Aetiology**: Linking the past and present.

3. **Management plan and goals**: Linking the present with the future.

LINKING THE PRESENT JIGSAW PIECES TO MAKE THE PRESENT JIGSAW PICTURE: DIAGNOSIS

Formulation and Classification is a summary of the picture, not a label of the person. Yet we all do it! We label each other. We may summarise a situation using words like 'weird', 'breakdown', 'stressed out', or use a variety of personality types to describe someone. Within the church people may formulate/classify a situation in the context of someone being for example a 'backslider', or 'spiritually dead'. People helpers may use terms to describe causes of problems arising from the past such as 'parental inversion,' where the child takes care of the parent, or 'bitter root judgments,' where someone might make judgments of another in the context of early childhood problems. Professionals also use systems to categorise/classify including the well-known Diagnostic Statistical Manual (DSM) and the International Classification of Diseases (ICD).

Diagnoses indicate a group of *symptoms*. Symptoms are problems which we *hear* from the counsellee. Diagnoses also identify *signs* that are problems which we *see* when we look at the counsellee. Diagnoses are the signs and symptoms which are causing significant distress and dysfunction to the counsellee personally or in their social context. The diagnostic formulation describes the picture in more detail.

The diagnostic formulation can:

- summarise strengths and weaknesses and can graph the duration and amount or volume of problems and strengths
- prioritise the issues, as on a dartboard of importance, from the central important issues to the peripheral (not so relevant) ones and then on to the problems which are not present or relevant (off the dartboard). When describing a case, use the dartboard analogy to prioritise your presentation (as opposed, for example, to initially methodically going around all of the circles and sectors). Thus start with: 'The most important issues for this person are...'

How the Circles fit into the Diagnostic and Statistical Manual (DSM)

The DSM places issues on five axes.

Axes	The Circles
I:	Mind/behaviour diagnoses.
II:	Personality diagnoses.
III:	Physical (Soma: medical problems) diagnoses.
IV:	Social/external circles (includes aetiological).
V:	The Global Assessment of Functioning (GAF) equivalent to the vertical axis of the Square, from below the water level to above the water level.

Note: As DSM V takes over from DSM IV, some details of what follows may change. However, these changes can easily be accommodated by the circles and sectors.

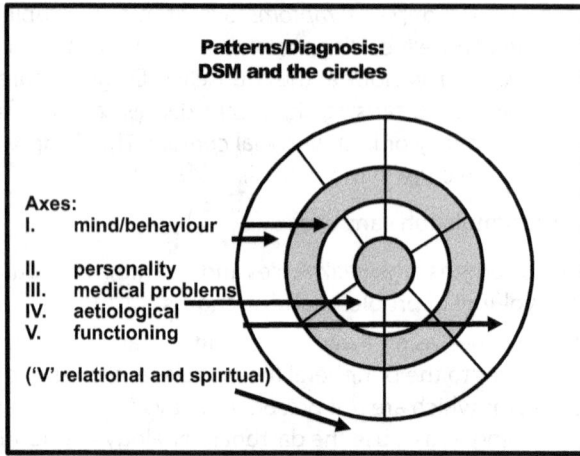

Patterns/Diagnosis:
DSM and the circles

Axes:
I. mind/behaviour

II. personality
III. medical problems
IV. aetiological
V. functioning

('V' relational and spiritual)

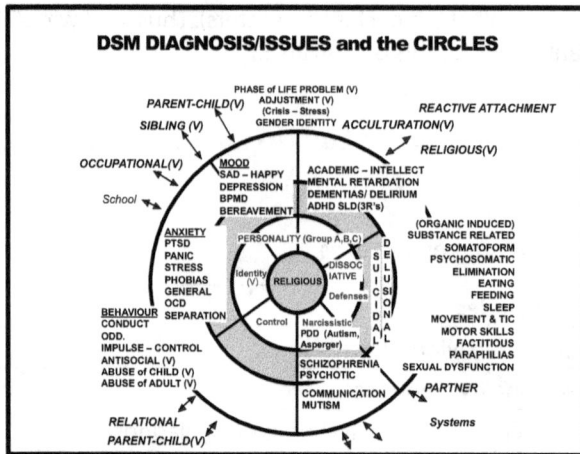

DSM DIAGNOSIS/ISSUES and the CIRCLES

The DSM diagnoses can be placed on the Circles. This is a complex picture and many more presentations can be based on this diagram, in applying the CWF to the issues.

How diagnoses fit into the Circles

We will commence with the outer circles and move inwards, looking at which diagnoses/issues fit which circles. Rather than a comprehensive review of diagnoses, it focuses on using the Circles to link the jigsaw pieces in the present (symptoms and signs) to make the jigsaw picture (diagnoses).

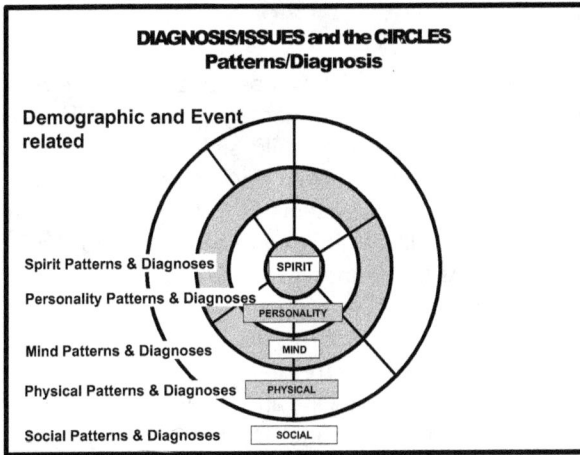

DIAGNOSIS/ISSUES and the CIRCLES
Patterns/Diagnosis

Demographic and Event related

Spirit Patterns & Diagnoses — SPIRIT
Personality Patterns & Diagnoses — PERSONALITY
Mind Patterns & Diagnoses — MIND
Physical Patterns & Diagnoses — PHYSICAL
Social Patterns & Diagnoses — SOCIAL

DEMOGRAPHIC: THE THREE BRUSHES RELATED DISORDERS

Age related issues

Age related issues may cause problems that result in the 'phase of life problems' (V code: a DSM low grade diagnostic category) diagnosis, which can impact on all of one's circles.

Gender related issues

Gender related issues become diagnostic only if there is a gender identity disorder, where in essence, one prefers to be the other gender in all of one's circles. This is different from sexuality related issues such as same sex attraction which is no longer seen to be a disorder within the DSM nomenclature.

Culture related issues

When culture related issues become problematic they can become a 'V' code diagnosis related to acculturation. The culture bound syndromes which are defined in other texts are not within the DSM system of classification.

EXTERNAL EVENT RELATED DISORDERS

The DSM tried to get away from causative defined diagnoses, but has not been able to do this successfully particularly in relation to diagnoses such as those caused by reactive attachment problems, trauma (with the diagnosis of Post Traumatic Stress Disorder: PTSD) and events (adjustment and pathological bereavement diagnoses).

Social Circle Issues

The two major social issues which will be reviewed in the context of the Circles are to do with families and marriages. The DSM 'V' codes particularly belong here, including parent/child, sibling, occupational, relational, partner and religious problems. The principles applied to these systems can also be applied to other systems including work, church and peer groups. They all function like a family with a mother figure, a father figure and various siblings. As the counsellor obtains information it equips them to clearly see the jigsaw picture of the marriage or family and there is a greater capacity for change. As soon as they are on the understanding step in relation to the system, it is much easier to move on to the response step. Thus, just as for the individual, locate and link where the issues are on the circles of the system (family/marriage). Defining the diagnostic metaphors (summary pictures) of the system, allows you to respond to the system in the right places (parts of the Circles) and help change what is happening in the metaphors.

UNDERSTAND–LINK WHERE THE FAMILY IS AT IN THE CIRCLES

LOCATING THE CIRCLES OF THE FAMILY

It is important to firstly locate the jigsaw pieces of the family in order to understand and then respond to the family. Technically, this should be in the Understand, locate section, but is placed here for continuity and to facilitate both the locating and linking phases of understanding the family system.

DEMOGRAPHICS OF THE FAMILY

The Three Brushes of the demographic issues of the family are as for the individual.

Gender issues

Families can be more male or female in terms of the predominant influence being patriarchal or matriarchal. Families may have been more patriarchal during the Middle Ages and various cultures of the world today are still leaning that way. Today in Western society it could be suggested that families tend to be more matriarchal while business and industry are more patriarchal. The ideal family is where there are both a male and a female influence working together in an interactive and synergistic way. Here, both influences can be expressed in a positive and godly (top right-hand quadrant) way. The single parent family has obvious challenges in terms of providing a balanced male/female influence. In this situation, there is an opportunity for the church to care as an extended family and facilitate the balance.

In understanding a family, ask yourself: What is the gender brush across this family?

Cultural issues

The culture of the family is related to the personality/heart circle of the family as expressed through the physical and social circles of the family (especially behaviour and communication). The culture of the family can include for example, the way a family expresses and behaves in relation to issues of closeness, values, identity and power related issues/hierarchies. Related to these are rituals which are spread out over time, from daily activities to the rites of passage, as one person or a part of the family moves onto another developmental stage. Families are different in various parts of the world and family culture differs from one generation to the next. The rate of change in family culture is accelerating over time. Whereas in previous centuries family culture did not change significantly, now each generation is different. This is reflected in the terms applied to subsequent generations of the past 60 years, like Baby Boomers, Baby Busters, Generation X or Y.

In understanding a family, ask yourself: What is the cultural brush across this family?

Age issues

Families pass through different developmental phases. The phases of a family can be defined in terms of their children, i.e. prior to having children, having young children, adolescent children, and young adult children and then the empty nest.

In understanding a family, ask yourself: What is the age brush across this family?

CIRCLES OF THE FAMILY

In addition to the three brushes across the Circles, the family can be defined in terms of various aspects of the Circles, just as for an individual. The major circles and sectors involved in this include:

The spirit of the family

It is the corporate experience and sense of the presence of God in the daily life of the family. A family where the members have been born-again and live a spirit-filled, Christ-centred life has a strong spiritual position.

In understanding a family, ask yourself: What is the spirit position of this family?

The heart of the family

This is like the heart of the individual.

- **Love sector:** the amount of love, worth, trust and connection.
- **Truth sector:** the clarity of roles and boundaries. There can be issues of respect and understanding.
- **Control sector:** a healthy family is neither rigid nor chaotic. As the children grow into adults, control is handed to them to enable them to 'stand on their own two feet.'
- **Centred sector:** a God-centred family will function very differently from a self-centred or 'other-centred' one.
- **Coping sector:** a family with an underlying commitment to one another faces issues through loving communication and copes with change in a productive way. This is compared to a family which copes by fight/flight, withdrawal and avoidance.

In understanding a family, ask yourself: What is the heart of this family?

The mind of the family

In particular the mood sector of the family i.e. is it sad/happy, anxious/ peaceful or are there angry/loving feelings? The energy level and intelligence level of the family are also aspects to consider.

In understanding a family, ask yourself: What is the mind of this family?

The physical aspect of the family

Aspects to take into account include things like health behaviours, use of time and communication capacities. In addition, the physical size of the family in terms of number of family members is important.

In understanding a family, ask yourself: What is the physical side of this family?

The social life of the family

How open or closed the family is to external social interactions including having contact with friends, family, church and neighbours.

In understanding a family, ask yourself: What is the social life of this family?

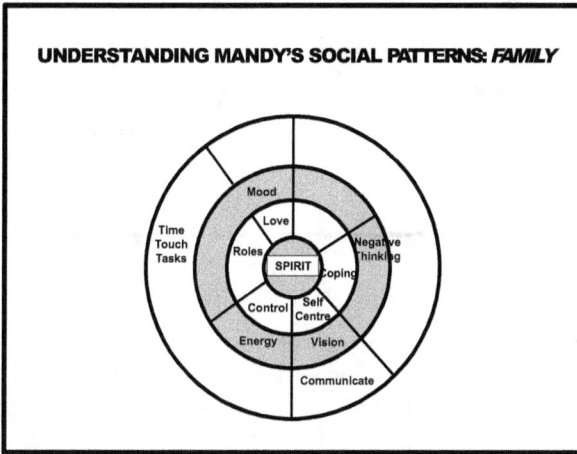

UNDERSTANDING MANDY'S SOCIAL PATTERNS: *FAMILY*

Mandy's family had problems in a large number of sectors.

A Diagnostic Metaphor of the Family

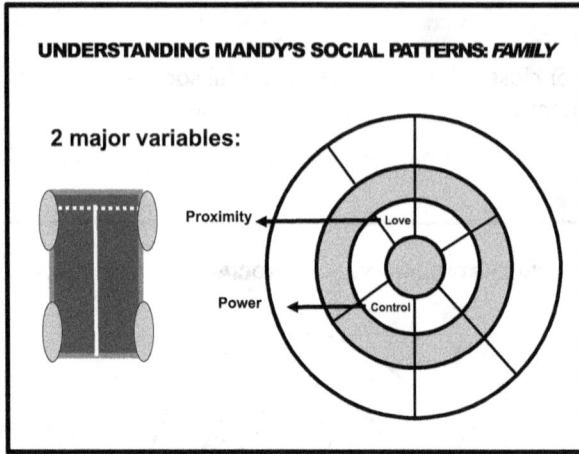

THE METAPHOR OF THE CAR IN RELATION TO THE CIRCLES

In addition to linking the jigsaw pieces, you can also formulate a 'diagnosis' or picture of the family using the structural metaphor of a car. The structure of the family can be likened to the structure of the wheels of a car. The wheels represent the people and their level of power/control, referring to the control sector of the family. The axles focus on proximity and the degree of connection as evidenced in the love sector within the family.

The wheels

The members of the family and the control sector

- **Front wheels:** The two wheels in the front represent the two parents in this example – a two-parent, intact family.
- **Back wheels:** The two wheels at the back represent the two children (although the number of wheels depends on the number of children).

Dysfunctional and problematic wheels

- **Number of wheels:** The CWF would accept that the *ideal* number of front wheels is two, not one (as in a separated couple), or multiple, as in the case of stepfamily situations. However, in *reality*, the situation is often very different.
- **Front wheels:** Parents. When a 'parent wheel' falls off in the context of separation, major structural changes occur within the car. In this

situation, especially if there is minimal contact with the separated parent, a four-wheel car has to adapt and become a three wheeler as the remaining parent attempts to fulfil both parenting roles. In a composite or stepfamily, there is an increase in the number of front and back wheels.

- **Back wheels:** Children. As a family increases its number of children, more back wheels (representing the children) are added. The family grows and eventually the children leave. At this point it is as if the back wheels have been removed, to be added to another car as they make their own car. A 'child wheel' may leave prematurely, for example when a 14-year-old leaves home as a result of child or family dysfunction. Conversely, a 'child wheel' may stay around longer than expected when a child is still living at home in their 30s. This may be because the child has a physical/mental disability, has not grown up psychologically or has a dysfunctional connection with a parent in a co-dependent way.

- **The wheel nuts:** The tightness/looseness of the wheel nuts represent the strength of commitment within the family (relates to the will involving the control sector). This particularly applies to the front 'parental wheels'. When the wheel nuts are too loose the whole car becomes unsafe. This is speaking about commitment within the family.

- **Position of wheels:** The further forward the tyre is situated on the car, the more power that tyre has (control sector). The person closest to the front of the car has the most power in the family. In the same way if the tyre is at the back it has to follow and it has the least power. In this way a highly aggressive or even anxious eight-year-old child can become too powerful in influencing and move forward towards the front of the car, taking the place of the parent's power in the family.

- **Size of wheels:** As well as position, tyre or wheel size can represent power (control sector). Wheels can be too big like a large truck wheel, representing dominance, or too small like baby cycle wheels, representing lack of power. The wheels of a child's bicycle are appropriate for a child, but not a parent.

- **Tread of the tyre:** Tread is a measurement of the tyre's ability to grip the road (control sector). A tyre is said to have poor tread when the rubber has been worn down and the grip has gone. In the family, this metaphor represents how worn down/out a person may be and how much grip they have on their situation.

The axles
The members of the family and the love sector

- **Front axle:** The axle between the parents represents the strength and proximity/distance of their connections. The longer axle indicates a greater degree of distance and a corresponding lowered level of connection within the love sector.
- **Back axle:** The axle between the children represents the degree of sibling connection.
- **Central axle:** The axle between the front of the car and the back of the car represents the parent/child connection and the parenting.

Dysfunctional axles

- **Number and place of axles**: There can be more than one central axle in families where the father and mother operate with different parenting styles. An example is when one parent is strict and the other is lax. Different parenting often arises when there is a lack of connection or communication between the parents (love sector). At worst, there may be virtually no connection between the parents. Instead there is a separate connection from the father to the child and another one from the mother to the child. This can occur in a family where animosity exists between divorced parents. This can also happen, even temporarily, within an intact family, when the parenting is not consistent.
- **Size of axles:** This indicates the strength of connection (love sector). An axle may be thin and distant, indicating a lack of connection and unhelpful independence, or thick and short, indicating a connection that is too close. Close tyres may be so close against each other that they cause heat (friction/hostility). This is similar to what is known as 'expressed emotion' or 'co-dependency', referring to too much closeness with a negative consequence. Tyres which are too distant are in an independent position. Interdependence is the ideal where the tyres have a sufficient closeness for connection but also sufficient distance to operate independently. In this way the tyres work together to move the vehicle forwards.

Locating and linking where the issues are on the circles of the family and defining the structure of the family will allow you to respond to the family in the right places (parts of the Circles) and help redefine the structure.

UNDERSTAND–LINK WHERE THE MARRIAGE IS AT IN THE CIRCLES

LOCATING THE CIRCLES OF THE MARRIAGE

Marital diagnoses, using the Circles: How do the Circles help to understand marital jigsaw pictures?

Locating the marital pieces: It's important to locate the jigsaw pieces of the marriage, in order to Understand and Respond appropriately to the couple. Technically, as with the family, this should be in the Understand–Locate section, but is placed here for continuity and to facilitate both the locating and linking phases of understanding the marriage system.

The 3 brushes of the demographic issues apply to marriage in a similar way as they apply to the family and also the individual.

DEMOGRAPHICS OF THE MARRIAGE

Gender issues

Marriages like families can be more male or female in terms of being dominated in a more male or female way. Couples can be mainly male influenced where a wife is little more than a servant, or female dominated as in a 'henpecked husband'. A balanced situation is where there is an integration of both the male and female influences. This is more in keeping with the character of God, who out of His image, made us to be male and female: *'Then God said, 'let us make people in our image to be like ourselves'* (Genesis 1:26).

Cultural issues

The culture of the marriage, like family culture is related to the personality/heart circle and it is expressed through the physical and social circles of behaviour and communication. The culture of marriage alters across time, generations and countries. As with the family, the culture of marriage can include the way a couple expresses and behaves in relation to issues of closeness, values and identity. This also includes power/hierarchy related issues.

Age issues

Marriages have a developmental aspect to them and change with age. Marriages can go through three phases or pendulum swings:

1. Initial position

The marriage may have a particular theme or emphasis in terms of how a couple copes. For illustration purposes there may be a pursuer/distancer pattern where a wife pursues her husband wanting closeness and he distances himself, wanting space.

2. Second position

The marriage may change at some point where the couple exchanges the role of pursuer and distancer. Here, often in the context of a crisis, a change of directions occur with the wife distancing and the husband pursuing. However, if the husband continues to distance himself the marriage can drift apart.

3. Final position

The third stage of marriage development, which some never achieve, is when a balanced position is obtained. This involves a healthy and steady balance between distance and closeness representing connection and individuality, which grows the love sector and the truth sector in the individuals and the marriage. The marriage is defined by a sense of value and respect as connection as well as healthy boundaries coexist.

In understanding a marriage, ask yourself: What are the three brush colours across this couple?

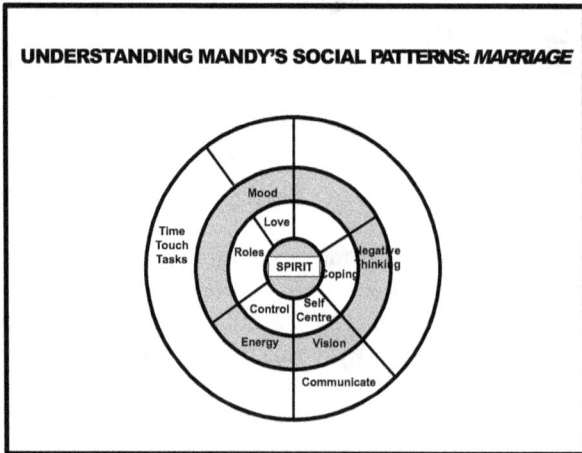

UNDERSTANDING MANDY'S SOCIAL PATTERNS: *MARRIAGE*

Just like for the family and the individual, marriage can also be defined in terms of locating issues in the Circles.

CIRCLES OF THE MARRIAGE

Spirit of the marriage

The couple that has a God-centred relationship is like a three stranded cord as opposed to a cord made of two strands. The third strand, symbolising the presence of God, adds a synergy to the power and strength of the relationship. There is more opportunity for one to be proactive toward the other, as they respond individually to the centrality of God in their own lives rather than reacting to the other person. From this position, true servant leadership can emerge as the husband takes a greater role as servant leader enabling his wife to take a greater role in being his helper. This must lead to a greater capacity to stay together.

In understanding a marriage, ask yourself: What is the spirit of this couple?

The couple which Prays together MAY stay together

Heart of the marriage

This is like the heart of the family and the individual.

- Love sector: The amount of love, worth, trust and connection.
- Truth sector: The clarity and types of roles and boundaries; issues of respect and understanding.
- Control sector: A healthy marriage is not defined by control/power struggles; it is built on a sense of love and respect from the underlying love and truth sectors.

- **Centred sector:** A God-centred marriage provides a balance between caring for the other person and oneself, God being the central point of the pendulum, allowing for a balanced 'to-ing and fro-ing.'

Coping sector

There are various patterns or themes of coping within the marriage which may change over time. This depends on how each individual copes and whether they are reactive or proactive towards each other. The options include the following patterns of interacting/coping:

- **Fight/flight:** One is aggressive and the other defensive. In a more passive way, this can be expressed where one pursues and the other distances.
- **Flight/flight:** Both people are distancing and withdrawing from each other and often the marriage drifts apart.
- **Fight/fight:** Both fight with each other resulting in a highly conflictual relationship.
- **Face/face:** Both face up to issues with each other and communicate in a constructive way which allows them to negotiate change and adapt to each other without losing themselves. This allows them to live the great commandment with each other, loving God and loving the other person as well as oneself, including their whole being i.e. all the circles: the spirit, heart, mind and strength.

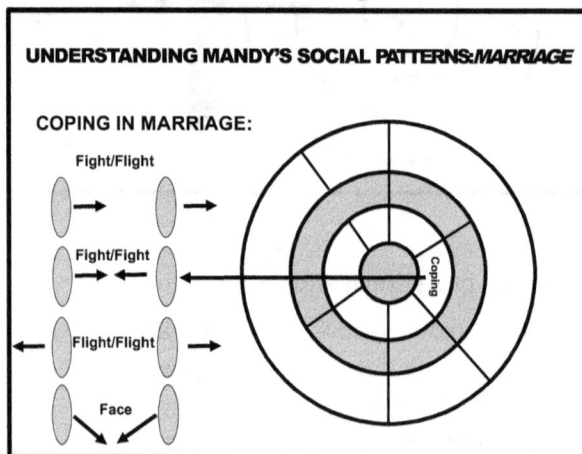

UNDERSTANDING MANDY'S SOCIAL PATTERNS:*MARRIAGE*

In understanding a marriage, ask yourself: What is the heart of this couple?

Mind of the marriage

As for the family, the mind of the marriage includes the mood i.e. sad/happy, anxious/peaceful, angry/loving feelings. The energy and intelligence level of the couple are also aspects to consider.

In understanding a marriage, ask yourself: What is the mind of this couple?

Physical aspect of the marriage

This includes how the couple use their time, their combined focus on health issues including diet and exercise, as well as the physical intimacy of the relationship in terms of sexual contact.

In understanding a marriage, ask yourself: What is the physical aspect of this couple?

Social life of the marriage

This relates to the degree of extroversion/introversion in the marriage, i.e. how social or isolated the couple is. It is about finding a reasonable balance between being by themselves and with others.

In understanding a marriage, ask yourself: What is the social life of this couple?

Diagnostic metaphors of the marriage

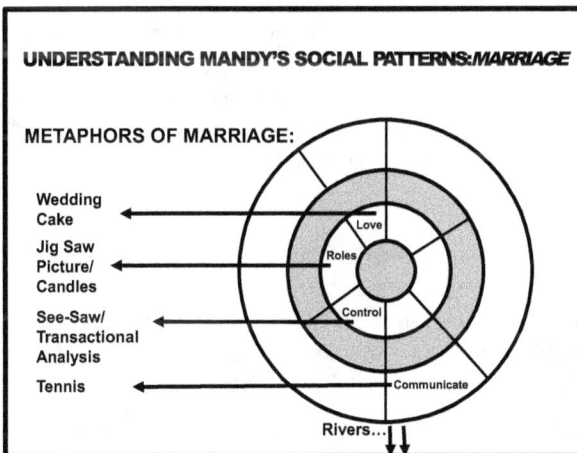

UNDERSTANDING MANDY'S SOCIAL PATTERNS:*MARRIAGE*

METAPHORS OF MARRIAGE:

Wedding Cake

Jig Saw Picture/ Candles

See-Saw/ Transactional Analysis

Tennis

Love

Roles

Control

Communicate

Rivers...

In addition to locating the jigsaw pieces of the marriage, one can also form diagnostic metaphors of the marriage. These metaphors can then be used for the understanding step as part of the process of marital assessment. Having a clear idea of the metaphors provides diagnostic summaries of the relationship which can then be used to inform the marital therapy on the response step. In this way these metaphors assist with understanding and change.

THE TRIANGLE AND THE THREEFOLD CORD: HIM, HER, GOD

The Christian marriage can be described as a threefold cord. It is an entwining of three individual strands and depicts a love relationship between the three cords representing a husband, his wife and God. The couple love the Lord their God and each other as themselves. God's life intertwines with theirs. Engineers would agree that a threefold cord is stronger than a twofold one. While the three cords are separate, they are one. The threefold cord illustrates the Triangle, moving through life with God.

THE THREE CANDLES, THE THREE CIRCLES, AND THE THREE RIVERS: HIM, HER, US

Three candles

My wife and I like candles. We chose to have three candles to symbolise the three 'people' within the marriage. A blue one, a pink one and a central white one representing the marriage. (In this analogy, the central candle represents relationship and the marriage rather than God.) At the beginning of our wedding ceremony, the outside blue and pink candles were alight. During the wedding, we lit the central white candle, but kept the outside two alight. The marriage is an entity in itself. *A man leaves his father and mother and is joined to his wife and the two are united into one* (Gen. 2: 24). The couple and the 'one' make up the three 'people'.

Three Circles

The three candles are the three separate circles of the relationship, one for him, one for her and one for the marriage. Each of these candles represents a whole circle as defined in the CWF. There are three circles, just like there are candles. There is also a loop of connection and communication (verbal and non-verbal) between his circles and her circles.

There are six points in this loop, and one can start the cycle at any point:

- The exit from her leading to the...
- Entrance for him, leading to his...

- Inner circles (especially his heart) which then...
- Exits from him, towards her...
- Entrance, which then enters into her...
- Inner circles. The message then again exits from her, and the loop goes on.

The loop of communication is three-dimensional. If it is a constructive/victorious loop, it will go in the *upward* direction like a soaring eagle, whereas if it is a destructive/vicious loop, it will go *down* like a whirlpool. A constructive part of marital therapy is to change the direction of the cycle from a vicious one to a victorious one. This can be done by facilitating change at some of the six points of the loop, from vicious to victorious particularly in the way messages are given and received.

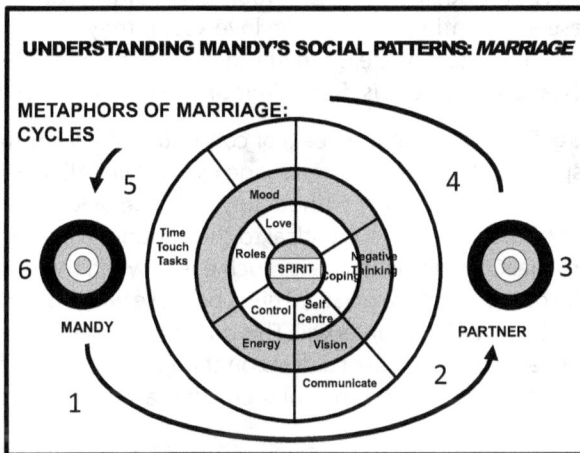

UNDERSTANDING MANDY'S SOCIAL PATTERNS: *MARRIAGE*

METAPHORS OF MARRIAGE: CYCLES

MANDY

PARTNER

Mood, Love, Time Touch Tasks, Roles, SPIRIT, Negative Thinking, Coping, Control, Self Centre, Energy, Vision, Communicate

Three Rivers

The two outside candles and circles develop over time and form the middle candle and circle. Likewise, the couple in the marriage have their own lives, like rivers. The rivers represent the background and life of each person. Each of them comes from a different set of parents and different influences and contributes to the life they share together. He has his river and she has her own river too. As the two rivers come together they form the third river (like the third circle and the third candle). There is a degree of turbulence, as is expected when two rivers meet. Turbulence can continue in some marriages, becoming unsafe rapids. In other marriages it subsides over time.

In marital counselling it is helpful to look upstream and compare the marriage of the couple with their own parents. This is particularly helpful at heart sector level to identify issues of love/connection, respect/boundaries and control. An additional exercise, to help find the themes or names of the rivers, is looking at what might have happened if his father had married her mother or if her father had married his mother. Finally, looking ahead in time downstream, it can be helpful to predict the course of the river as it flows into the lives of the children, clarifying themes of the river as it passes from generation to generation.

THE LOVE SECTOR AND THE WEDDING CAKE

There are a number of Greek words for love. Four of these are relevant to marriage. They can be likened to the four levels of a wedding cake. Although these are mentioned under the love sector they also apply to different circles and sectors of the marriage, including the mind and physical circles. Each layer of the cake is dependent on the one beneath it.

- **The base:** This is the *agape* (Greek) or commitment love or the 'I love you despite you love.' At times, marriage can feel like all there is left is the hard base to chew on, without any fruitcake or icing. It is often this layer of the cake which is critical to the continued existence of the marriage. Commitment love is much easier when there is the centrality of the presence of God. This is because when one responds to God as Lord, it affects one's will. This *agape* form of love is a love of the will, and much more of a decision than a feeling. Significantly this love is activated by the control sector. It is a love from proactive obedience.

- **The fruitcake:** This is the *philios* (Greek) or friendship love. This is the 'I like you' love; 'I like being with you,' 'we are friends'. The friendship is made so much more secure, based on the *agape* love they share. Philios love is about a sufficient degree of constructive overlap and difference between the two, particularly in terms of each other's mind, physical and social circles. It is about a couple being able to enjoy similar likes and dislikes of mental, physical or social activities.

- **The icing:** This is the *eros* (Greek) or erotic/ sexual love. This is the 'I desire you / I am attracted to you' love. This love is much more within the mind and physical circles where there is a feeling of love in the context of physical/sexual arousal. However, it does not only belong there. True sexual intimacy needs to span right from these outer circles of body and mind into the heart circle, where in an undefended way (coping sector), there can be heart love (love sector) in the context of respect (truth sector) without the interference of controlling behaviours. The icing or sexual intimacy succeeds when the underlying relationship and friendship are functioning well. Relationship problems (fruitcake issues) are one of the main causes of sexual difficulty (icing problems).

- **The decorations:** On the top of the cake are the decorations and figures. These stand for the *storge* (Greek) or parental love for children. The children arrive from a couple's sexual love and they are able to stand firm when no one else 'tastes the icing' in terms of an affair. When all four loves are present in the marriage the children are secure.

THE CONTROL SECTOR AND THE SEESAW

The higher one is on the seesaw, the more power one has. Equally, the lower one is on the seesaw, the less power there is and the greater the dependency and despair can be. It is hard to stay on a seesaw that is going up and down all the time or always on one angle. It is easier to stay on the seesaw when there is an equal sharing of power between both husband and wife, where the seesaw is equal.

THE LOVE AND CONTROL SECTORS AND THE CAR

As with the family, the marriage axle focuses on proximity and degree of connection (referring to the love sector within the family). The axles can be dysfunctional in terms of size and length of connection (love sector). The wheels (the people and their control sectors) can have dysfunction in terms of the wheel nuts, size (power issues) and the tread in terms of how much of the grip they have on life, as described for the family.

THE COMMUNICATION SECTOR AND COMMUNICATION TENNIS

Central to understanding a marriage is identifying the capacity of the couple to communicate. While communication tennis is in itself a Response tool, it is also an easy way to Understand how a couple communicates. An effective metaphor to convey communication is tennis. Playing tennis is the communication required to travel the CURE steps.

1. Connect: Agree to play: 'Let's play Communication Tennis!'

A marriage is not a war, it's a game. Marital communication is not a competition; the goal is to achieve a win for both players who agree about the:

- Place and time to play: The where and when to play?

It is best to communicate (especially if the issues are important) in a mutually suitable place, at an appropriate time, when the couple is not too tired.

The time together may be for a reasonable duration. Two minutes is too short and five hours is too long. Couples may need to compromise to make a meeting arrangement work.

• The court

The court is divided into two sides, one for each person. It is better to keep within the boundaries rather than jump over the net and attack the other person. The net is a boundary, not a defence mechanism/barrier. You have your side of the court, and the other person has their side. Couples who can differentiate and separate themselves from each other will play better tennis than those who lose their individuality and become lost in a marriage.

• The ball

The ball represents the content of the issues being discussed. The ball is not a missile, it is a ball! A loose leaf folder is a useful tool for tennis. Using one page per issue, which can be indexed at the beginning, this book can keep a record of the tennis communication. Many balls (issues) can be connected to other balls and as the couple starts to play one ball, they can easily move on to many others, taking the communication to a much deeper level.

During a game the ball in play (topic being talked about) may change in size and significance. Always keep your eye on the ball as it might change even between volleys. One way to monitor the changing balls is to score them between 1 and 5, depending on which circle it is associated with. The smallest ball, Size 1 ball, is an external/social one. This however may be connected with a Size 4 ball, which relates to the heart of the person (e.g. a 'Do you love me' type ball).

Size 1: Social/external. Talking about others.

Size 2: Physical/behavioural/activities. 'What are we going to do today?' 'Why do you squeeze the toothpaste tube from the top?'

Size 3: Mind. Feelings/thoughts; interests/ideas: 'How do you feel about that?'

Size 4: Heart. 'Do you love me; respect me; try to control me?'

Size 5: Spiritual. 'What difference is Jesus making in your life?'

These balls (issues) need to be played even prior to courtship progressing, right through marriage in an ever deepening way.

The ball, representing the issue, has a pink spot on one side, for her perspective on the issue. On the opposite side is a blue spot for his perspective. These are the different views about the same issue. When he looks at the issue, he sees the blue spot. When she looks at the issue, she sees the pink spot.

2. Understand

First set. The purpose of the first set is to be able to look at the other person's spot, and understand it, so that there can be a 360° view of the issue.

The Tennis Game: Take it in turns to play a game

*   Server

You can invite the other person to serve or initiate a serve yourself. 'Would you like to talk about this?' or 'Can I talk about this?' The person serving is the one who is expressing their opinion about their spot. The server shouldn't take too long (making their point). There is more than one serve/ opportunity in the game to get a point across. There may be about four to eight serves before the other person has an opportunity to serve. For the one who doesn't find serving (talking) easy, go first. For the one who does most of the serving, try receiving a few serves (listening).

*   The receiver

The receiver reflects back the ball, looking at the server's spot, not their own. It is a reflection of content and process. Content: 'So what I hear you are saying is ....' Processes may be: 'What I pick up is you may be particularly feeling....' The receiver does not catch the ball and serve it back (state his/ her own opinion) but rather attempts to return the issue. This is one of the most common mistakes in communication.

3. Respond

Second set. The purpose of the second set (which is by far the shortest) is to respond to the issue and attempt some kind of resolution. Once there is a good understanding this step will be much easier to stand on. Men often may try to 'fix it' and play the second set before the first set! The response can include brief practical problem solving, being together at the foot of the Cross, or challenging the other (and oneself) to move more towards the right-hand quadrant of the Square.

4. Engage other help

A Referee: If communication becomes too hard between the couple, the best thing is to engage other help. There is a Pyramid of support from people watching the tennis game.

> » A trusted friend or couple, but take care that this does not compromise the friendship. They need to be the referee, who remains neutral.
> » A trusted small group leader.
> » A people helper from the church.
> » A paid referee (Marriage counsellor).

THE FIVE BLESSINGS

Here is a portion of the speech I gave to my son, Daniel and his wife Sarah on their wedding day.

"Daniel and Sarah, you are two different people yet you are a connected unit. I have five blessings to give to you both as you enter the commitment of marriage. These blessings are for you to listen to, talk about, think on, take to heart, and act on for a lifetime.

1. The Cord

   May you be an ongoing threefold cord, strong, individual yet connected, loving God, each other and yourselves.

2. The Cake

   May you be a growing wedding cake of four loves. May you know the foundation of God's *agape* love, a love that loves 'despite' everything; the friendship of *philios* love which is the essential ingredient and basis for the growth of romantic *eros* love which needs to be exclusively guarded, and which is the foundation for *storge* love, designed for parenting.

3. The Candelabra

   May you be a shining candelabra which has two different outside candles, yet is a connected unit. You can only be one if you are two and that makes three. By remaining connected to The Light you can proactively give light to one another, and your marriage.

4. Communicating Tennis

   May you use your differences to grow through communicating, using the tennis metaphor and walking the CURE steps:

- Connect: Invite the other safely to play; identify the balls not bullets.
- Understand: The purpose of the first set is to look at the other persons spot, taking turns to listen one game at a time.

- Respond: The second set is easy because the game/issue is 90% resolved already on the Understanding step. In other words, good understanding generally results in a resolution. If the issue gets too hard you can always...
- Engage other help: Use your Pyramid of family and friends, church, ministry and professionals to support, referee and coach. (Remember I am a professional!)

5. The Cross

   May you know the place to bring your failures and falls, where you can exchange your shame for unfailing love, your guilt and lostness for forgiveness and faith, your despair for Freedom and hope. So in returning to the Cross you might resume your communication (tennis), and relight your candle and turn darkness into light; remake your cake of the four loves; rebraid your threefold cord, and be strongly connected to the unit which is who you are together.

Daniel and Sarah Warlow, may the Lord bless you with the five blessings of the cord, the cake, the candelabra, communicating tennis and the Cross. May He keep you, make His face to shine upon you as you live in His presence, and may He be gracious to you, as you receive His unfailing love. In His presence, may your differences make you a connected unit. Do five things with these five blessings: Listen, talk, think, take to heart, do, for a lifetime. We love you both,

Thank you, Dad/John."

Locating and linking where the issues are on the Circles of the marriage, and defining the metaphors of the marriage, allows you to move on to respond to the marriage in the right places (parts of the Circles) and to help change what is happening in the metaphors, as described later on the Response step.

In conclusion, the two major social issues of marriages and families have been reviewed in the context of trying to understand them using the Circles. Various metaphors from cars to tennis have been used to enhance your understanding of marriage and family issues. If you can see the marriage and the family through the Circles and sectors, then you can get a clear picture from which a comprehensible direction of change will follow.

UNDERSTAND: LINK WHERE THE PERSON IS AT IN THE CIRCLES

Physical Circle Issues

Mandy has issues in the following sectors of the physical circle:

- Appearance: not a significant problem.
- Behaviour: Particularly in the use of her time, doing less in general and less Activities of Daily Living (ADL), such as the household duties.
- Communication: Her effective communication (verbal communication) is less in quality and quantity. She is speaking less clearly, consistently, cooperatively, considerately, and less constructively.
- Soma: she has problems with her sleep, keeping her body healthy (with exercise) and her sexual activity is reduced. In addition, she has problems in terms of increased alcohol intake, a deteriorating diet and thyroid dysfunction.

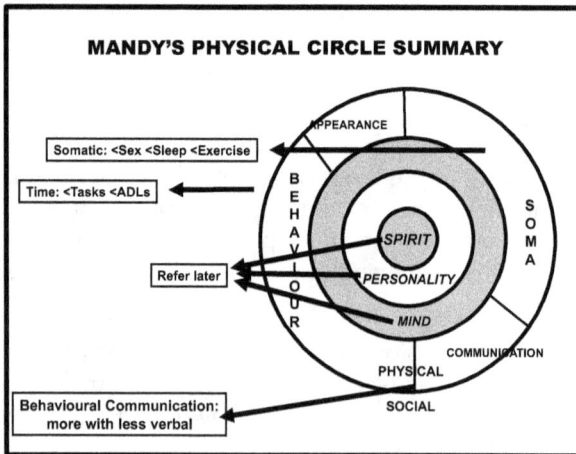

MANDY'S PHYSICAL CIRCLE SUMMARY

Somatic: <Sex <Sleep <Exercise

Time: <Tasks <ADLs

Refer later

Behavioural Communication: more with less verbal

APPEARANCE
BEHAVIOUR
SOMA
SPIRIT
PERSONALITY
MIND
COMMUNICATION
PHYSICAL
SOCIAL

(< is less of, or worse. ADL: Activities of Daily Living)

DIAGNOSTIC PATTERNS FOR THE PHYSICAL CIRCLE

Mandy has a thyroid disorder. Disorders in the physical circle include medical conditions and psychological disorders with a significant somatic aspect.

Physical circle disorders

Somatic Sector: Physical related problems such as organic induced mental disturbances, disorders related to substance, somatoform, elimination, eating, feeding, sleep, movement/tic, motor skills, and sexual dysfunction. In addition, there are the communication disorders of expression and reception.

Behaviour Sector: All disorders have a behavioural component. It can be helpful to place disorders involving anger (mood/emotion) in this sector, as they are especially expressed through behaviour, and can also be accessed through behaviour therapy tools.

Communication Sector: These refer to communication disorders particularly related to difficulties in receiving and expressing communication, amongst other dysfunctions.

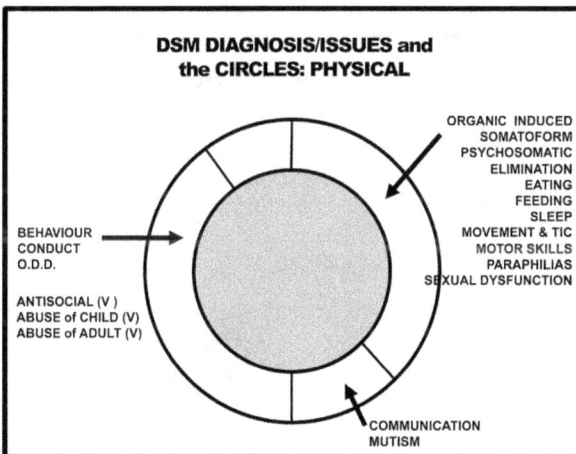

Mind circle issues

Mandy has issues in the following sectors of the mind circle:

- **Mood:** a lowered mood and obsessive, anxious thinking.
- **Volition:** lowered.

- **Perception:** she has strange experiences in her sleep, which are likely to be hypnagognic hallucinations and not part of a psychosis.
- **Thinking:** She has suicidal ideas and some persecutory thoughts though not to the strength of being delusions. She is sensitive in a negative way about how others think about her.
- **Cognition:** Her concentration and memory are not so good.

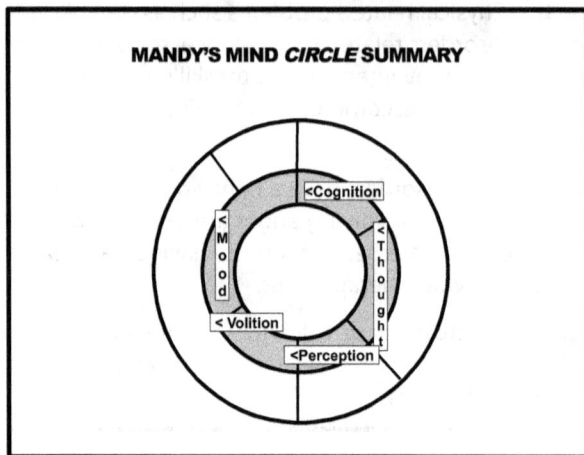

MANDY'S MIND *CIRCLE* SUMMARY

(< is less of, or worse)

DIAGNOSTIC PATTERNS IN THE MIND CIRCLE

These diagnoses, while being predominantly located in one sector, generally have issues in multiple sectors as defined below. The DSM diagnoses can be placed on various sectors of the mind as follows.

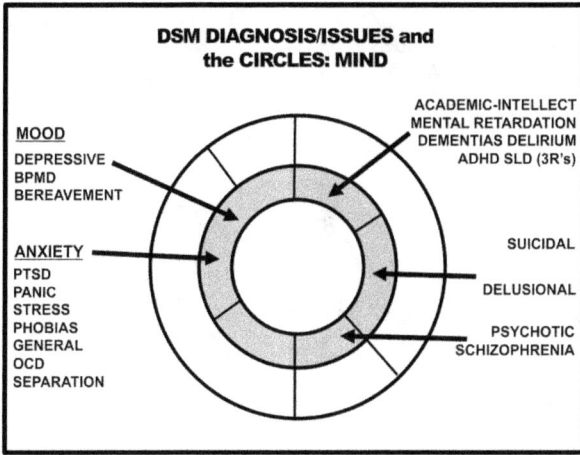

DSM DIAGNOSIS/ISSUES and the CIRCLES: MIND

MOOD
DEPRESSIVE
BPMD
BEREAVEMENT

ANXIETY
PTSD
PANIC
STRESS
PHOBIAS
GENERAL
OCD
SEPARATION

ACADEMIC-INTELLECT
MENTAL RETARDATION
DEMENTIAS DELIRIUM
ADHD SLD (3R's)

SUICIDAL

DELUSIONAL

PSYCHOTIC
SCHIZOPHRENIA

MOOD SECTOR

Aggressive disorders

DSM categorises these as behavioural disorders, which on the Circles would fit more in the physical circle in the behaviour sector. These include the Oppositional Defiant Disorder and Conduct Disorder. Interestingly, when someone with a Conduct Disorder becomes 18 years old their condition moves from an Axis I disorder to an Axis II disorder where it becomes an Anti Social Personality Disorder.

Anxiety disorders

Including panic, generalised anxiety (Generalised Anxiety Disorder: GAD), phobias, obsessive compulsive (Obsessive Compulsive Disorder: OCD), separation and traumatic stress disorders (Post Traumatic Stress Disorder: PTSD). In relation to the CWF we will focus on OCD, GAD and PTSD.

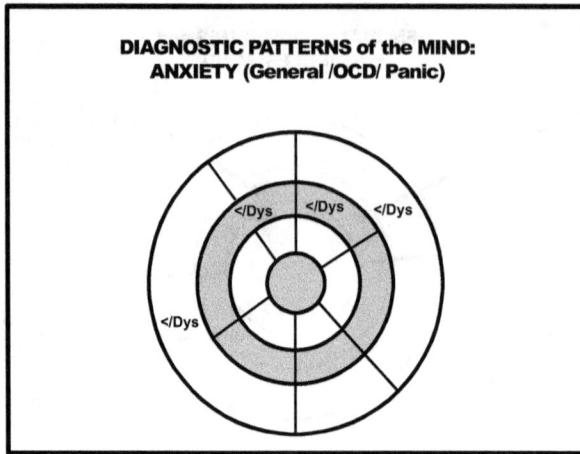

**DIAGNOSTIC PATTERNS of the MIND:
ANXIETY (General /OCD/ Panic)**

Legend: Dys: Dysfunctional / < worse

1. **Obsessive Compulsive Disorder:** Includes dysfunction or reduction in capacities in the following sectors
   - Mind
     » Mood and thought: Obsessions are a composite of mood and thought sectors, having anxious thoughts. However OCD is defined more as an issue of the mood sector rather than the thought sector, being an anxiety disorder.
   - Heart
     » Control: Compulsions are a problem of over control as opposed to impulsiveness where there is under control.
   - Physical
     » Behavioural: Compulsions are also the behavioural response to the obsession.
2. **Generalised Anxiety Disorder:** Includes dysfunction or reduction in capacities in the following sectors.
   - Mind
     » Mood: Increased anxiety which can also be connected with the other two negative moods, irritability and sadness. Generalised Anxiety Disorders may have significant aggressive or depressive components in some people.
   - Volition
     » The anxiety often saps away energy and motivation.

- Thinking
  - » The focus of thoughts is often stressful with catastrophic and What if...? thinking.
- Cognition
  - » Concentration and memory are often affected.
- Physical
  - » Soma: the muscles are tenser and the rate of respiration is often higher. Sleep and appetite may be affected.

3. **Post Traumatic Stress Disorder (PTSD):** Although it is related to an external event, PTSD is defined as a stress related disorder. PTSD is a diagnosis defined more by aetiology (cause) than by phenomenology (symptoms). One of the criteria for diagnosis is that the person must have experienced a significantly traumatic causative event. This creates a problem in relation to the varying degrees of sensitivity (entrance/conflict sector) of people to events. It is possible, though less usual, that a highly traumatic event has no significant effect on someone while others are incapacitated by a less stressful event. Likewise and again less common, an event which would not cause PTSD in most people can result in the same symptoms described in PTSD in another. These symptoms are located in following sectors.

- Mind
  - » Mood: PTSD is an anxiety (stress) disorder marked by an increased anxious activation caused by re-experiencing the trauma from outside reminders or from internal memories. Symptoms in other mind sectors which tend to overlap with depressive symptoms are:
  - » Volition: Often a loss of motivation.
  - » Thinking: The sense of a short, unhappy future.
  - » Cognition: Reduced concentration.
- Heart
  - » Coping: Avoidance of anxiety/stress producing situations.

Sad/Happy Disorders

Includes Major Depressive, Dysthymia and Bipolarity.

Major Depressive Disorder

Includes dysfunction or reduction in capacities in the following sectors.

The main circle:

- Mind
    - » Mood: Lowered and also may be irritable and anxious.
    - » Volition: Lowered with reduced pleasure and energy.
    - » Thinking: Increased negativity.
    - » Cognition: Reduced concentration and memory.

The other circles:

- Heart
    - » Love: Reduced self-esteem.
    - » Truth: Lowered self concept.
    - » Control: Increased despair and lowered sense of confidence.
- Physical
    - » Soma: Reduced sleep and appetite (although in atypical situations both may be increased).
- Social
    - » More withdrawal.

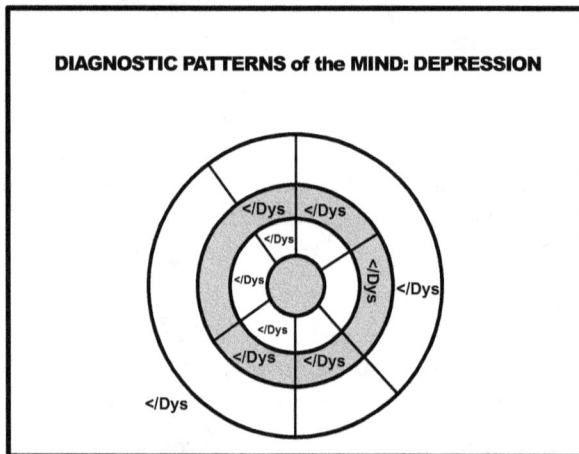

DIAGNOSTIC PATTERNS of the MIND: DEPRESSION

Legend: Dys: Dysfunctional / < worse

PERCEPTUAL AND THOUGHT SECTORS

Psychoses, Schizophrenia, Delusional Disorders

The active symptoms of psychosis in the thought sector are predominantly delusions, and in the perceptual sector hallucinations. In a psychosis the negative symptoms that develop include reduction in the volition sector (avolition), and the communication sector of the physical circle (alogia).

COGNITIVE SECTOR

Mental Retardation; Dementias, and Delirium; Attention Deficit Hyperactivity Disorder (ADHD); specific learning disorders (problems with 'Three Rs': reading, writing, arithmetic); academic/intellectual problems and Pervasive Developmental Disorder. ADHD in particular is focused on.

Attention Deficit Hyperactivity Disorder (ADHD):

Includes dysfunction or reduction in capacities in the following sectors.

- Mind
  - » Cognition: Capacity to concentrate, remember and be organised is diminished.
- Heart
  - » Control: impulsivity, which is a problem of under control.
- Physical
  - » Soma: motor hyperactivity.

ADHD is a developmental and biological disorder and as such arises from the soma sector of the physical circle. The symptoms are largely due to brain changes in a large number of areas, including the frontal lobes.

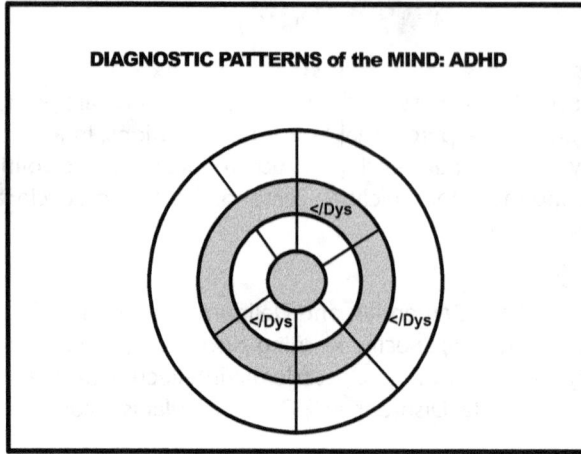

DIAGNOSTIC PATTERNS of the MIND: ADHD

Legend: Dys: Dysfunctional / < worse

Personality Circle Issues

The Personality Disorders; Impulse Control Disorder; Dissociative Disorder (coping sector).

Personality refers to the core/heart circle. The terms personality, core and heart can be used interchangeably.

Mandy has issues in the following sectors of the heart circle:

- Love: A reduced sense of worth.
- Truth: A reduced sense of direction accompanied by confusion.
- Control: Despair.
- Centredness: self-centredness/altruism in the past.
- Coping: Withdrawal instead of facing issues (flight).
- Conflict: The entrance of her heart is more sensitive to negative input.

Mandy does not have a personality disorder, but she has personality related issues.

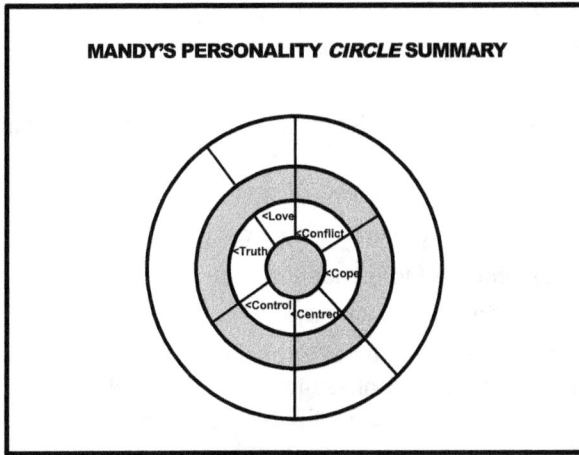

MANDY'S PERSONALITY *CIRCLE* SUMMARY

(< is less in amount or worse/dysfunctional)

DIAGNOSTIC PATTERNS IN THE PERSONALITY CIRCLE

Diagnostic and problematic issues arise in the context of dysfunction or reduction in capacity in the following sectors:

Safety issues

There is an umbrella over the whole of the circle of personality to do with a sense of safety vs insecurity. Some people are more secure while others are less so. Safety applies to all circles. There is a need for social, physical and mental safety as well as safety of the heart/personality. The foundation of safety in the personality circle is especially located in the love sector.

The Four Selfs

The 'Four Selfs' of **Self-esteem, Self-identity, Self-control** and **Self-centredness** reside in the love, truth, control and centred sectors. Significantly these parameters of 'the four Selfs' are pervasively and continually lowered in Antisocial Personality Disorder (ASPD) and Borderline Personality Disorder (BPD), the cluster B disorders of the DSM. In these contexts, there is an underlying low self-esteem, marked identity confusion with an external locus of control with impulsivity. The foundational issue in these situations is a lack of love, correlating with dysfunctional attachment in early childhood. In addition, there is a high degree of self-centredness in people with these disorders.

- **Love:** A core deficit/dysfunction in Personality Disorders.
- **Truth**: Compromised in identity related problems (a 'V' code in the DSM).
- **Control**: Where there are disorders of compulsiveness vs impulsivity. In this sector there are also personality variables relating to:
  - » Conscientiousness vs Irresponsibility.
  - » Choleric vs Phlegmatic.
  - » Dependency vs Independence.
  - » Organisation vs Spontaneity.
- **Centredness**: The Narcissistic Personality Disorder (NPD) is in many ways the extreme of selfishness. Narcissism and self-centredness are also features of ASPD and BPD. Although they would extensively refute it, people with NPD have an underlying dysfunction and reduction in the love, truth and control sectors. In contrast, people with Pervasive Developmental Disorders like Autism have a biological disturbance in their capacity for empathy. Unlike the narcissistic personality, there may not be significant damage to the underlying sectors of love, truth and control. It is in the context of centredness that it is appropriate to consider ASD.

Autistic Spectrum Disorders (ASD)

ASD affects the heart (personality) in a significant way. However, it is predominantly seen as mind based, rather than a personality disorder. It is largely biological and includes Autism and Asperger's Syndrome. The predominant sectors affected by ASD include:

- Heart

Centredness sector: ASD is largely a disorder of empathy. This equates to biological/brain deficit rather than heart/personality narcissism. The autistic person has a lack of reciprocity in relationships and tends to be more comfortable living in their own world. This does not mean that a person with ASD does not have a love sector and is incapable of connection.

Control sector: There is a compulsiveness or over control which is again biological rather than heart/personality based. It results in a tendency towards rigid thinking and people with ASD find change difficult and distressing.

- Physical

Communication sector: In Autism as opposed to Asperger's Syndrome, there are deficits of communication and dysfunction.

Coping: Coping styles

» Externalising vs Internalising: A well-known underlying difference between people.

» Novelty seeking.

» Harm avoidance.

» Open vs closed.

» Histrionic.

» Dissociative: One of the better ways of coping with severe childhood trauma.

» Factitious: Where medical symptoms are displayed for some kind of secondary gain.

» Repression and suppression: pushing down or away out of one's attention. Repression is unconscious (like pushing problems 'under the carpet' or in the 'compost'), while suppression is a conscious act of putting a problem to the side to wait for a more appropriate time to deal with it (putting the problem 'in the fridge' or 'in the drawer').

The five 'F's' of coping: (can you think of any more!)

» Faking and performance: (Christians are very good at this).

» Fighting: in an active or passive way.

» Flight and withdrawal/avoidance:

» Freaking: an anxiety response can be seen as a coping mechanism.

» Flop: a depressive response can be seen as a coping mechanism.

Constructive ways of coping include:

» Facing issues

» Fun.

For couples, a healthy way to maintain a positive relationship is to spend designated time together each week, alternating how that time is spent between doing something fun one week and having a coffee/meal facing and talking about issues the next week.

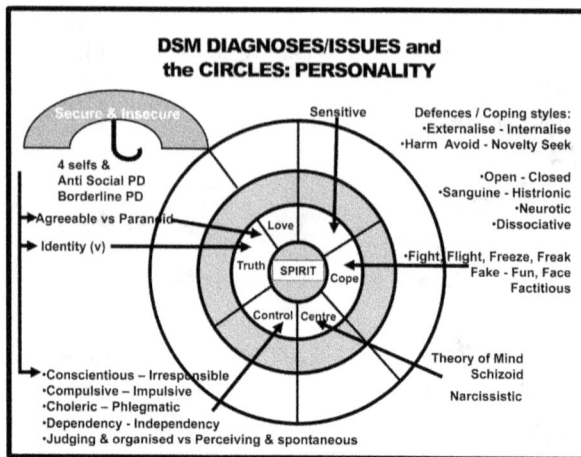

DSM DIAGNOSES/ISSUES and
the CIRCLES: PERSONALITY

Spirit circle issues

Mandy has forgotten her underlying spiritual position as a result of the loudness and dominance of her current experience. She tends to believe her incongruent (hypocritical) practice/experience rather than her spiritual/positional status. This refers to what happened in her spirit circle when she became a Christian, under the crossbar of the Cross. For Mandy, the *reality, relevance and relational* aspect of her spiritual life has diminished. Her spiritual life has become more dormant and dry. Significantly though, Mandy is not spiritually dead because she has been born-again.

Mandy's spiritual disciplines (outworking of the spirit) have been affected by her outer circles. She has become obsessive in her reading of scripture (up to three hours per day) and withdrawn from the larger experience of church (Sunday church). Despite all of this, there have been no changes within her spirit, positionally. She continues to have the presence of God with her, His purposes for closeness, and His provisions of *unfailing love, forgiveness, freedom* and *His fullness*. Nevertheless, the Holy Spirit, although present in His fullness is restricted in His expression. The Holy Spirit is like a guest coming to your house. You can allow Him entrance to some rooms and not others. Although the whole guest, the Holy Spirit may be present, He may not have access to the whole house.

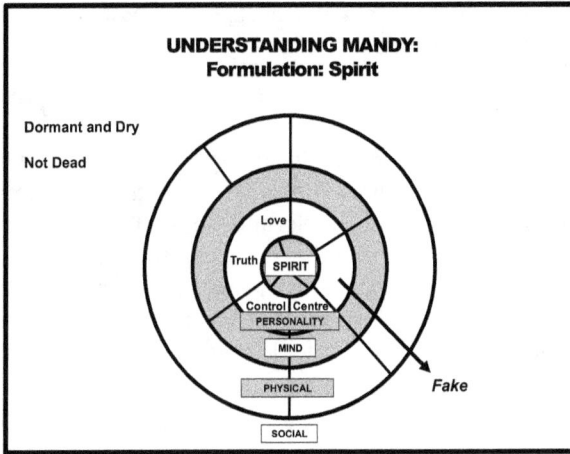

UNDERSTANDING MANDY:
Formulation: Spirit

Mandy's spiritual life, while not dead, is dormant, dry and fake in its influence in her life.

So far, we have sought to understand the following questions relating to the present jigsaw pieces to make the present jigsaw picture (diagnosis).

- What are the uses and abuses of classification?
- What are the possible problems/diagnoses in the sectors of the Circles:
  » Social
  » Family
  » Marriage
  » Physical
  » Psychological/Mind
  » Personality/Heart
  » Spiritual

LINKING THE PAST WITH THE PRESENT: AETIOLOGY

The two central questions are:

1. What are the general causative factors arising from the five Circles?
2. What are the linear and circular causative patterns?

In relation to Mandy, the relevant aspects of the *past* circles which have links with the *present* include the following:

SOCIAL CIRCLE

- **Family**: Significant dysfunction including a lack of love and a sense of rejection resulting in difficulties with connection/attachment. Her father was punitive and had affairs and her mother was avoidant towards her at times and on other occasions they had an overly close relationship. She felt caught up in the marital dynamics and that she had to side with one against the other in a form of triangulation. She felt blamed by her parents for the disruption she caused in the marriage.
- **School**: Mandy was fairly obsessive in her schoolwork, wanting to please the teachers. She did not have a behaviour problem and there were a number of moves to new schools during her childhood.
- **Friends**: She was a loner.

As Mandy grew up, but continuing to look in the social circle:

- **Marriage**: There was not very much in the way of healthy communication. It was characterised by a pursuer/distancer relationship where Mandy pursued while her husband distanced from her. Intimacy was lacking and the relationship was a power struggle at times and sometimes she mothered him.
- **Parenting**: She was enmeshed (too close) with her children.
- **Church**: She felt used by the church because of her obsessiveness, need to please and hard work.

PHYSICAL CIRCLE

- **Soma**:
  - » Genetics: There was a family history of depression.
  - » Illness: Mandy had had a thyroid problem.
  - » Substances: Increased alcohol consumption.
- **Behavioural**: She had been influenced by the way her parents have modelled relationships and life.
- **Communication**: She had had ongoing difficulties communicating with her husband and this has worsened since she became depressed and less communicative.

MIND CIRCLE (PSYCHOLOGICAL CAUSES)

The following issues from her recent past moving into the present have amplified and fed back on themselves and kept Mandy in depression.

- **Mood**: Depression and anxiety.
- **Volition**: Lack of motivation.
- **Thinking**: Especially her negative and slightly persecutory ideas (thoughts of people being against her).

Significantly Mandy's higher IQ has been a protective factor for her psychological wellbeing.

PERSONALITY CIRCLE

Likewise, the following issues arising from the personality circle have amplified and fed back on themselves and kept her in depression.

- **Love**: Low self-esteem.
- **Truth**: Identity confusion persisting from her teenage years beyond normal.
- **Control**: Taking excessive responsibility (an excessive internal locus of control).
- **Centredness**: Altruism expressed as a tendency to enter other people's lives.
- **Coping**: Perfectionism resulting in Mandy losing her sense of self. While these coping mechanisms have served her well in the past, they are now less effective.

SPIRIT CIRCLE

She has considerable spiritual strength having previous positive experiences. In the past she has been aware of her spirit position as a Christian. She recognised and knew God to be a father in a different way to her earthly one. She also had close spiritual friends.

WHAT ARE THE GENERAL CAUSATIVE FACTORS ARISING FROM THE FIVE CIRCLES?

These can be relevant in the past and present. The Circles are like the Cross-section of a tree. The Circles have risen continuously from the roots and go on to produce the shoots. The roots can be seen as the connection to previous generations and the shoots grow forward into future generations. In other words, the larger the past influence is, the greater the impact will be on the present and future. The passing of issues from one generation to another and from the distant and recent past into the present comes through influences from the various circles as follows:

The whole of circle influences

Across the Circles are the three brushes of age, gender and culture. The three brushes will colour the developmental pathway. In addition, they may become causative influences in themselves. Transitions within age, gender and culture can also cause significant problems.

Age: Transitional stages of life such as teenage and midlife, can be sufficient stressors in themselves. Adolescence has become a much longer stage over the last century. A large number of psychiatric disorders arise in adolescence, partly illustrating the challenges of this period. For example anorexia nervosa is an expression of the multi circle challenges which often arises in the context of adolescence.

Gender: Being male or female has a considerable influence on all sectors. For example being female increases the likelihood of depression and being male increases the likelihood of substance abuse. If there is a gender identity related issue and the person is changing from one gender identity to the other they will experience major stress as they transition.

Culture: Various modern cultures have greater capacity to function and cope than others. There are disorders known as 'Culture Bound Syndromes' which are specific to one culture. An example is Anorexia Nervosa, which is largely a western phenomenon. Transitioning across cultures or culture shock is recognised as highly stressful. Children acculturated to a host culture, while living in a family that maintain traditions and allegiances from their culture of origin, often live in a place of tension. They are straddling two different worlds: the culture of their parents and the culture of their peers.

Social circle influences
- Safety vs Abuse.
- Stability vs Change.
- Attachment vs Rejection.
- Gain vs Loss.
- Conflict and Triangulation (caught between parents, having to side one against the other).
- Acknowledgement vs Disrespect.
- Clarity regarding what one is and isn't responsible for vs Blame.

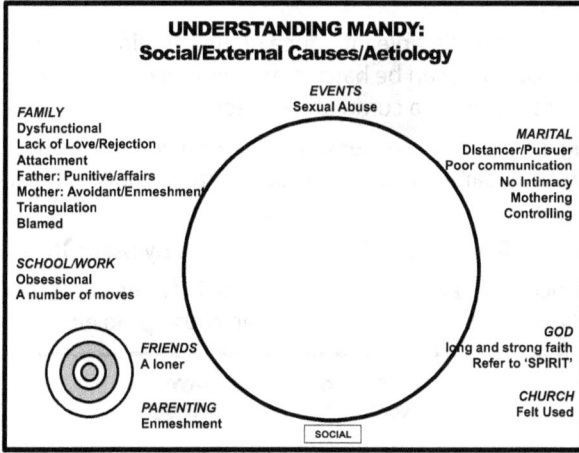

UNDERSTANDING MANDY:
Social/External Causes/Aetiology

Physical circle influences

- Behavioural influence through modelling, especially by parents.
- Somatic influences through genetics and illnesses.
- Communication dysfunction. For example families where there is mainly non-verbal or confused/incongruent communication such as between action and word e.g. 'Do what I say, not what I do' or inconsistency between things spoken from one discussion to another, leaving the person unsure how to respond.

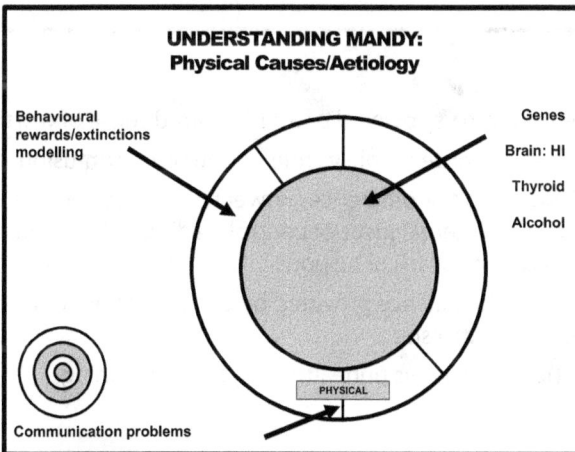

UNDERSTANDING MANDY:
Physical Causes/Aetiology

Psychological (mind) circle influences

- Volition: Has considerable influence on functioning. If someone has run out of petrol, it can be hard to move forward and upward and over time this can have an a cumulative effect.
- Thinking: i.e. optimism vs pessimism, realism vs catastrophe and unreality (paranoia) or mood dominated thoughts (anxiety/depression).
- Present mindfulness vs thoughts dominated by past/future.
- Intelligence: This is a significant influence in terms of coping. Extremes of intelligence (too high or too low) can cause problems.

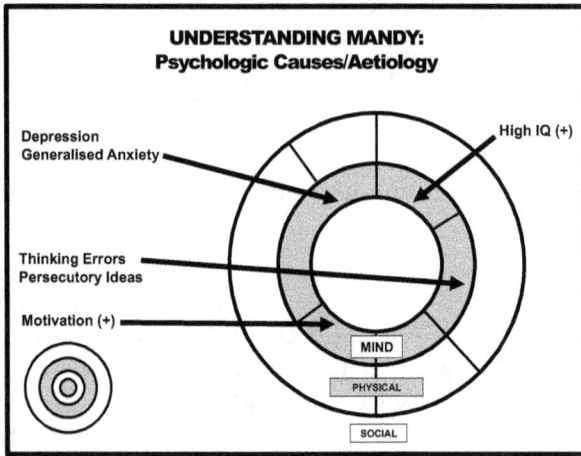

UNDERSTANDING MANDY:
Psychologic Causes/Aetiology

Personality circle influences

- Love: Self-esteem vs Lowered or a self-centred sense of worth.
- Truth: Clarity of sense of role vs role or boundary confusion.
- Control: Knowing the difference between what you can and cannot do vs an excessive internal locus of control leading to blame or external control leading to a lack of responsibility.
- Centredness: The balance provided by Christ-centredness vs narcissism and altruism.
- Coping: healthy ways vs unhealthy ways of functioning.

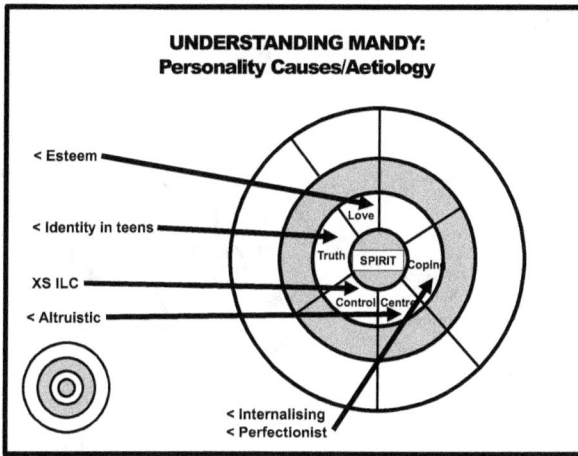

UNDERSTANDING MANDY:
Personality Causes/Aetiology

Legend: < is worse or less

Spirit circle influences

There is a significant advantage in accessing one's spirit position. Here, the presence of God can provide such a deep connection that it can override external influences. The provisions of God can impart internal buoyancy bags and cause the bird to fly in terms of exchanging negative influences for positive in the following heart sectors.

- Love: The unfailing love of God can be exchanged for shame and aloneness.
- Truth: God's forgiveness can be exchanged for guilt and confusion
- Control: God's freedom can be exchanged for our despair
- Centredness: Sacrifice, servanthood, stewardship, submission and surrender can be exchanged for our narcissism.
- Coping (exit of the heart): The capacity to fight the fight of faith.
- In the spirit circle: God's fullness can be exchanged for our emptiness.

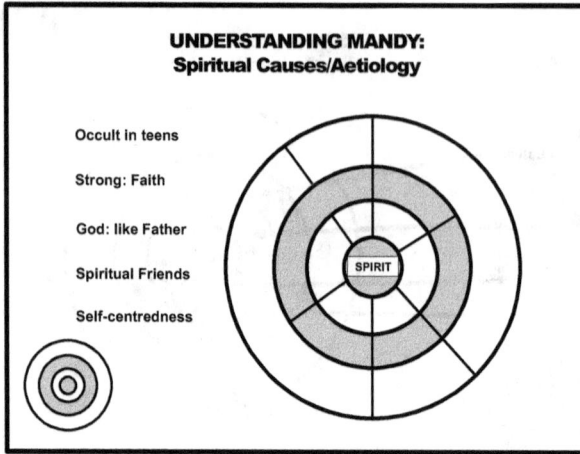

UNDERSTANDING MANDY:
Spiritual Causes/Aetiology

Occult in teens

Strong: Faith

God: like Father

Spiritual Friends

Self-centredness

SPIRIT

A critical part of the formulation is linking the past with the present (aetiology), and seeing which way on the road the person is likely to head without any intervention (untreated prognosis).

In reviewing this, two questions have been addressed:

1. What are the general causative factors arising from the five circles?
2. What are the linear and circular causative patterns?

THE TWO WAYS THE PAST AFFECTS THE PRESENT (AETIOLOGY) AND THE FUTURE COURSE (PROGNOSIS)

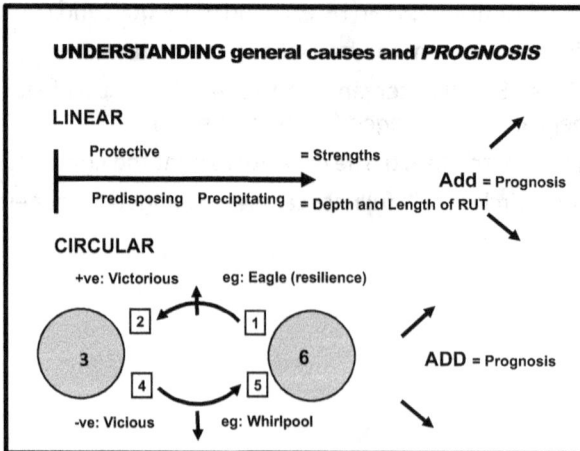

UNDERSTANDING general causes and *PROGNOSIS*

LINEAR

Protective = Strengths

Predisposing   Precipitating = Depth and Length of RUT

Add = Prognosis

CIRCULAR

+ve: Victorious   eg: Eagle (resilience)

3   6

-ve: Vicious   eg: Whirlpool

ADD = Prognosis

Linear: the past affects the present i.e. a causes b

Linear causality is where one thing worsens another, which in turn worsens another unrelated issue, resulting in a linear deterioration over time. The distant and recent past of both positive and negative influences can combine to give an impression of the overall influence of the past. The greater the influence and the longer its duration, the harder it will be to change in the future (prognosis). An analogy of the road/rut one makes through life, explains the influence of positives and negatives. For people going well in life, the journey is on a solid and developing road. There may be positives which keep the road strong and functional. For those who have struggled the road has become a rut, which has deepened over time. This process may have begun in an earlier generation with dysfunctional parents. A measurement of the extent of the impact of past influences is illustrated by the breadth (depending on how many circles are involved), depth (the severity of problems) and length (duration of influences) of the rut. The deeper and longer the rut, the harder it is for the person to escape the impact of the old past influences on their present life. Also, the condition of the rut provides an indication of what may lie ahead (prognosis). Generally speaking, the worse the past has been, the worse the future, especially without intervention.

Circular: one issue affects the other issue which in return affects the original issue i.e. a causes b which worsens a

Circular causality is where one thing worsens another, which feeds back on the first influence and amplifies the circular deterioration. These influences from the past can be positive and negative. They can be from within the different parts (sectors) of the person or from outside (other people). If the influence is positive the person rises and the spiral goes up. If it is negative the spiral goes down, and the course of life deteriorates. The overall balance of positives and negatives will determine whether the person sinks or swims, falls or flies (prognosis). Three illustrations help clarify this idea.

The boat: Positive influences from the past function as buoyancy bags (protective aspects). Negative influences are like holes in the boat that allow water in (predisposing aspects from the distant past and recent precipitating issues). The buoyancy of an individual is gauged by adding the influence of positives and negatives, the amount of buoyancy bags and number of holes. Significantly the more water the boat takes on, the more it sinks. This is the circular aspect in that the boat is susceptible to sinking with additional water and similarly as the boat rises, the more likely it is to stay afloat and weather the storm.

The soaring bird is an analogy for the person or system (e.g. marriage/family) who circles upwards, going from strength to strength.

The sinking whirlpool is an analogy of the person or system whose situation is deteriorating. Their life is going round and round as it spirals down the drain.

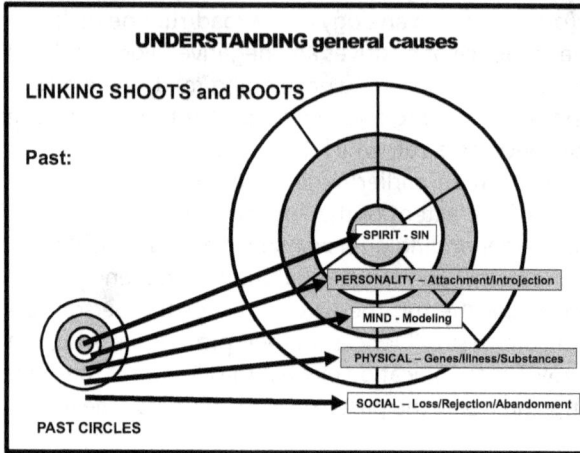

LINKING THE PRESENT WITH THE FUTURE: MANAGEMENT PLAN

The Questions of this section:

- What are five aspects of feedback to a counsellee?
- Goals: How can the management plan be defined using the Circles, the Square and the Triangle?
- What plans for change can be located in the various circles?

The core issue is to provide a link between the present (understood in the context of the past) and the future, and identify the problems and the possibilities. The accurate linking of these will enhance the likelihood of change on the basis of ongoing connected therapeutic linking between the counsellee and the counsellor.

There are five aspects regarding where to go to proceed with the counsellee regarding the management plan. They include:

- A Goal: The Why? Where are we heading?
- People: The Who? Who should be involved in the process?
- Place: The Where? Where are the best places for help?
- Timing: The When? What should happen in the immediate, short and long term?
- Tools: The What? What therapeutic modalities should be used and in what sequence?

A GOAL: WHY? WHERE ARE WE HEADING?

The overall goal as defined by the CWF is in the:

Triangle
To love God and others as oneself. The Great Commandment (Mark 12:30, 31).

Circles
To be centred, in other words to live out from the inner circle of the spirit as opposed to being led by influences from other sectors/circles. This is in line with what Paul prayed, 'May the God of peace sanctify you through and through. *May your whole spirit, soul and body be kept blameless.*' (1 Thess: 5, 23).

Square
To seek to live in the top right-hand quadrant, moving towards the top right-hand corner to the place of God-centred positive living.

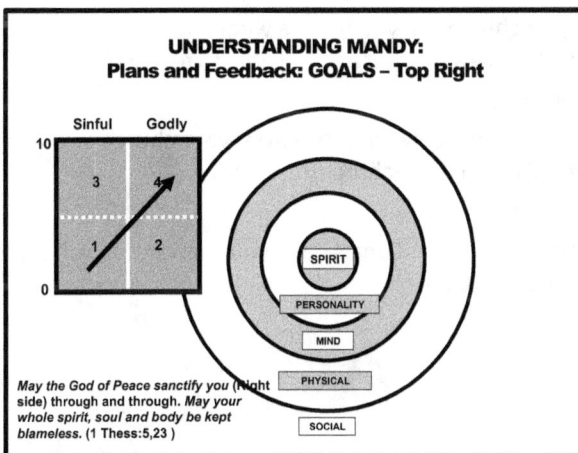

UNDERSTANDING MANDY:
Plans and Feedback: GOALS – Top Right

Cross
To live from one's spirit position at the foot of the Cross, accessing what is already ours in Christ.

Pyramid
To be in the centre of a supportive Pyramid.

PEOPLE: WHO? WHO SHOULD BE INVOLVED IN THE PROCESS?

This is illustrated by the Pyramid. The more the counsellee can stay within the context of a supportive Pyramid, the safer and faster their progress will be. The less the counsellee is in a Pyramid, the slower the progress. Including a review of the Pyramid when you are with a counsellee is a very helpful way of having some guidelines for the future prognosis.

A supportive Pyramid has the corners of:

- Friends and family
  - » Ask: Do you have any friends who know that you are here seeing me? Do they know what's going on for you? Do they ask: How are you? and Where are you at in yourself? Are you able to fellowship/pray with them about these things?
- Church
  - » Twos and threes: Are you linked with anyone in the church who can journey with you?
  - » Small-group: Are you in a small group and how safely open are you able to be with them?
  - » Bigger church: Do you go to a weekend church? What are you able to give and what are you able to receive?
- People Helpers
  - » Ask: Do you receive ministry from your church or other ministry organisation (Para-church)?
- Professionals
  - » Ask: Which professionals have you seen and how helpful/unhelpful has that been?

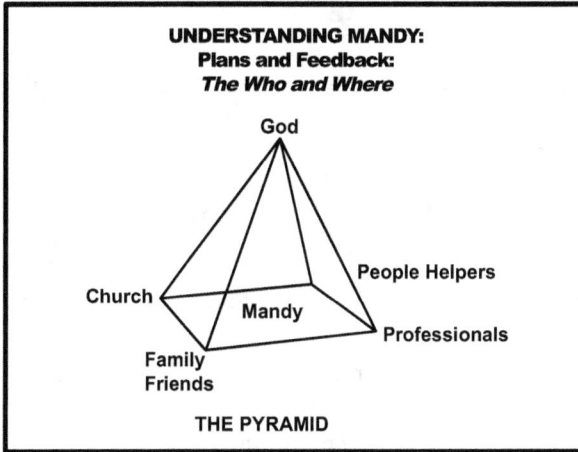

UNDERSTANDING MANDY:
Plans and Feedback:
The Who and Where

God

People Helpers

Church

Mandy

Professionals

Family
Friends

THE PYRAMID

PLACE: WHERE? WHERE ARE THE BEST PLACES FOR HELP?

Places to consider, depending on need include:

- Hospitalisation, especially if there is a suicide risk or the family is beyond coping
- Day program involvement
- Group program
- Retreat opportunities
- Virtual opportunities: telephone/text messaging and computer based contact.

TIMING: WHEN? WHAT SHOULD HAPPEN IN THE IMMEDIATE, SHORT AND LONG TERM?

It can be quite helpful to have a time based grid to plan the future options, especially when used as a guideline.

Interventions	Immediate	Medium	Long-Term
Social			
Medical/Physical			
Psychological			
Spiritual			

TOOLS: WHAT? WHAT THERAPEUTIC MODALITIES SHOULD WE USE AND IN WHICH SEQUENCE?

The tools that change can be selected from the tool bag of the Circles as follows:

Social Tools
- Marital, family, church, group interventions.

Physical Tools
- Soma: physical health checks, medications, substance use control, diet.
- Behavioural changes, in terms of activities, use of time and what one does.
- Communication skills i.e. communication tennis.

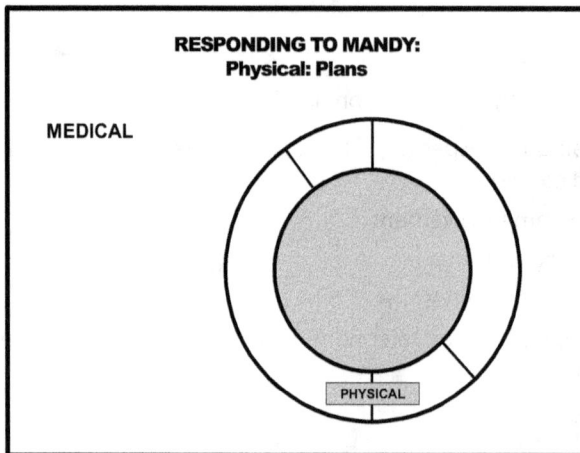

RESPONDING TO MANDY:
Physical: Plans

MEDICAL

PHYSICAL

Psychological Tools
Especially:

- Cognitive based therapies
- Personality based therapies

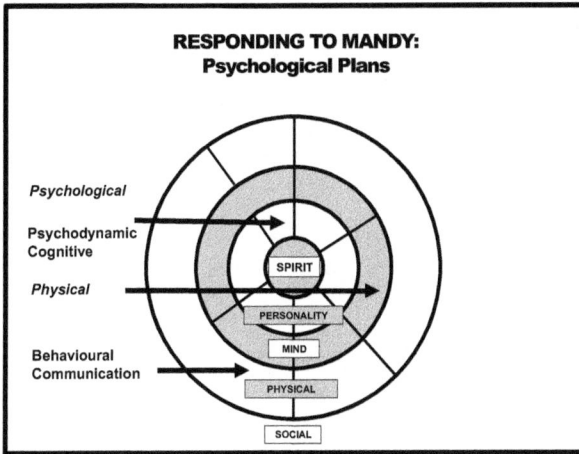

RESPONDING TO MANDY:
Psychological Plans

Psychological

Psychodynamic
Cognitive

SPIRIT

Physical

PERSONALITY

MIND

Behavioural
Communication

PHYSICAL

SOCIAL

Spiritual Tools
- Integration of the above with spiritual issues (which the CWF invites)
- Ministry
- Using the CWF in twos and threes, and in small group

The questions which have been addressed include:

- What are the five aspects of feedback to a counsellee?
- Goals: How can these be defined using the Circles, the Square and the Triangle?
- What plans can be located in the various circles?

SUMMARY OF UNDERSTAND–LINK

This linking section should be done in the context of having located the jigsaw pieces in the present to produce the jigsaw picture. The influence of the Circles is from the distant roots of the tree and the recent past. From this picture of the Circles over time, some guidelines can be obtained for the ongoing direction of the future shoots of the tree (prognosis). Looking at the management plan is looking at what alternative directions these shoots of the tree can have if linked in with agents of change, in contrast to what would happen without any help.

The linking section is normally done in the context of reciprocal feedback with the counsellee, as mentioned at the beginning of this chapter.

SECTION V:
RESPOND

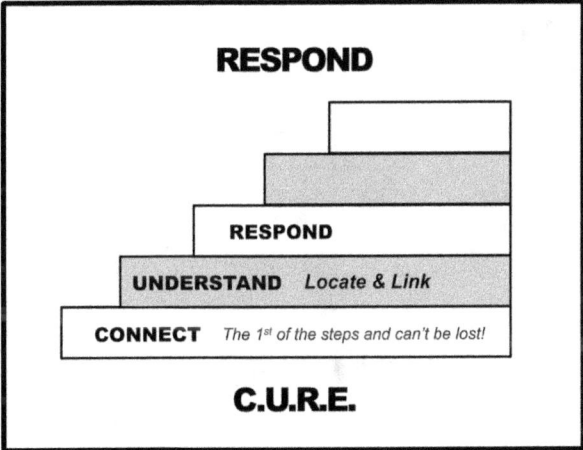

7: THE RESPONSE STEP – THE FIVE TOOL BAGS

Responding, or applying therapeutic and counselling strategies for change, is now safely able to be established on the connection and understanding steps. Apart from the greatest danger to the response step being an inadequate foundation, the other risk is for counsellors to go beyond their capacity, training or level of supervisory support. This section helps provide a way of understanding where various therapeutic strategies (tools) fit, especially in relation to the Circles. The response step helps one to locate which approaches are suitable for which levels of training, as well as to have a sequence or hierarchy of approaches for various therapeutic challenges and complexities. This allows the counsellor to be aware of which group of tools to apply for which problems, and at which stages of therapy. In essence, the deeper the issues, the more need for the tools from the inner circles (bags). The peripheral tools are generally quicker and easier to use compared to the inner ones.

The issues of this section:

- How can I be a better therapist?
- What makes the difference between a good therapist and an expert therapist?

The CWF suggests that the critical issue is the linking of the

- **Problems** with the **possibilities**.
- **People** involved, the counsellee, with the counsellor and God.

The emphasis of the CWF is to provide a framework rather than a model. In order to facilitate change and to be able to do therapy, it is important to be up-skilled generically in various therapeutic modalities and be able to integrate these with the CWF.

The CWF Tool Bag

The tool bag is based predominantly on the Circles as mentioned in the management plan. In this tool bag, you can place your own therapeutic tools, models and approaches. The tool bag enables you to retain a broad therapeutic approach as opposed to becoming narrow or restricted. The CWF also allows for specialisation, which means you don't have to have all the tools and therapeutic models and you can see what you can and can't do. The CWF enhances breadth, allowing one to consider both:

- Psychological and Spiritual.
- Supernatural and Natural.
- Affective and Cognitive.
- Shallow and Deep.
- Inside and Outside.
- Individual and Systemic Group Issues.
- Brief and Long term Interventions.

Map

Provides a direction and a sequence for change. On this map, you can:

- Drive your own car (therapeutic process).
- Go in the direction you choose as opposed to being totally led by the counsellee, like two lost people wandering around. The invitational posture ensures the counsellee remains in a central place in therapy.
- Have direction for each session and the whole of therapy.
- Find the freeways and avoid the side roads (unless you need them).

The map allows you to start any session from wherever the counsellee begins and head centripetally (towards central) into the inner circles (like roads heading into the central business district). It allows internal changes to come out of the heart of the person such that there are actual behavioural and external changes from therapy. This general direction of moving inwards and ideally upwards to God, and then outwards is the overall direction of therapy and also the guideline for each session.

Thus when Mandy comes in for therapy, she starts to talk about her outer circles in terms of what has happened in the various social aspects of her life: what she has done (behaviour) or said (communication). You can then pick up the more centrally located issues so there can be a centripetal movement into her heart. This centring can be facilitated by asking centring questions like, 'How's that for you?' 'What's that like for you?' 'What was the impact of that on you?' and 'What did that mean to you?'

The 5 Steps

The response step is the third of the 5 Steps and is based on the preceding understanding (locating and linking) step which is based on the ongoing foundation of the connection step. Remember each of these steps is dependent on and sits on the previous one. They are not rungs in a ladder where the previous rung can be discarded once past. They are applicable throughout the counselling process, as well as to each individual session. If a session is not proceeding well, it is often helpful to walk back down the steps, even to the point of reconnecting, if that first step has been lost.

The speed limit for the journey

How fast, far or deep one goes in a session is determined by the invitational posture. While retaining a connection (the first step), it is critical to move on into the journey of therapy with the counsellee giving full consent and therefore retaining power and choice (control sector). However, the counsellee has come to you for expertise. Being an expert is based more in the truth sector than the control sector, and indicates knowledge (mind), skills (physical circle) and professional attitudes (heart circle). Expertise does not have to mean dominance.

Remember, the invitational posture consists of the therapist:

- being one step beside (retaining the connection)
- being one step behind (allowing the counsellee to lead)
- looking ahead (having more knowledge about the counselling aspect of the map than the counsellee who has more knowledge about their own issues)
- showing the options, empowering the counsellee
- not going ahead in terms of:
  - » dragging the counsellee in the direction you choose
  - » kicking the counsellee from the back to hurry up
  - » bashing the counsellee on the head (even with the Bible!).

This invitational posture is highly ethical, providing for counsellee consent throughout the process of counselling. The approach Jesus had to the woman at the well and the woman caught in adultery is characterised by connection and understanding, followed by a joint moving towards a response. Jesus was very directive at times, particularly with the Pharisees (top left-hand quadrant people), confronting them about their hypocritical, incongruent approach. One can still be on the response step while providing assertive options and challenges.

THE QUESTIONS FOR THE RESPONSE STEP ARE:

- How do the Circles broaden one's 'tool bag'?
- How do the Circles provide a 'map' for therapy?

The 5 Tool Bags

1. Social
- The church
  - » How can the church be a worshipping and a therapeutic community, a community of change?
- The family
  - » How are the Circles and the car metaphor used to bring change?
- The marriage
  - » How can circular causality be used for change?
  - » What are the metaphors of marriage, and how can they be used for change?
  - » What are the hierarchies of intervention?

2. Physical
- What tools are located in three of the four physical sectors?
- How can behaviour change the three negative moods?
- Behavioural tools and integration: What are the issues?

3. Mind
- Where do eight aspects of cognitive change fit on the Circles?
- What are five ways we think?
- What are five core questions we ask and where do they fit in the Circles?
- What are five core beliefs we hold and where do they fit in the Circles?
- Cognitive tools and integration: Who are some of the authors who have used these?

4. The personality
- Where do six aspects of psychodynamic change fit on the Circles?
- Transference: What is it, and what are its uses and abuses?
- Psychodynamic tools and integration: Who are some of the authors who have used these?

5. The spirit
How do the five sectors of the personality link in with:

- Spiritual provisions?
- The purposes of the spirit?

- Our spiritual positioning?
- Repentance?

What 10 benefits do the sectors of the personality receive from the spirit?

REMEMBER MANDY

Mandy is a 40-year-old Caucasian woman with two children and she works in a pharmacy. She is in the process of separating from her husband after 20 years of marriage. She came to see you because she has been suicidal, depressed and anxious. Although she does not feel her Christian life is very active, she still has a strong underlying sense of faith. She feels unsupported by her church. This is aggravated by the fact that she is involved in an affair outside of her marriage.

When Mandy comes to a session, the tool bag and the map will help you to be with her, and find a way into her heart, regardless of where she starts. So, you join with her and walk the journey into her heart and out again into her everyday life. She may start a session with any of the following issues:

- Church…
- Family…
- Alcohol…
- Her health…
- Her sadness…
- Her long devotions…
- Wondering why she is coming…
- Nothing in particular…
- Feeling out of control…
- Feeling confused…

Use centring questions which start the journey into the heart:

- 'How is that for you?'
- 'What does that do to you?'
- 'Where does that leave you?'

The purpose of this section in the tool bag is not to give a complete guide to the various models of intervention and therapeutic tools within each part of the bag. It is more to show the need for a broad approach to interventions and helping change, which is facilitated by seeing the Circles as a tool bag. The CWF provides a framework more than a model for change.

To find out the models and approaches to change in each of the compartments (circles and sectors), it is important to refer to the standard texts in those disciplines/areas, as well as accessing the knowledge and skills you already have. The CWF will allow you to be clearer about which tools you have, and which tools you don't have. As you become more aware of the therapeutic tools of your tool bag, you will be spurred on to find out (network with) those who have these skills so that you can refer your patient/client/counsellee to such people. In addition, you may also be more directed in terms of where your areas of growth need to be, and which tools you yourself need to be mastering.

8: THE SOCIAL TOOL BAG

For training purposes, the capacity to use the church
tools *is expected at all levels of learning.*

For training purposes, the capacity to use the marriage and
family tools *is expected at advanced levels of learning.*

The social tool bag is so named because we are looking at using the social circle to promote change. The social tools covered in this section are primarily concerning finding opportunities for change in the areas of church, family and marriage. As a result of that change within the social circle, (e.g. in the marriage) changes can occur within individuals who are part of that system.

The aim of change in the social circle is to facilitate the whole system to move individually and together towards the top right-hand corner of the *Square*, living from the foot of the *Cross,* and accessing the *Pyramid.*

A significant amount of change can occur in the context of changes arising from church, family and marriage. The principles and practices of change in these contexts can be applied to other situations where relationships are involved, such as with peers and co-workers.

MANDY'S SOCIAL CIRCLES

Social

- Work: She is managing in the pharmacy, but not performing as well as previously.
- Friends: She is withdrawing from social contact, but maintaining a couple of long-term friendships.
- Family: She has little support from her parents and siblings.
- Intimate relationships:
  - » Spouse: Mandy is in the process of separating from her husband after 20 years.
  - » Affair: She is involved in an affair of one year duration, which has become sexual.
- Counsellor: She has experienced a breach of confidentiality.

Social: past

- Family: Mandy grew up in a dysfunctional family where there was:
  - » Love sector: A lack of love.
  - » Truth sector: Role reversal where she had to look after her parents and triangulation where she was used in the marital dynamics by one parent against the other.
  - » Control Sector: A sense of being blamed.
- Friends: Largely a loner with no intimate relationships during her teenage years.
- Church: Felt used by church, partly because she was obsessively helpful.
- School: Somewhat obsessive in her work and had a number of moves of school.
- God: A long and strong faith.
- Events: One episode of being sexually abused.

For Mandy, positive changes can occur as a result of changes in her social circle including the church, the family and marriage.

CHURCH AND CHANGE

To be a relevant place of change for Mandy, the church has to be a place for safe relationship, where she can Connect, be Understood (in all of her 5 Shapes) so that then she can make changes with appropriate responses from those around her.

Question: Can the church be both a worshipping and a therapeutic community?

THE CHURCH AS A PLACE FOR CHANGE?

The church has the potential to be the largest therapeutic organism there is. As an agent of change, the church needs to be a place for healing and wholeness. For this to occur, it needs to be primarily a relational body and in this way an organism rather than an organisation although this is also important. For relationship to take place, the church has to be a safe place for connection and understanding.

THE CHURCH AS A PLACE FOR RELATIONSHIP?

A critical dimension of safe relationship is size. The 'S' of S.A.F.E.T.Y, required for connection refers to 'size' or the number of people involved in the connection. Size is important! The smaller the size the safer it will be.

The body is the most common metaphor used in the Bible for the church. The body is made up of parts, called systems, such as the cardiovascular, gastrointestinal or nervous system. The body has systems of various sizes operating on five different levels. These levels include the individual *cell* being contained within the *cluster of cells* that surround it, which are then contained within the *organ* (e.g. the heart), contained within the *system* and all are then contained within the whole *body*.

In the same way the church can be seen to have various levels and sizes of relationship. If the church is meant to be predominantly relational and all levels of the church are important, it makes sense to have a hierarchy of the levels within the church. Begin with the size that is most likely to promote relationship. The extent a counsellee can experience relationship with Connection and Understanding is inversely proportional to the size of the group. Smaller is always safer and generally, it is at the smaller level that one can *trialogue* in deeper ways.

Trialogue is not about being alone, focussing just on a horizontal, social relationship with another, nor only a vertical, spiritual relationship with God. Trialogue is connecting in SAFETY with another person and God. In its essence, it is 'share and prayer'. It is an example of loving the Lord our God with all of our heart, soul, mind and strength and our neighbour as ourselves" (Mark 12: 30, 31). It can occur with another person, and is best when there is a sufficient overlap of circles (particularly where the two people can get on with each other). It can also occur in a small group and healthy Christ-centred couples can practise it in their relationship.

Trialogue can occur at various levels in connection with another person and with God:

- **Social**: Just being together, all three.
- **Physical**: Doing things together and talking together.
- **Mind**: 'Mind it', meaning sharing one's mind, including sharing feelings and intuitions, passion and interests, vision and imagination, ideas and inventions, between you, the other, and God.
- **Heart to Heart**: Undefended sharing: love vs aloneness, who I am vs confusion, choice vs despair

Trialogue happens in the context of S.A.F.E.T.Y, and where there are 'You' questions like 'What difference is God making in your life?' This is a spiritual 'You' question. Others include entry questions, centralising questions, appropriate linking questions and responding questions (rf. Connection).

The sizes of relational levels within the church (going from small to big) are:

- **Twos and threes**: This is where you connect with another one or two people, sharing at a deeper level (heart to heart, going more into the central aspects of the Circles) in the presence of God, in other words trialogue.
- **Small-group**: This grouping can be up to about 12 people, meeting every one to two weeks, possibly around a particular focus like study, prayer and areas of interest, or just meeting with each other and God.
- **Weekend church**: The weekly service.
- **The local denominational level**: This for example can be a quarterly meeting of people within the area who share a similar worship style.
- **The local whole body**: All of the churches within the area.

Some people feel safer in a large group, such as the weekend service, but that may be because connection at any deeper level feels unsafe. Many churches emphasise the weekend church service and overlook the importance of the places for greater connection like the twos and threes and small groups. They also may neglect the larger expressions of the body of Christ like the local denominational and whole-body level. To have a healthy and balanced church life, it makes sense to connect across all of the levels of church. Ideally the priority given to meetings in the body of Christ should be proportional to the capacity for relationship at that level.

In this way one would meet with:

- One or two others more than the…
- Small group, more than the…
- Weekend church, more than the…
- Local denominational level, more than the…
- Local whole body of Christ.

Rarely would you hear a preacher say, 'If you are too busy to go to a small group, you are much too busy to come here to weekend church!' Significantly, church has become more weekend and stage centred. Church needs to become a more relational place so that it can become a place for wholeness. The church is a very important part of the Pyramid, but it is not the whole Pyramid or the whole body of Christ. The other corners of the Pyramid also contribute:

- Family and friends.
- The people helping arm of the church (Para-church).
- Christian professionals who specialise in coaching and counselling.

The church should be helping people to move to the top right-hand corner of the Square. This is the place of God-centred, positive living. The church is not primarily a counselling centre although some counselling centres are based in churches and mental health issues can be addressed there. It is especially in the smaller groups that one can use the common language of the 5 Steps and the 5 Shapes of the Christian Wholeness Framework to facilitate change and growth. One can use the 5 Shapes to grow in understanding and change at the level of twos and threes and small groups regardless of the overt reason (e.g. Bible study/women's groups) for the small group.

Checklist for CWF in twos and threes and small groups

The following notes can be used as a checklist/reminder for twos and threes and small groups as they look at facilitating depth of relationship, movement towards a God-centred positive life and being a follower of Jesus in the context of the church as the body of Christ.

WHY USE THE CHRISTIAN WHOLENESS FRAMEWORK?

- To live the Great Commandment (Mark12:30,31) and the New Commandment Jesus gave us (John 13:34).
- To grow as a follower of Jesus, rather than of yourself (Mark 8:34-37).
- To grow the body of Jesus, the church (Eph. 4:12-16).
- To become holy whole (1 Thess. 5:23) in your:
  - » Spirit
  - » Soul/heart changing from:
    Shame to love and connection
    Lost to known and understood
    Despair to hope, response, freedom and choice
    Defended and stuck to being open, growing and changing.
  - » Mind
  - » Body
  - » Social functioning:
    Family
    Friends
    Church
    Work /school
- To do the Great Commission (Matt 28:19,20).

THE WHAT, WHY, WHERE, WHEN, AND HOW TO CHANGE, USING THE CWF

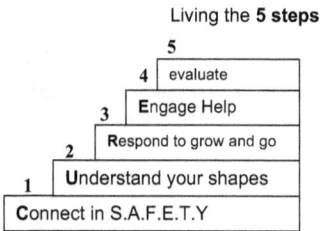

Living the **5 steps**	Living the 5 **shapes**
5	How are we really living?
4 evaluate	How is your Pyramid?
3 Engage Help	How can we grow and go?
2 Respond to grow and go	How are your (and my) 5 shapes?
1 Understand your shapes	How are we connecting?
Connect in S.A.F.E.T.Y	

Square: Centredness (I, other = sin vs God) Success --- Suffering
Triangle: God, others, self
Circle: Five levels: Social, Physical, Mind, Heart, Spirit
Pyramid: Apex: God; Four Corners: family/friends, church, ministry, professional.

Cross: Below the bar = spirit position: dead in sin vs dead to sin and born-again; disconnected vs connected in the Trinity, in God's family and in God's kingdom where there is:

- Unfailing love
- Forgiveness
- Freedom;
- Fullness; for the
- Fight above the bar

Speed of travel: The Invitational Posture:

- One step beside and behind
- See ahead but don't go ahead

Step I: **Connection: 'How is it going...?' 5 Shapes**

Square: Which quadrant is our connection in?
Triangle: Who do we connect with? (monologue, dialogue, trialogue)
Circle: How deep do we go?
Pyramid: How are our other connections?
Cross: Do we meet together at the Cross?

SAFETY

Size Smaller = safer: twos and threes, small groups, church.
Attitude Care, Confidentiality (How private is this?), Consent ('What do you want?').
Face How real are we? (Fake, Flight, Fight, Freak, Flop).
Empathy 'What is it like in your shoes, eyes, head, and heart?'
Time Do we have enough consistent time to connect?
You 'You' Questions: Entry questions: 'How are you?' 'Where are you?'
...move up to Step II

Step II: **Understand your (and my) 5 Shapes**

Square: Which quadrant are you in with...?
Triangle: God, others, yourself.
Circle: Ask Centralising Questions: 'What is that like for you?' Linking Questions 'Does this link with the past/other situations?'
Pyramid: Four corners: How are they going?
Cross: 'What difference is God making in your life?'
...move up to Step III

159

Step III:	**Respond in all 5 Shapes, together: Think, How can I help you...?**
Cross:	Live from your central spirit position and from the foot of the Cross?
Square:	Move towards the top right corner in your Triangle, Circles and Pyramid?
Triangle:	In your three connections, with God, others, self?
Circle:	In your five circles: Live out from your central circle, through all your circles.
Pyramid:	In your four corners: How are they growing? How are you a part of other Pyramids? ...move up to Step IV

Step IV:	**Engage other help**
Pyramid:	How can I be a part of your Pyramid? Who else do you need in your Pyramid? How can you grow to be part of other Pyramids?

Step V:	**Evaluate each step**
	How are we journeying on the 5 Steps and 5 Shapes?

GROUP THERAPY

Groups can provide a sense of connection and belonging, resulting in a sense of, 'I am not alone in this' and 'I do belong'. Particular groups which are helpful in a church context include Recovery Groups and the Search for Life programmes. Groups for specific populations (women, mothers, special interest groups for specific areas of need) can be very helpful. The Alcoholics Anonymous movement and especially the Christian version have been immensely powerful agents for change.

HOW DO GROUPS WITHIN THE CHURCH DIFFER?

Within the local church corner of the Pyramid, there are the small groups. These may be defined by demographic variables like gender, age, individual/family/couples or by areas of interest (prayer/Bible study/sport). Church based groups are specifically for receiving and giving, as part of a local church.

In another corner of the Pyramid there are people helper/Para-church groups. These groups run more specific programs for developing skills and assisting change. These may be for general or more specific areas of need such as addictions, mood related problems, relationship issues. People helper groups also include general recovery groups or groups defined by a specific demographic variable like marriage, parenting, personal development and gender specific ministries. These people helper and ministry groups are over and above men's/women's church based small groups which fit more into the local church.

HOW DO I DO GROUP THERAPY?

There are a range of methods of group therapy and each one can be based on a variety of theoretical approaches. The CWF does not set out to provide a specific method of group therapy but rather allows the use of the 5 Steps and 5 Shapes in the context of group therapy as in any other situation.

For Mandy, by being in a CWF informed church, she can find a safe place for connecting and being understood. In this safe place, she can then move on to a greater likelihood of responding to her own issues with the appropriate responses of those around her. The 5 Steps and 5 Shapes of the CWF can help facilitate the process of groups in the church, Para-church ministries or in group therapy.

FAMILY THERAPY

Family therapy is dependent on a thorough understanding of the family. Family therapy can be quite complex because there are a number of individuals involved and multiple lines of interactions between them. Considering this, it may be helpful to have more than one therapist. This will make it easier to understand, not only the content of what is talked about, but also the process of how the members in the family relate at any particular time of the interview. In this context, one (or more) of the therapists can be present in the room or observing through a one-way window. It also may be helpful to schedule extended sessions to be able to understand the content and process, for example one and a half hours instead of 50 minutes.

It would be ideal to have individual time with each member of the family first but that can be time consuming. This will enable you to get a good idea of the shapes (especially the Circles) of each person. The family ideally needs to be seen together in order to get the view of the shapes (especially the Circles) of the family system without necessarily having details of the individual shapes which surround and make up that system.

For Mandy, family therapy is going to be particularly relevant because her children are feeling the impact of what has been happening in her life. They are also affected by the possible separation of their parents.

Question: How can the Circles and the car metaphor be used for change?

THE GOALS FOR FAMILY CHANGE/FAMILY THERAPY

For Mandy and her family, the main goals are to:

- Rise from their sufferings (below the water level) and get back to being a functioning family (above the water level) in a God-centred way (right-hand side in the Square).
- Be a family which is safe from breaking up, where there is love and respect in an empowered and God-centred way. They need to be able to cope in a much better way as a family. (This refers to the circle of the heart: love, truth, control, centredness and coping sectors).

In order to conduct successful family therapy, it is important as a therapist to have a clear view of where you are going and where the family wants to go. This requires a clear understanding of what a 'top right-hand quadrant family' looks like. The ultimate goal of therapy involves change in all the people and the system. For internal changes to be realised, they must be shown and expressed through the physical circle i.e. by behaviour and communication change. For holistic change to be genuine and enduring there has to be deep, inner change. Having clear goals will clarify and facilitate direction for change in the various circles.

As mentioned, there are a variety of family therapeutic tools or methods available to realise these changes. It will depend on your training, preference, and on what is considered to be best for the particular family with whom you are dealing. The methods and tools for family therapy are generic and not specific to the CWF. To do family therapy effectively, you have to receive training in the family therapy approach you prefer and integrate that into the CWF.

The intention of the CWF is to increase your capacity to conduct family therapy in whichever modality/method you prefer.

THE SEQUENCE AND PRIORITY OF FAMILY THERAPY RESPONSES

Physical change

- Behavioural change occurs more quickly than in-depth change. For a system to be able to change at behavioural level in a lasting way, it is best to focus on behavioural management first, rather than in-depth changes which take longer. External changes will result in internal changes over time. Having said that, normal living is ideally from the inside out. This is particularly true when change is driven from the transformation of the inner circle, which is the spiritual position of the individual or system.
- Communication is central to facilitating change and the 'first port of call' in marital therapy.

Cognitive change

- Cognitive change in the family particularly involves being able to deal with problems as problems as opposed to personalising them. Affect regulation or controlling the level of feelings within the family is also important.

Psychodynamic change

- Psychodynamic change focuses on changing the storyline coming down from the previous generations and especially from both sets of families. The ongoing narrative passing on to the children becomes the predominant storyline. Matters of family transference where things from the past are transferred into the present family must also be identified and dealt with.

Family Therapy Models: It is often easier to start at the outside

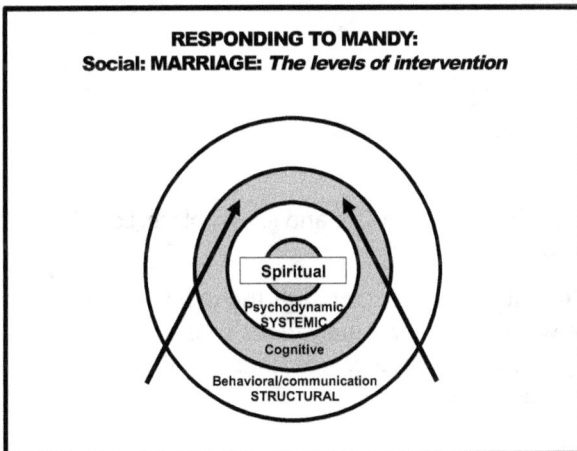

RESPONDING TO MANDY:
Social: MARRIAGE: *The levels of intervention*

Spiritual

Psychodynamic
SYSTEMIC

Cognitive

Behavioral/communication
STRUCTURAL

CHANGING THE CIRCLES OF THE FAMILY

Here is the tool bag and framework for intervention based, for the sake of clarity, on the Circles of the family, from inner to outer. Goals of change and possible methods for change are outlined.

While family therapy is in the social and peripheral circle, it is considered to be more for advanced counsellors. You may prefer to skip this section and return to it after looking at change in the inner circles of the individual.

Changing the spiritual circle of the family

Goals: Encouraging family members to become God-centred again (especially within the marital subsystem). This can be achieved with spiritual disciplines including prayer and scripture in the context of casual conversation and family gatherings.

Methods: Through the expression of individual spiritual changes in and through the family and out to others. The more family members whose spirit has changed *position* through repentance and justification (rf. spirit circle), live out that change in *practice* (by repentance and sanctification), the more the whole family lives in the Spirit. The more the fruit of the Spirit is expressed within the family, the more it will be expressed out from the family to others.

For Mandy and her family, a greater degree of change through all of the circles of the family can occur as the individuals become Christ-centred and Spirit-filled.

Changing the heart circle of the family

LOVE SECTOR CHANGES

Goals: For the family to be a safe and loving place. Love is the foundation of the heart of the family.

Methods: Connection grows through the practise of SAFETY. This takes time as the whole family and the various subsystems (marital, parenting, sibling) within it, come together, do things together and communicate together (using tennis communication).

For Mandy and her family it is going to take time and practice to achieve these things.

TRUTH SECTOR CHANGES

Goals

- Boundaries and roles: The family should be a place of understanding and respect where boundaries and roles are acknowledged. The individuals within this family need to be seen as separate identities with their own set of Circles, including opinions and ways of doing things. Each person is able to have their own space where possible and their own time as appropriate. Clarity of the role of each member is important, particularly the parents taking the lead role in the family, which is critical to family functioning.

- Identity: Develop a family history with memories which say, 'This is our family,' as opposed to being just any family. This will increase the sense of identity and respect for the family and the sub systems within it.

- Limits: Promote clear limits for individuals, subsystems and the family as a whole, clarifying what is okay and what is not, what is acceptable and what is not. These limits may change as the family develops.

Methods

Implementation of the goals through understanding and encouraging the various needs and roles of individuals. Doing things like spending time together, recording (written, photographic) and reminiscing about events, as well as developing family rituals or habits, such as various celebrations and significant days, weeks and years. It is important to have clear guidelines and rules that will enable the family to function effectively.

For Mandy and her family, implementing the goals and sustaining them will be a challenge.

CONTROL SECTOR CHANGES

Goals

Order and flexibility are required in the family so that it isn't chaotic or rigid. The family also needs constructive parenting so the children can live in an environment with external controls which they can adopt as they grow up. This way they can be in control of themselves as they move out of the family and into adulthood.

Methods

Implementation of the goals through rules which are clear and relevant and by encouraging individual, subsystem and family proactive initiatives as appropriate.

For Mandy, this will be particularly important to work on with her husband, specifically in relation to parenting.

CENTRED SECTOR CHANGES

Goals

With each individual being God-centred, there is a much greater capacity for proactive rather than reactive relationship.

Methods

Implementation of the goals through modelling God-centred living and promoting a culture of living and talking about where an individual, a subsystem, or the whole family is, in relation to the two columns of the Square i.e. self-centred vs God-centred.

Mandy and her husband, in the context of their supportive Pyramids, can find their own ways of becoming more God-centred in all parts of their family.

COPING SECTOR CHANGES

Goals

The coping sector is also the exit of the heart. It is the sector where the heart is expressed out into the other circles. If the family can live the great commandment of loving God, each other and themselves, in a committed way using healthy communication to face the issues, then they will be able to adapt to change and grow. If the family copes in dysfunctional ways, particularly employing fight/flight mechanisms (either active or passive) they will proceed along a destructive path which will erode the love sector and advance the collapse of the other sectors (truth and control).

Methods

Implementation of the goals through promotion of attitude and action in facing issues using communication skills (communication tennis).

For Mandy and her family learning communication tennis will become a key to change.

Changing the mind circle of the family

Goals
The importance of the mood of the family cannot be overstated, especially in seeking to promote the mood and the fruits of the Spirit (love, joy and peace instead of anger, sadness and stress). Thought processes and topics of discussion need to be healthy and constructive. Intellectual growth needs to be promoted as much as possible.

Methods
Implementation of the goals through promotion of times of closeness, fun and activity together. Making sure topics of conversation are heading towards the top right-hand corner of the Square. Making time to learn (e.g. school based or through IT/TV, minimising distraction).

For Mandy and her family, setting up time to grow the mind of the family, will be a challenge in the context of the busyness of life. In addition they will have to change their minds from the negative, destructive patterns to positive, constructive ones.

Changing the physical circle of the family

Goals
Promoting the health of the family including diet, use of alcohol/substances and level of fitness. Developing behaviour and activities the family can do together, including chores and leisure activities. Ensuring the communication (a physical circle activity) has healthy content and that it is clear, constructive, cooperative, consistent and considerate.

Methods
Implementation of the goals through things like shopping for healthy food and beverages. Meal management (meal times, shared preparation, participation and clearing up), making exercise a part of the family timetable and where possible doing it as a family. Making time for chores and fun, and getting enough rest and sleep will also help reach the goals.

For Mandy and her family these changes will grow the physical side of their family life.

Changing the social circle of the family

Goals
Promoting healthy socialising as a family and also with other families including visiting and inviting people over.

Methods
Implementation of the goals through choosing times for family gatherings that work with family members (weekly, monthly, annually) and making time for friends and extended family. Also getting involved in church based activities individually and as a family...

For Mandy and her family it will be important to find people with whom they can be real. These relationships are important in the context of finding meaningful and safe places in their social circles.

CHANGE: USING THE DIAGNOSTIC METAPHORS OF THE FAMILY

Change can occur using the diagnostic metaphors of the family. This involves changing the structure of the family using the car metaphor. In order to facilitate change and move onto the response step with the family, it is important to remember we need a good connection and understanding of the family, as we have already established.

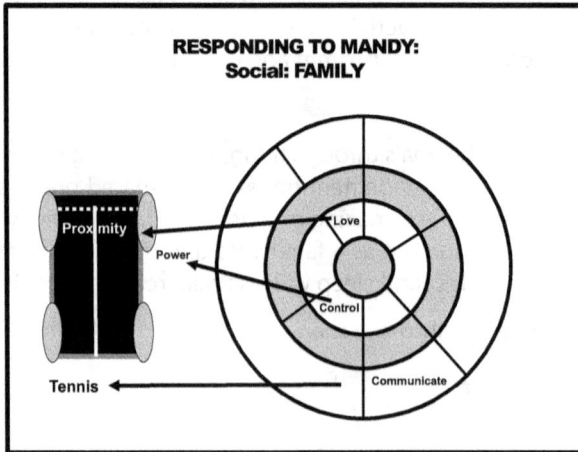

RESPONDING TO MANDY:
Social: FAMILY

The structure of the family car metaphor particularly relates to two sectors of the heart circle, the issues of love and control. It is a helpful way of looking at a structural approach to family therapy. The love and control sectors within the heart circles of the family are critical to understanding the psychological structure of the family. The love sector particularly refers to the proximity/distance between the wheels. The control sector refers to the power attributed to a wheel/person (more powerful if they are bigger in size and closer to the front of the car).

CHANGING THE WHEELS (THE PEOPLE AND THEIR CONTROL SECTORS)

Changing the front wheels
Goals: One of the best things parents can do for the family is to stay connected and remain as the front wheels, in the position of leadership. It is inappropriate for the children to be in a position of power in the family.

Methods: Family therapy involves promoting the power of the parents and positioning the children so that they are children, without any form of parental role. The stability of the car is ensured by making sure that the wheel nuts (commitment) do not loosen and fall off the front wheels (marriage).

Changing the back wheels
The back wheels of the sibling subsystem are an important aspect of the family. Time spent together as siblings in a positive way is clearly an important goal.

Changing the wheels (size and shape)
Size: Size represents power (control sector). Goals in therapy include making sure that the parents are both effective and empowered to provide the same limits. Another goal is allowing the children's wheels to grow in proportion to their age and stage, having greater liberty and more distant limits, as they take more responsibility.

Tread: The tread of the tyres can become worn. There needs to be periods of restoration/retreading of the wheels through positive times together and alone. Things like regular family meals on a weekly basis and annual holidays work well for the family. Where possible finding opportunities for the parental couple to get away without the children and have times when one parent spends time doing an activity with each of the children separately. This retreads the wheels and builds up the axles.

Growing the axles (love sector)

Help the axles have the right distance, so that they are neither too close (co-dependent) to cause friction, nor too distant (inappropriately independent) to become disconnected.

Front axle: Helping parents maintain connection through walking the CURE steps strengthens the front axle and enhances the individuality of the wheels.

Back axle: Promoting connection between siblings so they have constructive times together.

Central rod: The rod connecting the front of the car to the back represents the parent/child connection and the parenting. Growing this axle through coordinated and connected parenting will make the family car function better. To do this the parents need to spend time with each other and have an agreed approach with the children. By clearly communicating that approach consistently they can make a strong parent/child connection for their children.

Mandy and her husband are responsible for what their car is like and what the production line of future family cars (the children's families) will become.

The CWF can assist family therapy by seeing the family as a system, particularly through the shape of the Circles. Various sectors can become targets for change. The metaphor of the car especially highlights the love and control sectors of the heart of the family. Having a clear framework for understanding the family allows one to apply various therapeutic strategies through communication, behavioural, or psychodynamic approaches.

MARITAL/COUPLE THERAPY

Remember Mandy's marriage

MANDY'S CIRCLES

Social: **Intimate relationships**
Spouse: Mandy is in the process of separating from her husband after 20 years of marriage.

Affair: She has been having an affair over the last year which is now a sexual relationship.

Marital therapy is dependent on a thorough understanding of the marriage. As with family therapy, the CWF assists couple therapy. The CWF sees the couple as a system in itself and uses the 5 Steps and especially the shape of the Circles to assist in the process. As with families so with couples, the CWF allows you to apply various therapeutic strategies. These strategies can be applied through communication, behavioural, or psychodynamic approaches. Marital therapy, like family therapy is about responding to a system.

Marital therapy is similar to family therapy in terms of understanding the Circles of the system (in this case the couple), through locating and linking the issues and allowing right responses.

This therapy applies to couples who are courting, are married or are separating/separated.

The goals for the couple are change through couple therapy. If Mandy and her husband can own these goals, they are much more likely to succeed. The goals are to promote the:

Triangle: A threefold cord is so much stronger than a twofold one.

Circles: A couple with Christ in the centre of their own individual lives and in the centre of their relationship will have the centre of rotation in the centre for all the circles of their marriage This will give them a smoother ride.

Square: Moving towards the top right-hand corner in all of the circles of their relationship: social relating; physical health and intimacy; mind; heart and spirit circles.

Cross: Being able to come together at the foot of the Cross.

Pyramid: To have a joint support network including mutual family and friends and a church where both feel at home and where both can give and receive. The Pyramid also provides them with people who can minister to or help them as a couple, in their journey towards Christian wholeness with things like marital retreats, courses and more personalised assistance. When they are more in the top right-hand corner, the couple will be able to minister and help others. In this way they can be part of other peoples' Pyramids.

The methods and tools for couple therapy are generic and not specific to the CWF. The development of tools requires training in whatever form of marital therapy you prefer and integrating that with the CWF.

The tool bag and framework for interventions is based on the Circles of the marriage, moving from the inside out. Again, as with family therapy, goals of change and possible methods for change are outlined. In addition, changes occur through addressing the diagnostic metaphors of the marriage.

While marital therapy is in the social and peripheral circle, it is considered to be more for advanced counsellors. You may prefer to skip this section and return to it after looking at the inner circles of the individual.

In order to facilitate change, and to move onto the response step with the marriage, it is important to have a good connection and understanding of the marriage, as noted previously

THE SEQUENCE AND PRIORITY OF MARITAL THERAPY RESPONSES

As for family therapy, so in couple therapy, behavioural change occurs more quickly than in depth change. If a system can change at the behavioural level in a lasting way it is best to first focus on behaviour rather than aiming for in-depth change that takes longer. It is intended that the external changes will result in internal changes over time. Nevertheless, change ideally and normally, occurs from the inside out. This is particularly true when that change is driven from the transformation of the inner circle, the spiritual position of that individual or system.

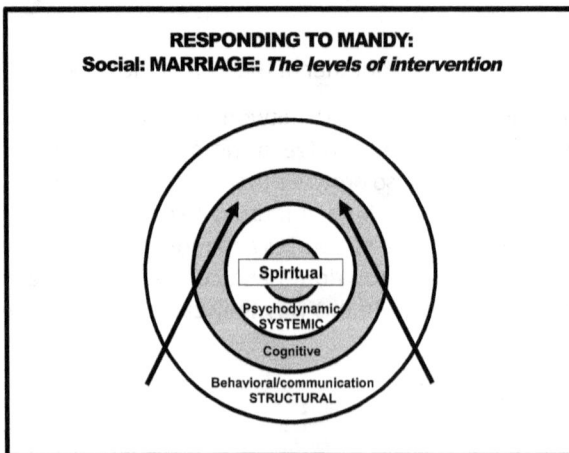

RESPONDING TO MANDY:
Social: MARRIAGE: *The levels of intervention*

Spiritual

Psychodynamic
SYSTEMIC

Cognitive

Behavioral/communication
STRUCTURAL

Here is the tool bag and framework for interventions based, for the sake of clarity, on the Circles of the marriage from the inside out. The goals of change and possible methods for change are outlined.

CHANGING THE CIRCLES OF THE COUPLE

Using the Circles of marriage as a tool bag for change.

Changing the spirit circle of the couple

Goals
As with families, to encourage the couple to become God-centred in position as well as in practice.

Methods
As with families, individually and collectively, by putting their spiritual position into practice. The couple can do this by repentance, expressing the fruit of the Spirit, and practising spiritual disciplines together and then turning that outwards to others.

For Mandy and her husband, their spiritual life will be central to the change in their marriage. Couples who truly access their life in Christ have that central threefold cord and the advantage of the central axis to the wheels of their marriage.

Changing the heart circle of the couple

LOVE SECTOR CHANGES

Goals
As with families, for the marriage to be a safe and nurturing place of love.

Methods
As with families especially through the growth of connection through the practice of SAFETY. This involves spending time as a couple (size is small), having fun and facing issues especially through empathic communication, asking things like 'How are you?' and 'Where are you at?' Love of the heart,

which is deeper than loving feelings, grows with time. It is significantly enhanced when each person experiences the *agape* love of God in the times when they fail and fall.

For Mandy and her husband, growing the SAFETY in their relationship will be essential. It will be especially difficult as they come out of the context of an unsafe relationship where there has been an affair.

TRUTH SECTOR CHANGES

Goals
As with families, the marriage should be a place of respect where boundaries are acknowledged. The marriage needs to enhance the identity of each person as an individual and their identity as a couple. Where there is an equality of worth (love sector) there can be appropriate difference and clarity in roles.

Methods
This can be achieved through understanding and encouraging various individual needs and the God-centred individuality of each person. Developing an identity as a couple in the same way the family identity is grown i.e. by spending time together, remembering past events, as well as developing rituals or habits around events, times of the day, week or year and various celebrations. All these things help couples move towards their goals.

For Mandy and her husband the recovery of respect for each other after the challenges in the marriage will not be easy. They will need a supportive Pyramid around them.

CONTROL SECTOR CHANGES

Goals
A relationship defined by power and control issues is unhealthy. It is important for couples to be releasing and empowering of each other. There needs to be a sharing of decisions, as much as possible. There also needs to be a division of responsibilities, depending on each other's strengths, gifting and skills.

Methods
Implementation of the goals can be achieved through clear communication regarding responsibilities and focusing on building intimacy and re-

spect rather than who has the power. Having a heart that seeks to release, promote and lift up another will also help.

For Mandy and her husband, it will be important for them to move from a restrictive relationship to one that is releasing. Once again, this will be difficult after the affair.

CENTRED SECTOR CHANGES

Goals
For the individuals that make up the identity of the couple to be God-centred. If they are able to be God-centred there is a much greater capacity for being proactive rather than reactive in the relationship. This is almost more important than with families because there is a greater possibility of finding the balance between addressing one's own needs and those of the spouse. It is as if God becomes the fulcrum of the pendulum, allowing each person to swing in a balanced way between their own needs and those of their spouse.

Methods
Implementation of the goals is achieved by each person seeking to be a follower of Jesus in his/her heart. They can achieve this by applying the processes of justification, repentance and sanctification. The couple can share the journey of sanctification (from the left- hand to the right-hand side of the Square) through spiritual disciplines and outward expressions of their God-centred life together.

For Mandy and her husband, their individual and joint relationships with Christ are central to any change.

COPING SECTOR CHANGES

Goals
As with the family, the coping sector is also the exit of the heart, the place where the heart flows out and influences the other circles. So, if the couple can live the great commandment, (loving God, each other and themselves) in a committed way, using healthy communication to face the issues, they will be able to adapt to change and grow. Alternatively if the couple copes in dysfunctional ways, for example using fight/flight mechanisms (actively, which is more likely with men and passively with women), they will end up on a destructive course. This will feed back into the *erosion* of the love sector and the compromise of the other main sectors (truth and control).

Methods

Implementation of the goals is through promotion of attitudes and actions that face the issues. Developing communication skills and designated times for discussion (using communication tennis) is vital. Having fun together and promoting activities and rituals of love, commitment and growth will also contribute to achieving change in the coping sector.

For Mandy and her husband, changing from their old ways of coping to the new ways will take time and courage and knowing they are not doing it alone.

Changing the mind circle of the couple

Goals

As for the family, the goal is to promote the mood and fruits of the Spirit: love, joy and peace instead of anger, sadness and stress. Regulating the levels of mood of the couple ensures there is a more stable ride through hardships as opposed to a rollercoaster experience. Maintaining healthy and constructive thought processes and stimulate intellectual growth where possible.

Methods

As for the family, implement the goals through promotion of times of closeness, fun and quiet activities together. Ensure topics of conversation head towards the top right-hand corner of the Square. Make time to study for intellectual development.

For Mandy and her husband, they need to put aside time for all these things.

Changing the physical circle of the couple

Goals

Similar to the family the goal is to promote the health of the couple with things like healthy eating, controlling use of alcohol/substances, increasing exercise to improve fitness and increasing the sexual intimacy of their marriage. Developing activities the couple can do together including chores and leisure activities. Enhance the content and processes of communication by making it more clear, constructive, cooperative, consistent and considerate.

Methods

Implementation of the goals through methods used for the family, as well as developing appropriate levels of sexual intimacy in the context of the various stages of relationship in marriage:

- Pre-marriage
- Early marriage
- Pregnancy (pre, during and post)
- Ongoing relationship
- Later life

For Mandy and her husband it may take a while to restore the sexual intimacy. Growing the other physical aspects of their relationship will help.

Changing the social circle of the couple

Goals

As for the family, promoting healthy socialising as a couple with other couples,

Methods

Implementation of the goals through spending time weekly, monthly and/or annually with other couples, doing church based activities together and individually. Developing leisure activities with other couples like dancing, walking and sport.

For Mandy and her husband, change will accelerate if they find other couples to be with and as they have their own social life together.

CHANGE: USING THE DIAGNOSTIC METAPHORS OF THE MARRIAGE

These metaphors have already been used for the understanding step in marital assessment. It is from this position that the response step and change can occur.

STRENGTHENING THE TRIANGLE AND THE THREEFOLD CORD

Goals
This highlights the importance of individuality and togetherness in retaining a connection with God.

Methods
Having regular individual and collective time doing spiritual disciplines on a daily, weekly and even longer on a quarterly/annual basis.

GROWING THE 3 CANDLES

The two become one and then the two are three. The 3 candles, the 3 circles, and the 3 rivers, refer to the two individuals and the one marriage.

Goals
Promotion of the growth of each individual particularly in relation to the 5 Shapes, regardless of what the other one is doing.

Methods
Each person individually seeks to contribute to the growth of the middle candle, the relationship.

DEVELOPING THE 3 CIRCLES

Goals
In particular the therapist will want to move the heart of the marriage towards the top right-hand corner to a place of God-centredness.

Methods
The middle circle represents the marriage. The couple therapist is more concerned about this middle circle of the marriage than the individual circles (his and hers) on either side. As discovered in understanding the couple, in the outer circles there is a loop of connection and communication (verbal and non-verbal) between his circles and her circles. On the response step, change needs to happen in the relationship, particularly moving from a destructive/vicious loop to a constructive/victorious loop in the upward direction.

Change has to happen at some of the six points in this loop, such as:

1. The exit from her: Change can happen with what she says and does.

2. His entrance: Change can happen with how he perceives the incoming messages.

3. His inner circles (especially his heart): Change can happen with how the incoming messages are experienced by him in the context of his own story and life journey. This may require him to implement some personal changes so that the incoming messages are not contaminated by his own issues.

4. The exit from him: Change can happen with what he says and does.

5. Her entrance: Change can happen with how she perceives the incoming messages.

6. Her inner circles (especially her heart): Change can happen with how the incoming messages are experienced by her in the context of her own story and life journey. This may require her to make personal changes so that the incoming messages are not contaminated by her own issues.

The purpose of this process in therapy is to address individual actions, words, perceptions and experiences. Setting aside individual time to look at the experiences of the inner circles may need to be done as an addition to the marital work.

For Mandy and her husband the candles have nearly blown out. Their interactions have spiralled down in a vicious cycle. Ahead of them is the rebuilding of their own candles, so that they can also keep the middle candle burning. Ahead of them is the change they both need to make to the six points of interaction.

RIDING THE THREE RIVERS

This metaphor provides a tool to help the couple understand the normality of turbulence at the beginning of marriage and motivate them to take the bridge/shortcut across the turbulent river by using effective communication as opposed to going the long way around each tributary, which would involve extensive individual therapy for both of them!

For Mandy and her husband, unless they really learn to take the short cut of communication (with the assistance of communication tennis) they both have a very long journey up their tributaries, to get around the river of their current turbulence.

GROWING THE LOVE SECTOR AND THE WEDDING CAKE

The base: Promotes commitment love assisted by sexual purity, being with others with a similar value system, staying away from temptations and staying close to God. Growth of the friendship is a strong protective factor for unfaithfulness.

The fruitcake: Represents spending time in a positive way (overlapping each other's circles) doing things together and being with each other, being mindful to address conflicts that could come up and eat away the fruitcake.

The icing: Ongoing growth of the sexual aspect of the relationship. Once again being very careful to address and deal with anything which would get in the way particularly other relationships or sexual temptations including pornography.

For Mandy and her husband, each level of the wedding cake has been so badly damaged that the whole cake has crumbled and nearly collapsed. In many ways they have to make all three levels again.

THE CONTROL SECTOR AND THE SEESAW

Goal
To promote equality of power as much as is possible. The aim is to help the couple sit on the seesaw, relating to each other 'adult to adult', as opposed to 'parent to child'.

Method
This is primarily achieved through increased communication and respect (truth sector) where power is not a focus of the relationship. (In other words, deal with the power sector in the relationship, by equalising it as much as is appropriate, so that it becomes neutralised and no longer an issue in the marriage!)

For Mandy and her husband it is easy to live a destabilised life, with the seesaw swinging from one position to another, particularly fuelled by the hurt of the marriage. The more they stabilise the seesaw and relate to each other as adults as opposed to parent/child, the faster they will progress.

THE LOVE AND CONTROL SECTORS AND THE CAR

This is about linking the couple's subsystem with the family. Remember the front wheels and the axle of the car relate to the marriage. This metaphor includes issues of proximity, power and their role as a couple in relation to each other and the children. The importance of the size and tread of the wheels as well as positioning, size and length of the axles is the same for the couple as it is for the family.

In terms of therapy tools, the goal for the couple is to strengthen their:

Axle: Alliance/connection/proximity through marital therapy. Making sure the axle is the right length, not too far apart or too close. If it is too close the wheels will rub together in a state of friction. Promoting a single axle (united and agreed approach to parenting) connecting the parents to the child subsystem.

Wheel nuts: Commitment. The nuts need to be securely tightened so they do not loosen and make the car unstable.

Size: The size of the tyres speaks of promoting individual/mutual growth and equality as a couple.

Tread: Representing enhancing individual growth.

For Mandy and her husband growth in their connection and commitment will increase the sense of safety particularly for the two back wheels of the car, their children.

THE COMMUNICATION SECTOR AND TENNIS

Using the metaphor of tennis not only helps in understanding the couple's communication as mentioned, but also provides clear tools for coaching and refereeing to improve the communication. In couple therapy this may mean the therapist has quite an active role refereeing and at times physically sitting beside one of the two people in the relationship. With individual coaching, be mindful to do the same with the other person to maintain neutrality. Neutrality allows the therapist to focus on the marriage primarily rather than the individuals.

Mandy and her husband need to play plenty of games of communication tennis. They need to be careful not to play any big balls (deep and meaningful issues) without a referee/coach present.

In conclusion, we have focused on change within systems and within individuals through tools which are located in the social circle. These changes will promote further changes in the other shapes, particularly with the individuals and the system (church/family/marriage) moving towards the top right-hand corner of the Square, living at the foot of the Cross, and accessing the Pyramid. Remember the family does not only have an individual Pyramid around each person, but also a Pyramid of other families around them as a system. As mentioned, principles and practice of change can be applied to any situation where relationships are involved, such as with peers and at work.

9: THE PHYSICAL TOOL BAG

For training purposes, the capacity to have a basic familiarity *with the* somatic tool bag *is expected at all levels of learning.*

For training purposes, the capacity to use *the* behaviour and communication tools *is expected at all levels of learning.*

Physical tools are therapeutic strategies located in the physical tool bag. They are:

- Somatic Tools
- Behavioural Tools
- Communication Tools

This section contains the somatic, behavioural and communication tools of the physical tool bag. It is not intended to give a complete guide to things such as medication and behavioural therapy. The CWF is a broad framework more than a model for change. Use relevant texts for in depth information regarding medication and behaviour management.

MANDY'S PHYSICAL CIRCLE

Physical: present
- Healthwise, she is not well in her 'soma'/body. She is eating less overall and what she does eat is often junk food. Mandy has increased her alcohol consumption to three units of alcohol per night.
- Sleep and exercise levels have deteriorated along with sexual activity with her husband.
- Behaviourally, Mandy is doing less with her time, including not keeping up with activities of daily living (ADL). Significantly, she is spending up to three hours a day reading her Bible and praying.
- In general Mandy's communication has diminished as she has become more socially withdrawn.

Physical: past
- In the past Mandy had been reasonably physically well.

Mandy will rise more quickly above the water level if she uses physical means alongside tools from the other circles to change.

The tools in the physical circle are from the following sectors:

SOMATIC TOOLS

These include having a medical check up and treatment. In particular things like checking thyroid function, medication and diet/alcohol control. Ongoing regular exercise and sleep are central to somatic health. Mandy needs these.

Despite the fact God made the brain, it can become unwell just like any other part of the body. God has given us the knowledge to develop medications that treat and heal the brain. Medical management of physical depression can actually enhance a person's spiritual experience. Medications may not brighten the 'Son' but they can remove the clouds.

MEDICATIONS AND THE CIRCLES

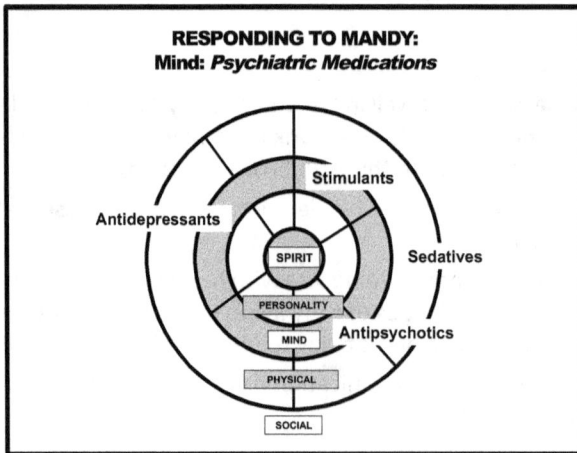

RESPONDING TO MANDY:
Mind: *Psychiatric Medications*

Stimulants

Antidepressants

SPIRIT

Sedatives

PERSONALITY

MIND

Antipsychotics

PHYSICAL

SOCIAL

Medication can assist in the treatment of psychological problems in various sectors including:

Physical circle

» Soma sector: Sleep problems helped by sedatives.

Mind circle

» Mood sector: Depression and anxiety helped by antidepressant medication. Mandy may need an antidepressant.

» Perception and thought sector: Psychosis helped by antipsychotic medication.

» Cognitive sector: ADHD helped by various medications including stimulants.

BEHAVIOUR TOOLS

Behaviour therapy includes a range of strategies such as:

* Response Prevention and Exposure (RPE): Preventing a response to anxiety especially in the context of exposure to the stressor.
* Relaxation: Slow breathing (10 breaths per minute) and muscle relaxation to prevent anxiety.
* Rewards and withdrawal of Rewards (Operant Conditioning): Shaping behaviour by the outcome.

Mandy's marriage can grow as they deposit positive behaviours into their marriage bank and into each other. The outside behavioural changes will impact the inner parts of themselves and their marriage.

Behaviour therapy has caused concerns amongst Christians in that it could imply we are more like an animal, able to be externally manipulated with diminished internal responsibility. The implication is that we have no spirit or soul, like one of Pavlov's dogs or Skinner's rats used in the early development of behaviour therapy. Other Christians have highlighted behavioural approaches, including Jay Adams. The Old Testament focuses on rewards and punishments, as well as the importance of action and behaviour. All these things are about behavioural management. From a CWF perspective, behaviour therapy is a powerful tool in the behaviour sector tool bag. It can be used in the context of a holistic Christian framework.

Behaviour can help a range of issues in the following circles and sectors.

Spirit

The Bible emphasises the importance of behaviour and putting faith into works (e.g. Book of James) The spiritual disciplines (including prayer and Bible reading) also involve behaviour.

Heart

The heart is expressed through attitudinal behaviours. Mandy's heart will change from the outside in, as she chooses actions which link into the sectors of the heart.

- Her love sector will grow as she performs acts of care for her husband.
- Her truth sector will grow as she works on being Mandy and her roles as wife and mother.
- Her control sector will grow as she submits herself to Christ and His Lordship, reviews the choices before her and makes decisions to change.
- Her centredness sector will change, depending on who she serves: herself or Christ.
- Her coping sector will change as she communicates and faces issues instead of withdrawing.

Mind (mood sector)

- Sadness and happiness levels of Mandy can change depending on things like what she does with her time.
- Anger (aggressive behaviour) can be significantly influenced by behaviour management. Use of distraction and finding alternative actions (e.g. walking away, finding a friend/teacher in the case of children) can be effective.
- Worry, fear or stress. Recognising how worry behaves is half the battle (avoidance and withdrawal and repetitive compulsions). Then being real about the fears/worry and gradually exposing oneself to the worry/fear until you are disobeying and overcoming the anxiety. The inhibiting of response to anxiety is called 'response prevention.' It's about trying to face the worry rather than avoiding it or stopping the repetitive compulsion. Being aware that anxiety will initially get worse to start off with makes the battle easier. It would help Mandy to prevent her response to her anxiety of compulsive Bible reading, by actually reducing this behaviour. (Bible study is good, but not as a compulsive behaviour.)

Physical

- Somatic behaviours including sleeping, exercise, eating and sexual activity. Behavioural management can be relevant when dealing with these issues. Learning these would help Mandy.
- Behaviours or activities of daily living are also useful to behaviour modification strategies. Activity can be therapeutic.
- Behavioural communication (non-verbal communication), often used in social skills training, can also fit behavioural therapy/management strategies. This could help Mandy in the way she communicates.

COMMUNICATION TOOLS

Communication tennis is the central metaphor for effective communication. Communication is one of the sectors of the physical circle. Helping Mandy to communicate using the communication tennis approach is a core physical approach to change. Essential to this is the counsellor's capacity to connect with Mandy in SAFETY and understand (which helps her to understand), her 5 Shapes. That will help her communicate about her issues. This has been elaborated upon under Understand–Link, as it is not only a Response tool, but also a way of understanding how a couple (or anyone) communicates.

So for Mandy, her health can improve, her sleep and sexual activity with her husband can improve. She can start to change old behaviour patterns. She can use this to change from the outside in. As she changes physically in the context of good communication, she can also start to change from the inside out, including her mood as she becomes less sad, stressed and irritable.

10: THE MIND TOOL BAG

For training purposes, the capacity to use the cognitive tool bag *is expected at Counsellor Level of learning.*

COGNITIVE THERAPIES

Mind tools are therapeutic strategies related to the mind circle. The main tools in this circle are related to cognitive therapy, as they are to do with the mind and thinking. (In my opinion, 'cognitive' as in cognitive therapy is a loose definition for the thinking or thought focused therapy.). Cognitive therapy is actually a composite of techniques which are located in a number of sectors from differing circles, all impacting and focused on the thought sector (rather than the cognitive sector). This is different from tools in the social and physical circles, which not only focus on, but are also based in and arise from those circles. Cognitive therapies are here defined as those which are focused on, rather than coming from the mind circle. For a more complete approach to CWF informed cognitive therapy, refer to the book, *Wholly Coping*. (This was written initially as a cognitive therapy book, *You can cope!* by my colleague and psychologist Peter Stebbins.)

The tools and techniques for the counsellor to equip the counsellee which impact on thought are:

- Problem Clarification
- Perception Changes
- Thought Changes
- Feeling Recognition
- Sensitivity Management
- Control Location and Management
- Physical Management (Relaxation)
- Problem Solving

The major tool reviewed in the mind tool bag is cognitive therapy. This section is not intended as a complete guide to cognitive therapy. Remember the CWF provides a broad framework more than a model for change.

The cognitive tools used here are from general cognitive therapeutic approaches, which can be further studied in standard texts on the subject.

The role of the mind is highlighted in the Bible, particularly in relation to our thinking. Christians who are particularly fluent in the cognitive approach to counselling include Larry Crabb and Selwyn Hughes.

MANDY'S CIRCLES

Mind: present
- Mood: More sad, irritable, anxious and obsessive.
- Volition: Experiencing less fun, pleasure and passion.
- Perception: Experiencing the sense of an evil presence some nights when going to sleep.
- Thoughts: More negative with some suicidal ideas and feeling a little bit 'got at' by others. She also has some distressing blasphemous thoughts.
- Cognition: Diminished memory and concentration, even though she has a reasonably high IQ (intellect).

Mind: past
- Experienced depression, anxiety and suicidal tendencies in the past.

As mentioned previously, when Mandy comes in for therapy, she would normally start with the outer circles in terms of what has happened in various social aspects of her life and what she had done (behaviour) or said (communication). The therapist then uses centralising questions like, 'How's that for you?' 'What was the impact of that on you?' 'What did that mean to you?' Don't forget to monitor her suicidal thinking.

COGNITIVE TOOLS

The questions responded to in this section:
- Where do eight aspects of cognitive change fit on the Circles?
- What are five ways we think?
- What are five core questions we ask and where do they fit in the Circles?
- What are five core beliefs we hold and where do they fit in the Circles?
- Cognitive tools and integration: Who are some of the authors who have used this approach effectively?

When you are with Mandy it is important to follow her, rather than the sequence defined by the Circles. The eight cognitive tools are laid out on the circles in the diagram here to help clarify where you are at on the map. Start with the easiest and most peripheral, and move initially in a central direction and then back out to the problem. Mandy will be helped by using and practising all of these tools. Change is promoted if the counsellee has:

Problem Clarification

- The counsellee having a clear idea of what the problem really is and where it lies.

Perception Changes

- Changing the way the counsellee perceives the problem.

Thought Changes

- Helping the counsellee become aware of how s/he thinks, what she questions and believes, is central to (at the core of, thus 'core beliefs') cognitive therapy.

Feeling Recognition

- Helping the counsellee become aware of her feelings to increase her own control over them, rather than letting the feelings have control.

Sensitivity Management

- Helping the counsellee in managing what gets into the heart particularly with more sensitive people. Guarding her heart.

Control Location and Management

- Helping the counsellee find the balance between accepting too much or too little responsibility for herself.

Physical Management (Relaxation)

- Helping the counsellee use the body to relax the mind.

Problem-Solving

- Helping the counsellee to have a realistic view of the problem and achieve a clearer perspective of the external problem, less contaminated by the internal issues as a result of going through the previous seven steps, Mandy can then assess the advantages and disadvantages (opportunities and threats) in relation to the problem.

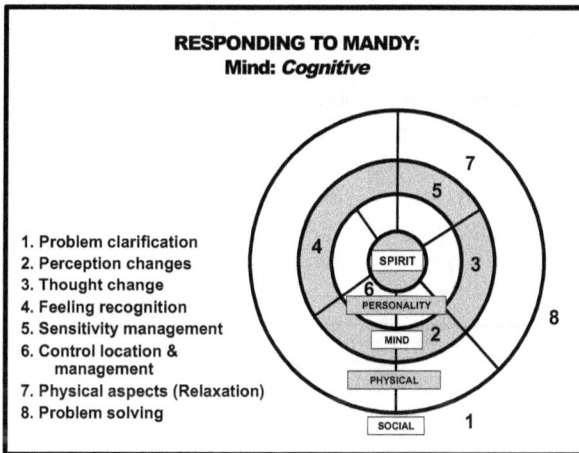

RESPONDING TO MANDY:
Mind: *Cognitive*

1. Problem clarification
2. Perception changes
3. Thought change
4. Feeling recognition
5. Sensitivity management
6. Control location & management
7. Physical aspects (Relaxation)
8. Problem solving

COGNITIVE TOOLS IN MORE DETAIL

Outside

PROBLEM CLARIFICATION: a clear idea of exactly where the problem lies and what it is.

First help the counsellee to locate the problem, in particular whether it belongs to you or someone else. If it belongs to you, it is helpful to externalise the problem without externalising the responsibility in order to see it for what it is and then overcome it. For example with anger, it is helpful to personify it (using a symbol/model of an angry figure) and then plan ways to detect it, beat it and prevent it from having power over you. Secondly define the problem in terms of its size, type, influence, advantages and disadvantages. For example anger can have the attraction of revenge while anxiety can have the benefits of withdrawal and avoidance.

Mind circle

PERCEPTION CHANGES: (Perception sector) changing the way the counsellee perceives the problem.

Problems can be seen through 'negative' spectacles. It's like the spectacles have negative slits that allow in only negative despairing, persecutory, anxious or depressive perceptions. A positive message that is real, hopeful, peaceful or happy cannot get through the negative slit. Counsellees who are depressed, angry or stressed, have mainly negative slits in their perception sector. As a result, they mainly take in negative messages, and even the positive ones are seen as negative.

An exercise might be to ask Mandy to cut out cardboard spectacles with cardboard messages which are positive or negative in shape. She will discover that the positive messages can only pass through the negative slit in the cardboard spectacles if the positive shapes are rotated and lie flat to look like a negative shape. Mandy learns that she does not perceive issues realistically but with a negative slant, through her negative slits. As a result, Mandy may be more prepared to change the slits in her glasses (from a negative shape to a positive one) to allow her to perceive both positive and negative messages.

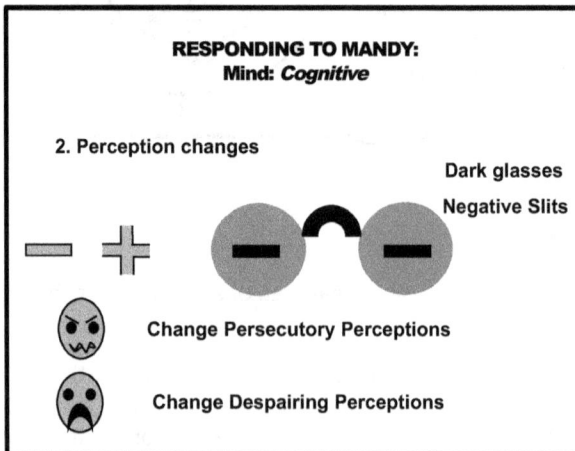

Another similar approach is to help the counsellee who mainly sees the bottle (the situation) as being half empty, to perceive it differently, and as being half full.

THOUGHT CHANGES: (Thought sector)

Helping the counsellee to become aware of the ways s/he thinks, what s/he questions and believes is at the core of the thinking problems ('core beliefs').

Thoughts are very important for Christians. In Romans it says that we should have our thoughts renewed. (Rom 12:2) Our thoughts are not God's thoughts according to Isaiah and they should be. (Isa 55:8). Philippians reminds us to look after our minds and keep our thinking positive. *Guard your hearts and your minds in Christ Jesus; Whatever is true, noble, right, pure, lovely, admirable, if anything is excellent or praiseworthy, think about such things* (Phil 4:7, 8).

Here are five examples of ways we think that in turn affect the way we think even more. By the counsellee addressing these thoughts, s/he can manage them more appropriately.

These thoughts can be:

• **Distant thoughts**

These are thoughts (like a kite) which go too far into the future (or even the past), and then get out of hand, especially when tossed around by 'What if...' winds. The core feature of mindfulness is being able to bring one's thoughts into the present. Living in the present is a strong emphasis in Christianity. Jesus tells us to beat anxiety by living one day at a time, 'Therefore do not worry about tomorrow, for tomorrow will worry about itself.' (Matt 6:34)

• **Catastrophic and Polarised thoughts**

These are thoughts where the only option is for an on/off switch as opposed to a dimmer switch. Where there can be a range of thoughts which are neither catastrophically bad nor excessively positive. A helpful strategy is to ask someone to put an on/off switch in one pocket and a dimmer switch in the other to remind them of this. Mandy may think her light has gone out, but seeing her circles at various levels of brightness is more realistic and helpful.

• **Personalised thoughts**

Where the problem has been taken to heart and it has penetrated into the heart circle and has been personalised (having entered the conflict/entrance sector of the heart). This increases the size of the problem as it raises new personal problems to deal with at the same time. Being aware of this can actually help a person to locate 'which problem is where'. They can differentiate between, 'my problem' and 'the actual problem.' Then they can manage the situation better. This is referred to below in the context of sensitivity management. Monitoring what she takes to heart will help Mandy.

- **Defended thoughts**

These are thoughts connected with the coping sector of the heart. These defensive thoughts distort and reduce reality. Paranoid thoughts are an example. They can include projected thoughts where we blame others, repressed and buried thoughts, rationalised and even spiritualised thoughts. Mandy needs to watch out for these.

- **Mood based thoughts**

These thoughts are connected with and driven by the mood sector. They make the problem more negative, anxious or frustrating, magnified, and unrealistic. Help Mandy to challenge unrealistic thoughts while also listening to what her mood sector may be 'saying'.

In addition (especially if she has had appropriate prayer ministry) it may be helpful to review if her blasphemous thoughts are more mood based thoughts or obsessions.

- **Heart based thoughts**

The thought sector can be an expression of the heart sectors. In particular ways of thinking can be fashioned and generated by one's underlying sense of safety, as well as the condition of the sectors of the four selves in terms of worth, identity, choice and centricity.

These thoughts that arise from the heart circle or the core of one's being (core beliefs), can then affect the way we think about problems. Being aware of the influence of the heart circle on the thought sector can allow one to see an external problem or situation more for what it really is, rather than a projection of distortion from one's own heart. Core thoughts can result in 5 core questions and 5 core beliefs. These are listed here in the order of the sectors with corresponding scriptures/biblical views which can be helpful to come alongside and challenge these questions and beliefs.

These are Mandy's thoughts, which can be challenged to change. Changing her thoughts and her meditations can have an impact inwards on her heart.

5 CORE BELIEFS

- What if? ...to ...You are my security.
- I must be loved! ...to... I receive your unfailing love.

- I am a nobody! …to …I am real about your view of me.
- I must be in control! …to… I respond to You.
- I am it! …to… You are my Centre.

We can think about and then challenge:

- Am I safe? ... to… *He has made my way safe* (Ps.18:32).
- Am I worth it? …to… Our Father loves us. (1 John 3:1).
- Who am I? …to… We are His children and we really are! (1 John 3:1).
- Can I? ... to … *I can do everything with the help of Christ* (Phil 4:13).
- Me first? to *Our old sinful selves were crucified with Christ* (Rom 6:6).

FEELING RECOGNITION: (Mood sector) Helping the counsellee to have more awareness of her/his own feelings ,increases control over them rather than letting the feelings having control.

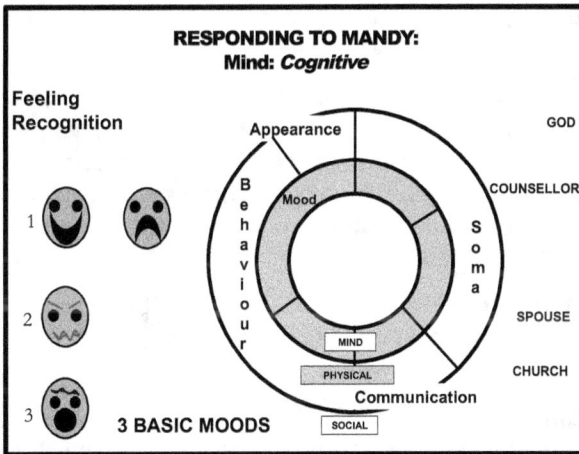

Being aware of the influence of mood on the way we experience problems allows us to deal with the problems more realistically. This is helped by knowing what moods there are (in particular the three negative moods of sadness, anxiety and anger) and that they can be influenced from any other circle/sector. This tool can help Mandy be real about feelings rather than having to respond to them.

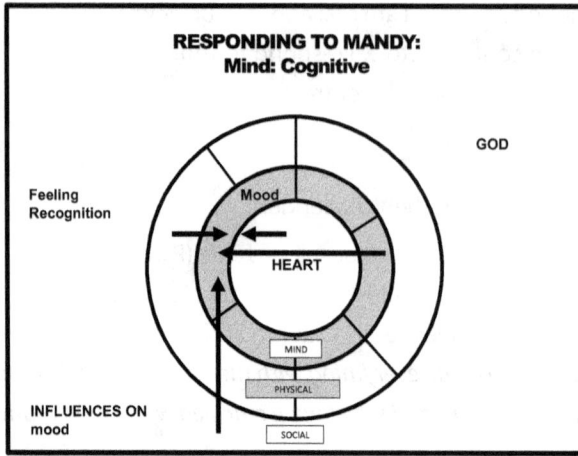

RESPONDING TO MANDY:
Mind: Cognitive

Heart circle

SENSITIVITY MANAGEMENT: (Entrance to the heart/conflict sector) Helping the counsellee to manage what gets into the heart, and to guard the heart. This particularly is relevant with more sensitive people.

Sensitive people like Mandy (a bit like eggs without a shell) can personalise problems and take them to heart more than thick-skinned people (like a soccer ball) who cope with a few bumps and scrapes. Being aware of this helps sensitive people protect and guard their hearts. In doing so they are able to place more problems outside of their hearts, without the contamination of their heart wounds, and deal with heart based thoughts.

CONTROL LOCATION AND MANAGEMENT: (Control sector) Helping the counsellee to find the balance between accepting too much or too little responsibility.

Problems can be dealt with a lot more easily without unnecessary blame (external locus of control) or inappropriately taking too much responsibility (excessive internal locus of control). A helpful example is to see control as a steering wheel. People with an external locus of control throw their steering wheel away and get into the boot or back seat. That way they feel they do not have to take the blame even if they crash! People with an excessive internal locus of control like Mandy feel responsible for other people's crashes and tend to take control not only of their own but everyone else's steering wheels! The balanced internal locus of control comes when the person sits in the driving seat of their own life with their own steering wheel. This allows for a better management of the problem in front of them.

HEART BASED THOUGHTS: (Safety and Love, Truth, Control, Centred sectors) has been mentioned above and is included here for emphasis. They are so important for Mandy to work on.

Physical circle

PHYSICAL MANAGEMENT: (Soma sector) Helping the counsellee to relax using the body to relax the mind.

The mind can deal with problems more effectively if it is not receiving anxious messages from the body. The body can be calmed down and relaxed through the physical strategies of slow breathing (10 breaths per minute) and standard relaxation techniques such as tensing and then relaxing various muscle groups. Regular practice will help Mandy.

Outside

PROBLEM-SOLVING: Helping the counsellee see problems in a more realistic way. As mentioned, there can be a clearer perspective on the external problem, less contaminated by the internal issues as a result of going through the previous seven steps. Now one is more able to look at the advantages and disadvantages, (opportunities and threats) in relation to the problem. Scoring the pros and cons of an issue will help Mandy to decide which options are best (although not 100% perfect).

As Mandy uses these approaches to deal with her mind circle she can experience change. In her mood: she may feel more joy instead of sadness, feelings of love instead of irritability, peace instead of anxious obsessiveness. She will be able to perceive things more clearly and think in more rational ways. She will be more able to address the problems for what they are.

11: THE PERSONALITY TOOL BAG

For training purposes, the capacity to use the psychodynamic tool bag *is expected at advanced level of learning.*

Personality tools are therapeutic strategies related to the heart or personality circle. The main tools in this circle are related to psychodynamic therapy. Tools of the heart, focus on the heart or personality sectors. The sectors are detailed in an anticlockwise order as follows:

- Love sector: 'Holding' and Attachment
- Truth sector: Narrative Responses
- Control sector: Dependency
- Coping sector: Linking.
- Coping sector: Letting Go.
- Transference. (Relates to all sectors)
- Integration (in the picture below) refers to bringing the secular and the Christian together.

THE PERSONALITY TOOL BAG: PSYCHODYNAMIC THERAPIES

Remember, the purpose of this section is not to give a complete guide to the tools in the personality bag, especially psychodynamic psychotherapy. The CWF provides a broad framework more than a model for change. The psychodynamic tools used here are from general psychodynamic therapeutic approaches, which can be further studied in standard texts on the subject.

MANDY'S CIRCLES

Personality
In her sectors of:

- Love: Self esteem: This has deteriorated, and she is becoming less caring of others.
- Truth: Self identity: She has become more confused as to who she is and where she is going. Associated with this is also a sense of guilt.

- Control: Self control: she has become more out of control, blaming herself and increasingly despairing.
- Centredness: Self Centredness: she has become more focused on herself whereas she was more altruistic previously.
- Exit of her heart/Coping: In order to cope, she has been 'faking it to make it', withdrawing and becoming more of a perfectionist.
- Entrance of her heart/Conflict: Sensitivity: she has become more sensitive than usual.

How do you move centripetally into Mandy's heart when she comes in for therapy? Remember, it is by using centralising questions such as, 'How's that for you?' 'What's that like for you?' 'What was the impact of that on you?' 'What did that mean to you?'

Once in the heart, it is a matter of collecting information from these sectors, especially the love, truth and control sectors.

Then link these sectors with the understanding you already have of her:

- Past memories in any of her circles
- Current situations in any of her circles
- Transference of these issues into relationship with yourself (the therapist) in the present

Then, be with her, in SAFETY, in a different way from her other experiences, where there is a place of worth, respect and hope, through real communication within herself, with you and with God, in the context of trialogue.

Questions responded to in this section:

- Where do the six aspects of psychodynamic change fit on the Circles?
- Transference: What is it, and what are its uses and abuses?
- Psychodynamic tools and integration: Who are some of the authors who have used this?

PSYCHODYNAMIC THERAPIES

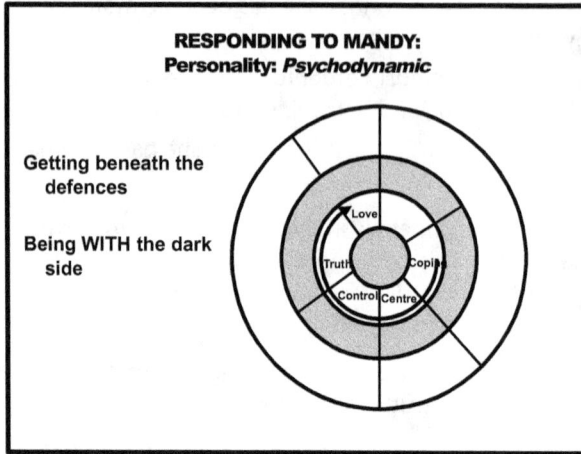

RESPONDING TO MANDY:
Personality: *Psychodynamic*

Getting beneath the
defences

Being WITH the dark
side

Love

Truth Copi

Control Centre

Psychodynamic therapies integrated with the CWF are interventions which allow one to go into Mandy's heart, into the past, centre into the spirit and go up to God.

Thus they facilitate Mandy to:

- More readily access the hidden and darker parts of her heart circle.
- Go down the 'memory shoot' (find the issues of the heart, take them to the memory sector, going back into the past and come out again into the heart but at a lower/younger level).
- Link her past story with the present to change the future. In this regard, it is considered that Narrative Therapy does have psychodynamic aspects in that Narrative therapy seeks to define and then re-author one's story.
- Link the present and past issues within the heart circle of the counsellee with what is happening in the counselling room (relating to transference).
- Let go and leave the past.
- Take her heart into the spirit circle and up to God in the context of in-depth trialogue (spirit circle).

It is noted that there are other Christian ministries (people helper corner of the Pyramid) who have focused on the past including:

- Leanne Payne

- David Seamonds
- John and Paula Sandford
- Ed Smith

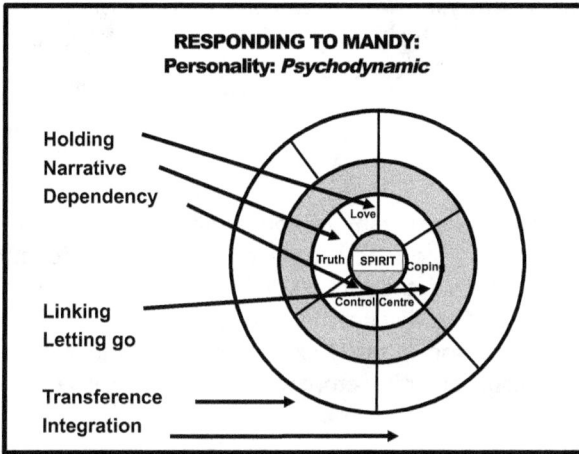

RESPONDING TO MANDY:
Personality: *Psychodynamic*

Holding
Narrative
Dependency

Love

Truth SPIRIT Coping

Control Centre

Linking
Letting go

Transference
Integration

Love sector: 'Holding' and attachment

Attachment is the glue between parent and child. It is the connection. Attachment is not only a psychological process but also affects the biology of the child's brain. Attachment is related to issues of the Love sector particularly in one's early childhood. There is an extensive body of literature on the subject of attachment. Winnicott, a paediatrician, referred to the mother providing a 'good enough' experience of a positive 'holding' environment for the child. Growing the Pyramid provides a safe place for someone like Mandy to be 'held' in the context of SAFETY This means she has safe connections and is understood by her family, friends, church, and people helper/ministry as well as in her professional counselling relationship. Her love sector can heal.

Truth sector: Narrative responses

We all have our own story which originates in our family tree. Narrative is relating our 'truth' or what is real to us. These truths are often based on our experiences which deposit and leave a residue within our heart which becomes a part of us. This results in us living a life in the present based on our past story and our present truths. Our storyline can originate from or proceed to the bottom left hand quadrant in a negative, unhelpful, or even self-centred and Godless direction. The Bible is a narrative/story in relation to how 'His story' can enter into our story so that we can develop an alternative history or storyline. Mandy can change her story line, particularly as she links her story with 'His story', and move towards the top right hand quadrant. Her truth sector can change.

Control sector: Dependency

During psychodynamic therapy or counselling at heart level, the counsellee may start to lean on the counsellor out of a need for support and strength. Dependency in the context of SAFETY allows for a temporary diminishing of controlling defences (due to low levels in the control sector). This enables the person to safely experience attachment (love sector) in the context of respect (truth sector), where the control is safely containing but not abusive. Mandy cannot do it by herself.

When any part of the Pyramid, especially the corners that assume more power such as health professionals, takes advantage of this position of control in a self-centred way, abuse of dependency can occur. The classic example is sexual acting out in therapy which results in re-traumatisation. Problems can also occur if the therapist encourages a dependency over and above what is appropriate or required in counselling. Safe counselling helps Mandy to grow her control sector in a balanced way.

Coping/exit sector: Linking

Linking as mentioned near the beginning of this book is fundamental to healing. Linking is placing two different things close together, and as a result, for one to change and influence the other. Linking allows for an exchange between the counsellor and the counsellee: from aloneness to love, darkness to light, 'the lie' to 'the truth,' despair to hope, and from the negative to the positive.

Linking is a healthy way of 'coping' and dealing with the problems of the person. Healing comes when there is holistic (all the circles) linking between: past and present, negative (below the water level) and positive (above the water level) and the counsellee with the counsellor. Linking comes from facing the issues in the context of openness and communication within oneself, the counsellor and God.

Linking comes from being real about the problems being addressed. For linking to happen, the 'truth' and reality of the negative and the positive issues need to be faced. Psychodynamic therapy encourages facing the negative 'truths' within the counsellee, where they can be seen as what they are because they are linked to a safe and different setting.

The Christian advantage is that linking can include the presence of God in the context of the body of Christ. For Mandy, healing will come as she is able to see how her past experiences are transferred into her relationship with others (transference).This mainly takes place with the therapist, but it is also possible with other parts of the Pyramid. Mandy can bring her past experiences into the presence of Christ and from here let go of the past, live in the present and move on into the future.

Coping /exit sector: Letting go the past and defences

Mandy has a lot of burdens to let go of and to grieve. Letting go is being able to let go the lies and pains of the past, live in the present and move on into the future. In addition, it is letting down barriers and defences which are past their 'use by date.' Defences are like road blocks in our lives. They are not put up for fun, they are erected to stop pain and bad experiences from getting in. However, defences not only block the entry sector but also the exit sector. This has the effect of preventing the pain and badness of what a person has taken in, from getting out.

True letting go the past comes when these issues are fully faced in an undefended way in the context of linking as mentioned. Letting go of the past may involve 'letting off' those who have offended. This is one of the most unfair, costly and expensive exchanges, and is otherwise known as 'forgiveness.' Change occurs as the counsellee moves away from dysfunctional defences/coping mechanisms (from flight, fight, freak, flop and fake to functional expressions of the heart including facing, fun and forgiveness). Safe counselling can help Mandy to live in the present, and move on into the future.

TRANSFERENCE (INVOLVING ALL OF THE HEART/PERSONALITY SECTORS)

Defining Transference

Transference is transferring or projecting the past experiences of relationships into present relationships, anywhere in the Pyramid. While transference is mainly talked about in the context of therapy, the CWF Pyramid helps one to see that it can occur with anyone.

Transference can occur in relationships with family, especially marriage but also in friendships, work and church relationships. In any church grouping like twos and threes, small groups, large church or with leadership and people helpers/ministry and in professional counselling. Transference even occurs with God at the pinnacle of the Pyramid, particularly if the experience of church has been injurious. Facing transference in relation to God is important prior to entering into the spirit circle. If the experience/ perception of God is not based on Biblical truth but rather one's own projections it is important not to proceed into the spirit circle. In other words, the therapist must deal with the counsellee's wrong thinking about God, and the reasons for it, before entering into the spirit circle.

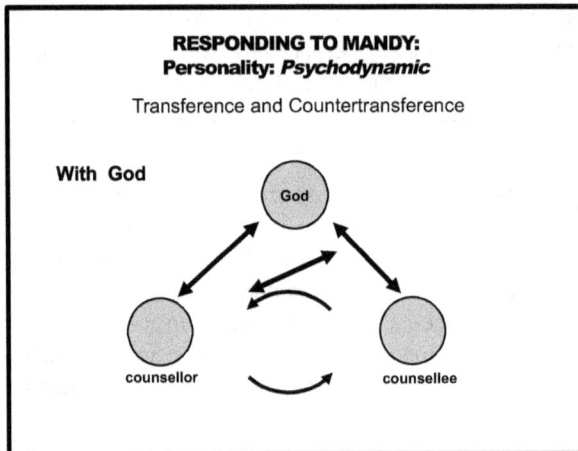

RESPONDING TO MANDY:
Personality: *Psychodynamic*

Transference and Countertransference

With God

God

counsellor   counsellee

The counsellee may experience God as an unsafe, unloving God who sees them as they were seen by people who may have abused, controlled and pushed them down. This is more likely to be the case if they have had abusive experiences from Christian parents or people in the church. In these situations, the 'gospel of saint counsellee' (heart theology) may not have a correlation with the 'gospel' in the bible. People may claim to have a theology, which is in fact more of a borrowed theology from a church denomination. However, the theology of their heart may be primarily shaped by their experience and they may not be fully aware of it until they face their own hearts in the way described here. If this is the case, and the counsellee wants to involve the spiritual as part of the holistic healing, it is important that the counsellee experiences a more theologically accurate view of God.

Mandy has had enough past issues (rf. Understanding step) which have affected her heart which will come out in transference, allowing her then to deal with them. Examples of transference include perceiving and projecting past experiences into the present especially regarding issues related to the:

- Love sector: Abandonment, betrayal.
- Truth sector: Lack of respect, not being heard or understood or taking on previous roles.
- Control sector: Feeling controlled.
- Coping sector: Using old ways of coping in the present, such as freezing like a victim or flighting in withdrawal, or fighting for control in therapy.

Detecting Transference

This can occur in any part of the Pyramid particularly when there are feelings/perceptions which do not add up when fully understood in the context of the present.

In therapy: Think transference before checking it out with the counsellee, whenever the:

- Counsellee says something about the counsellor.
- Counsellee experiences heart sector issues in the therapy session related to the issues mentioned as examples of transference.

The Therapist may have an experience or reaction with the counsellee over and above what would be expected from the content of what is being talked about. They may be current experiences from the heart sector and can occur in the counsellee or the therapist:

- Love sector: Aloneness and even hatred or being hated.
- Truth sector: Lack of respect/not being heard or understood.
- Control sector: Feeling controlled or being controlling.
- Coping sector: Using old ways of coping in the present like becoming very rational or clinical in a withdrawn way.
- Mind circle: mood sector: Feelings of sadness, anxiety, anger, chaos, boredom or eroticism.

In these situations, when the process and experience of the therapy session seem to be more than a reasonable adult/adult conversation, keep your eyes on the shapes (especially the Circles) of the counsellee and ask yourself as the counsellor:

What are these experiences telling me about the counsellee and myself in the:

- Present?
  » I might be tired/frustrated/erotic for my own reasons.
- Past?
  » The counsellee's issues may be tapping into my unresolved issues (which may need to be addressed in supervision.)

Then ask yourself:

- Who am I, or who do I represent for this person?
- Who are they experiencing themselves to be? (a child/teenager/protector/victim/abuser)
- 'What is happening between us in our session/therapy/connection which may be triggering past experiences?'

Detecting transference is best achieved through engaging other help, in supervision. Transference is often most visible when the observer is positioned one step away from the situation, i.e. to a supervisor. Thus, transference is most effectively discussed in the context of supervision. If your supervisor is not referring to issues of transference and there are relevant issues of the counsellee's past or the heart, you are missing out and your counsellee will not be benefiting either.

Use of Transference

Understanding transference: Transference is a stethoscope to the heart. It allows an understanding of insight into issues particularly in the heart sectors, as they are triggered and transferred into the present. Even if one does not outwardly use transference with interpretation, the glimpse one gets into deeper issues is in itself useful enough to promote understanding even as in the context of the examination of the physical heart.

Responding to transference

• Transference should not be acted out

The classic and most tragic example is where there is acting out of erotic (warm, attractive, buoyant) feelings by the counsellee. Initially, if the counsellor has not taken time to find out what the feelings might mean about the counsellee or themselves, they may not recognise transference and there is a risk that these feelings will be acted out in the therapy relationship. Because of the inherent power differential the counsellor is in a position of power over the client and thus any sexual acting out in therapy is seen to be abusive.

• Transference should be tentatively talked out

As transference is so often to do with the sectors of the heart, any discussion with the counsellee needs to be done in the context of maintaining the underlying and ongoing steps of connection and understanding. Analysis of transference is most accurate when there is already a basic understanding of the person's heart sectors and past circles. Interpretations drawn prior to obtaining a developmental past history are open to misunderstanding.

Examples of introducing transference into discussions with the counsellee could be:

» 'I was wondering if the feelings you are having may also be similar to feelings from the past…'

» 'I am wondering if what I am feeling (especially if it is tapping into any parts of the therapist's heart circle) may be relevant to the issues we are discussing….'

» 'What is going on between us that might remind you (the counsellee) of other situations back in the past?'

Before discussion with the counsellee, do not discount the possibility that your own issues are contributing to the situation (or may even be creating it). Thus, generally these questions are best initially thought out by the therapist prior to be spoken out loud.

Abuse of Transference

Abuse of transference occurs when it is unrecognised, and particularly when the experiences and feelings belonging to the therapist are put on to the counsellee. The injurious aspect of this is that the therapist is in a position of power and if transference is misused the counsellee risks being retraumatised.

In summary, using psychodynamic approaches for Mandy can allow her to access her heart circle in the present. She can then link the present state of her heart with what caused it to be so damaged in the past and present. Then she can more easily let go of the past and change as she is now not alone. She is in the Pyramid and she can move on into the future.

In this way Mandy can experience changes in her:

- Self esteem: Particularly as she now does not feel so alone or shameful as in the past and now can receive care for herself.
- Self identity: As it becomes clearer 'who' she is, particularly with increased awareness of what is hers and what is not hers and what has been put onto her from her past experience.
- Self control: As she has a greater sense of control over what is hers and a greater sense of freedom in the present.
- Self centredness: She is able to take her past and bring it into the present at the foot of the Cross because she is being held in a safe Pyramid.
- Coping: In order to cope, she was 'faking it to make it', withdrawing and becoming more of a perfectionist. Now she can face issues of the past with the present, the lies with the truth and find healing.
- Conflict/sensitivity: She is more aware of what she lets into her heart and how that affects her. She has an increased capacity to guard her heart.

12: THE SPIRIT TOOL BAG

For training purposes, the capacity to use the 'spirit' tool bag is expected at advanced level of learning. However, the use of trialogue, at the foot of the Cross, is available for anyone to use.

Spirit tools are strategies related to engaging the spirit circle. While accessing the spirit circle is open to everyone, Christian counsellors have the advantage of being able to assist the counsellee to bring issues raised in therapy from the outer circles into the spirit. This provides an extra circle to facilitate change, over and above the tools in the social, physical and psychological. In this section, we will look at how a Christian counsellee can access what they already have in their spiritual position, to activate their spirit to become the central source for change. Thus we will be considering:

Questions addressed in this section:

How do the five sectors of the personality link in with:

- Spiritual provisions?
- The purposes of the spirit?
- Our spiritual positioning?
- Repentance?
- What 10 benefits do the sectors of the personality receive from the spirit?

The purpose of this section is not to give a complete guide on how to change from a spiritual perspective. Remember, the CWF simply provides a broad framework more than a model for change. For Mandy, a lot of spiritual change will occur in the other parts of the Pyramid:

- On her own with God.
- With friends, and as her marriage improves, with her husband.
- In the church, in twos and threes, small groups and the larger church community.
- In the context of ministry, prayer ministry and safe deliverance ministry if appropriate.

MANDY'S SPIRIT CIRCLE

Spiritual: present

While her faith is still important to her, she feels that her relationship with God is now faltering and that God is less real to her and less relevant. As she is feeling increasing anxiety and guilt she is compelled to read her Bible more. This is aggravated by persistent and distressing blasphemous thoughts.

Spiritual: past

Mandy has had a strong and longstanding faith. She had experienced a sense of relationship with God which had been:

- Real.
- Releasing and freeing.
- Relevant.

How do you move centripetally into Mandy's spirit when she comes in for therapy?

The invitational posture is important to retain when moving into the circle of the spirit. This process must occur in the context of Mandy's willingness and her having an accurate view of God as opposed to a god of her own projections. There already would have been work done in the heart circle, with the assistance of the use of transference, exploring her perceptions and theology of God. She can now let go of lies about God, and have the opportunity of meeting the True God.

Gather from Mandy's peripheral issues any feelings, pictures, thoughts and memories that may have links to the heart circle. Connect them with what is going on in the heart.

At this point it may be helpful to ask a few questions:

- 'Can God be a part of this?'
- 'To what extent are you able to bring these issues into the presence of God and allow Him to come into these issues?'
- 'With your eyes open or closed, how would it be for you to have some time for yourself in this session with these issues and God?'
- If the answer is yes... 'Maybe after a minute or so, I could ask what's happening for you, or you could share it with me?'

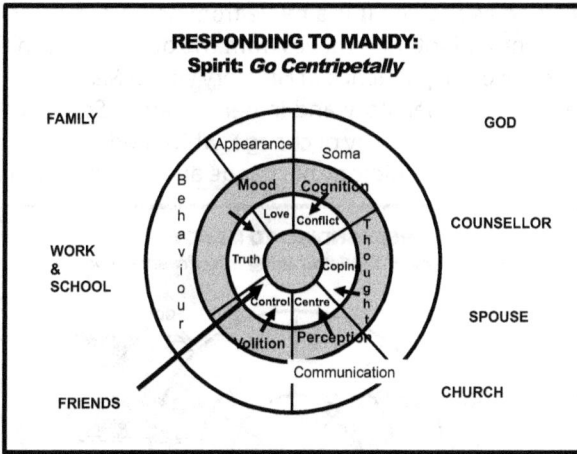

RESPONDING TO MANDY:
Spirit: *Go Centripetally*

MOVING INTO THE SPIRIT

Once the outside issues are gathered and brought into the presence of God, trialogue commences between the counsellee, God and oneself. In the context of therapy, this may involve giving the counsellee prayerful space. The counsellor takes the invitational posture, seeking to be responsive to what is going on with the counsellee and being sensitive to God. This is more a lingering with the counsellee in the presence of God, having arrived at the central place and just wanting to stay there as long as one is able in the constraints of the session time. This lingering, bringing aloneness and shame into love, darkness into light and despair into hope is how healing happens.

When the appropriate time comes, it is important to help the counsellee prepare for the end of the session. This can include a consolidation of what has happened by asking such questions as, 'How was that for you?' In addition, it is important to spend time considering how the internal changes may then be expressed into the heart, the mind, the physical circle and on to the outside.

While the activity in the therapy room is highly experiential, it needs to be based on a thorough and robust theology. In essence, you have the amazing privilege of being with the whole of Mandy, safely at the foot of the Cross in the presence of God. Here in the context of trialogue the most fundamental change can occur. (The trialogue and the Cross are highlighted in a CWF logo as shown.) It is a move from being self-centred to God-centred. The centre of rotation moves from the outer circles to the central circles. The power of the influence of His story within Mandy's life becomes central to a change in her story and in her narrative. So all of this occurs within the context of a theology of change, which needs to be as strong as a psychology of change, a biology of change and a sociology of change.

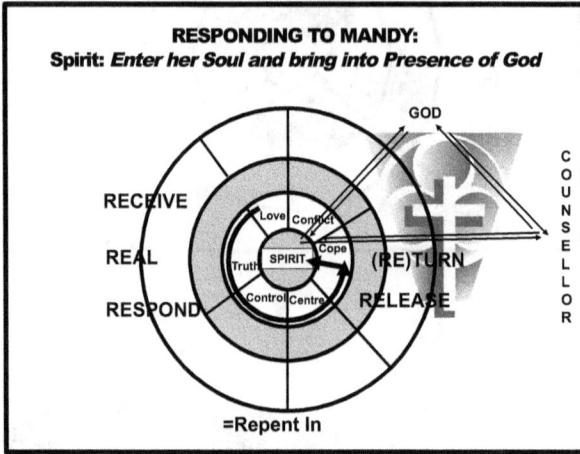

RESPONDING TO MANDY:
Spirit: *Enter her Soul and bring into Presence of God*

Mandy commences her process of repentance by moving into the centre of her being. In the counselling room, she can receive His love, be real about His forgiveness, respond to His freedom, be released from her self-centredness, and return to her central circle, to the God with and in her. Repentance can occur in the counselling room, as well as the rest of the Pyramid.

THE UNDERLYING BASIS FOR THE INFLUENCE OF THE SPIRIT ON THE PERSONALITY/HEART

Surrounded by SAFETY in the Pyramid, Mandy is more able to return to who she is in God and to His provisions for change from within, which she already has, as a Christian in her central circle of the spirit. She is now more ready to allow the Spirit to enter into the circles of her heart/personality and through her heart, her mind, actions and communication.

Spiritual holistic healing can occur at any of the four corners of the Pyramid, particularly in the context of a safe church experience (twos and threes, a small group and the big church), as well as through ministry which is safe and theologically sound. In addition, these spiritual changes can occur in the context of therapy where the therapist takes an invitational posture, and addresses the issues of the spirit in an ethical way as for any of the other circles. Likewise, it is ethical to adress Mandy's relationship with God, as one would address any other relevant relationship.

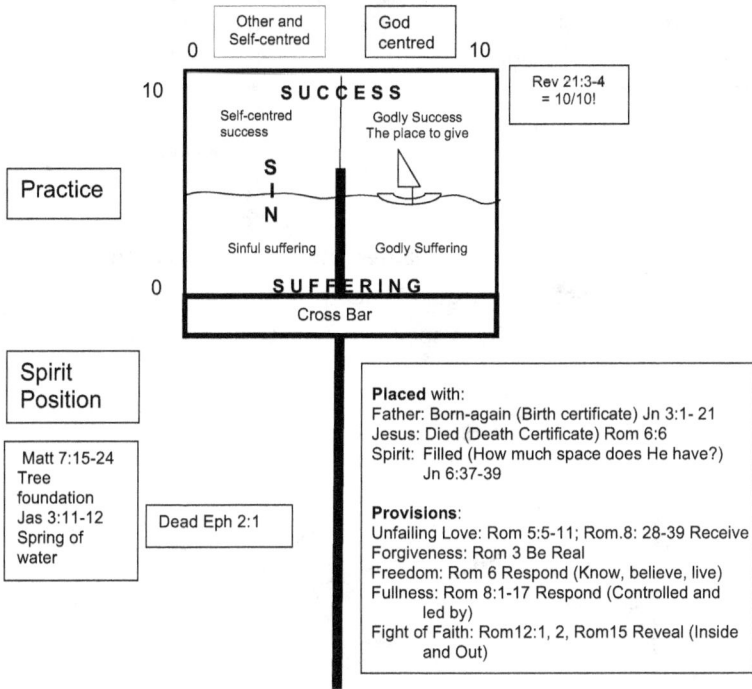

MANDY'S EXPERIENCE AND LIFE PRACTICE

Above Mandy's crossbar, sits the Square of the experience and practice of her life. Any of her experiences in any of the circles and sectors may be in any of the four quadrants. Prior to counselling there was a significant amount of her life in the bottom left-hand quadrant. In counselling, she can return again to the foot of the cross, and receive what is already hers, her spirit position.

MANDY'S SPIRIT POSITION

Mandy became a Christian many years ago. At that time she was born again, or in terms of the shape of the Cross, she moved in her spirit position from being dead in sin to being dead to sin. Despite the turbulence of her current life experiences below the waterline of the Squares, she has not lost what she already has, what she received when she became a Christian

In her central circle Mandy already has His...

- **Provisions of:**
    - » Unfailing love for the shame in her empty love sector.
    - » Forgiveness for the guilt in her truth sector.
    - » Freedom from the despair in the control sector of her heart.

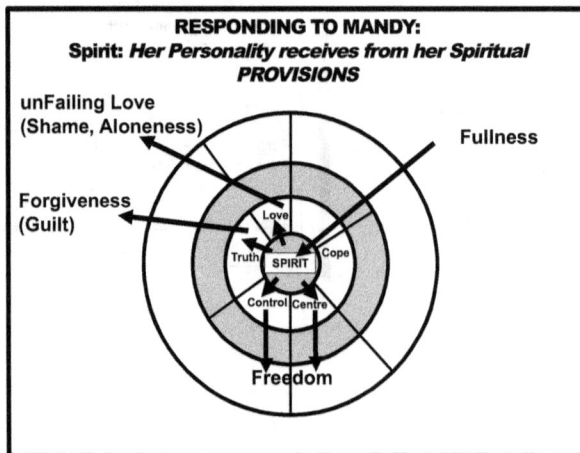

As she receives, His presence pervades her heart's sectors.

- **Placing her in the Trinity**: She is already...
    - » Born-again into a new family with the Father. She has a new identity. She is a child of God. She has a birth certificate.
    - » Identified and so connected with Jesus, that she has already died and risen with Christ. She has a death certificate!.
    - » Indwelt and filled with the Spirit.

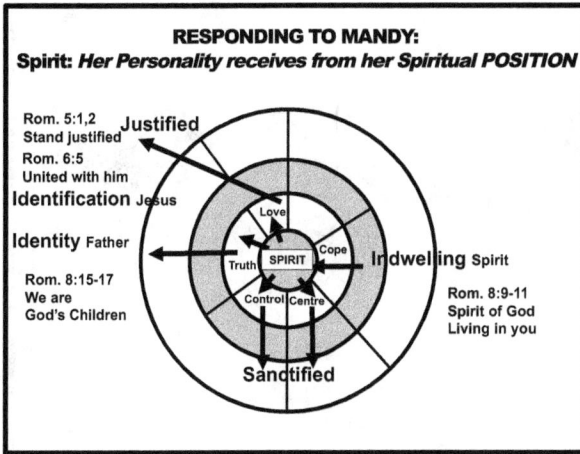

RESPONDING TO MANDY:
Spirit: *Her Personality receives from her Spiritual POSITION*

Rom. 5:1,2 **Justified**
Stand justified
Rom. 6:5
United with him
Identification Jesus

Identity Father

Rom. 8:15-17
We are
God's Children

Indwelling Spirit

Rom. 8:9-11
Spirit of God
Living in you

Sanctified

Love, Cope, Truth, SPIRIT, Control, Centre

- **Purposes**: Mandy already has His purposes...
  - » For Intimacy with Him, Imitation of Christ, Interaction with him: All things are from and to Him.

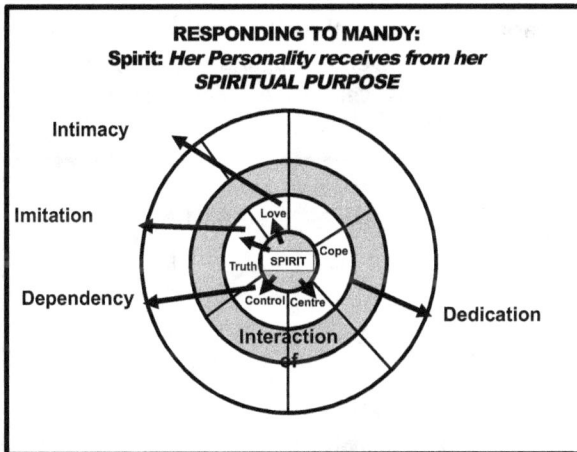

RESPONDING TO MANDY:
Spirit: *Her Personality receives from her*
SPIRITUAL PURPOSE

Intimacy

Imitation

Dependency

Dedication

Interaction of

Love, Cope, Truth, SPIRIT, Control, Centre

- **Presence:** Mandy has His presence within her, in particular, His abiding, communing and indwelling presence.

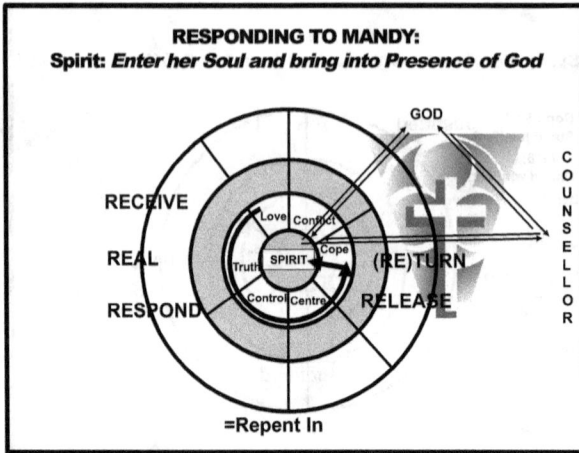

RESPONDING TO MANDY:
Spirit: Enter her Soul and bring into Presence of God

=Repent In

Change starts to move from Mandy's spirit out into her heart as she repents by firstly coming *in* to the presence of Christ. (This slide is repeated for emphasis.) In receiving, she can continue the process of repentance by expressing *out* into her heart circle the inner and central truth, which over time can increasingly dominate the other truths and lies she has taken to heart. In continuing to receive, be real and respond, she can replace her self-centredness with Christ-centredness and then reveal His presence through her other circles, out to others and God.

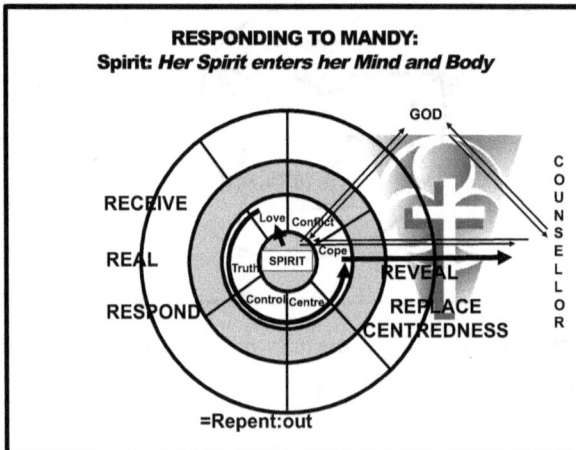

RESPONDING TO MANDY:
Spirit: Her Spirit enters her Mind and Body

=Repent:out

Her spirit position remains unchanged despite what has occurred in her experience/practice. Her spirit position is deeper than the dysfunction and distress of the other circles.

MANDY'S THEOLOGY OF CHANGE

In many ways, Mandy's experience and life practice, rather than her position in Christ, have dominated her life. The lies of her experience have shouted louder than the truth of Christ. In order to change this she needs to have participated in three aspects of the theology of change. (This is repeated from earlier in the book for emphasis.)

- **Justification:** (Rom. 5:1, 2)
  - » When Mandy became a Christian she moved from the left-hand side below the crossbar of the shape of the Cross to the right-hand side. That is where she has been ever since in her spirit position but not in the practice of her life, which has often been on the left-hand side of the Square above the crossbar.

- **Repentance:**
  - » When Mandy moves to the left-hand side of the Square, as she will from time to time, she can keep returning to the Cross and find again who she is, where her centre is, and what she has already received. Here Mandy can return to who she really is in God and allow the Spirit of God within to influence her again. She can then rise up from the Cross, into the right-hand or God-centred side of the Square, and practice a God-centred life.

- **Sanctification:**
  - » Living above the crossbar from a God-centred spirit circle, Mandy starts to change, inside out. She moves more to the right side of the square. Firstly her heart is affected, which can then change her mind, which can go on to change her physical life. Change then comes out into her social life. She is on her journey toward being sanctified... wholly.

3 stages			
	3. Journey		Sanctification
	2. Next steps		Repentance
	1st step		Justification

MANDY'S HEART CIRCLE CHANGES, INSIDE OUT

In all of this, Mandy's life practice and experience start to change and this change itself feeds back into her heart in a positive way bringing 10 changes. The first five heart changes are increased love, faith, hope, holiness and spiritual disciplines.

- Where there was hate and aloneness, love comes in the love sector.
- Where there was doubt and confusion in her truth sector, faith comes.
- Where there was despair in her control sector, hope comes.
- Where there was self-centredness, holiness and sanctification comes in the centred sector.
- Where there were dysfunctional ways of coping, Mandy can now cope better and let her heart be expressed through her exit/coping centre into the outer circles. This is facilitated by the practice of spiritual disciplines such as prayer and praise, the use of scripture, song, spiritual gifts and spiritual warfare and the participation in the sacraments of the Eucharist/communion.

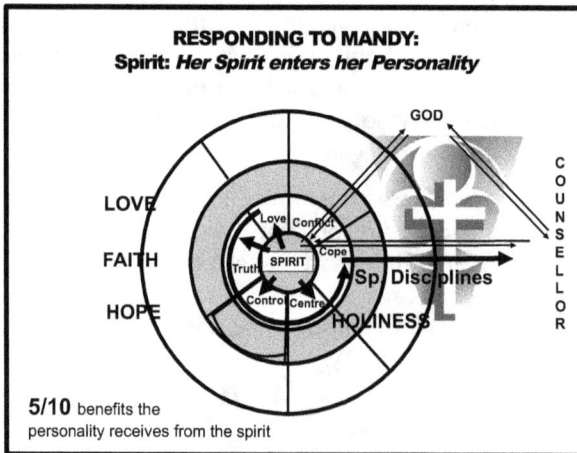

RESPONDING TO MANDY:
Spirit: *Her Spirit enters her Personality*

GOD

LOVE

FAITH

HOPE

HOLINESS

Sp Disciplines

SPIRIT

Love Conflict
Cope
Truth
Control Centre

COUNSELLOR

5/10 benefits the personality receives from the spirit

There is now love, faith and hope and the greatest of these is love (1Cor 13:13). Her heart can start to change from the inside, with a further five benefits:

- Care in her love sector.
- Clarity about herself/God/others in her truth sector.
- Choice in her control sector from the freedom she now has.

- Centredness on Christ.
- Coping in a differnt way, and living the Great Commandment.

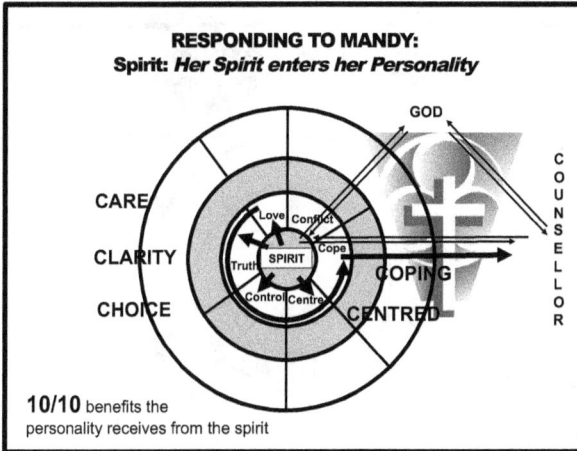

Mandy's heart circles continue to change.

Her Love sector receives:
- Love
  - » Provisions of unfailing love for shame and aloneness.
  - » Purposes of intimacy with God.
  - » Placement in a justified position with God (Rom 5:1, 2).

Her Truth sector receives:
- Faith.
  - » Provisions of forgiveness from the guilt.
  - » Purpose of imitating Christ.
  - » Placement of a new identity with the Father as a child of God (Rom 8:15-17).
  - » Identification with Christ to the point of being united with Him in his death, resurrection and ascension (Rom 6:5, Eph 2:6).

Her Control sector receives:
- Hope
  - » Provisions of freedom to respond to God.

Her Centred sector receives:

- Placement in a sanctified position set apart for God, crucified to the old life (Rom 6).

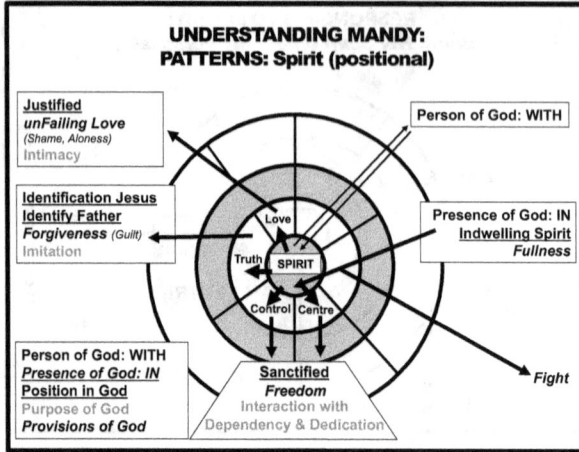

Her Coping/Exit sector is able to:

- Express/reveal the presence of God through all her circles.
- Live the great commandment and practice the great commission. (Mark 12: 30, 31)

Her Entrance (Conflict) sector is able to:

Be responsive to the presence of God within above other influences like self/others or the present and past.

MANDY'S MOOD CIRCLE CHANGES, INSIDE OUT

Feelings of love, joy and peace can arise replacing or at least influencing the anger, sadness and stress there. Her passion, imagination and ideas can be influenced and conformed to His presence as she is, 'transformed by the renewing of her mind' (Rom 12:2).

MANY'S PHYSICAL CIRCLE CHANGES, INSIDE OUT

Change comes in her physical circle and her behaviour where actions and words are more conformed to the image of Jesus. 'Offer your bodies as a living sacrifice,' (Rom 12:1).

So, Mandy changes from the inside out...

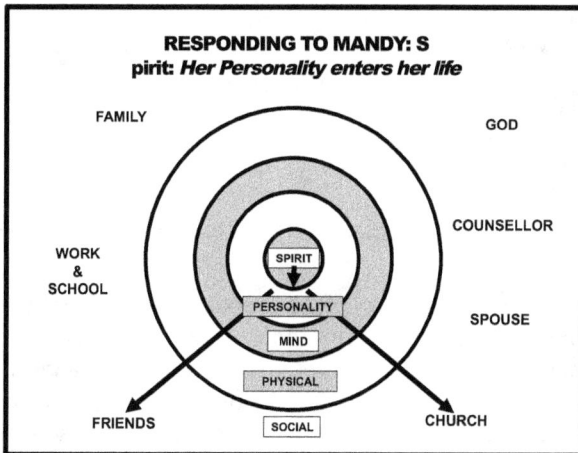

In summary, from the foot of the Cross in her central circle, Mandy can rise up and reappear, in the right-hand side of the Square. She will live for a period of time (often much too short), in a more God-centred way. Here she lives according to the Spirit rather than according to her selfishness.

Mandy will become more familiar with the act of repentance as it becomes a regular part of her life. The more often she faces where she is at when she is in the left-hand side of the Square, the more she can fall at the foot of the Cross. From there she is able to stand up again on the right side. As the process is repeated, the more Mandy changes in her overall direction from the left side of the Square to the right. This is the process of sanctification. She becomes more like Jesus, set apart from her selfishness for Him.

Mandy can now live out of her spirit position and experience a refreshing in her relationship with God. This is a place where God is more real and relevant to her. She is more free from anxious guilt as she falls often to the foot of the Cross and receives His love and forgiveness. Now when she reads the Bible, it is less an obsession and more about relationship with her God. Even in the times when she has obsessive, blasphemous mood based thoughts or an anxious 'false guilt', she does not have to access these feelings. She is able to experience God's love and forgiveness – not as an excuse, but as a place of freedom from which she can truly live.

13: THE RESPONSE STEP
– SUMMARY

What has been presented?

- The CWF and the need for generic training in various therapeutic modalities.
- A tool bag in which you can place your own therapeutic approaches and models of counselling. This tool bag will keep your approach broad and holistic. It will help you to participate in change, primarily from the inside out, but also from the outside in. In particular, the tool bag focuses on the social aspects of church, marriage and family; the physical components like medication and behavioural change; the mind realm of cognitive change; the heart/personality circle of psychodynamic change and lastly the spiritual circle of change. As you receive general training in these areas, you can recognise your own (and other's) limitations and abilities. From this foundation you can grow in a robust and holistic sociology, biology, psychology and theology of change.
- A map to provide direction for each session and the therapy as a whole. It allows you to be more efficient with your time. Specifically the map allows you to encourage Mandy to go to the heart of the matter, using centring questions with the invitational posture.

The response step is the third of 5 Steps and it has to rest on the ongoing connection and understanding steps.

The invitational posture allows therapy to be safe and inhibits the counsellor from going beyond the capacity of the counsellee.

For Mandy, helped by the responses to all her circles and being in the whole of the Pyramid, she can experience changes in her circles:

SOCIAL

- Work performance improvement.
- More open friendships.
- Family starting to come together.
- Marriage getting back on track.

PHYSICAL

- Control over her alcohol intake.
- Improved sleep and improving sexual activity with her husband.
- Managing activities of daily living and not as compulsive with Bible reading and prayer.
- More open communication.

MENTAL

- Mood: more joy, peace and loving feelings.
- Volition: more fun and pleasure.
- Perception: a diminution of the sense of an evil presence when going to sleep.
- Thoughts: More positive and greater control over obsessive blasphemous thoughts.
- Improved concentration.

PERSONALITY

- Self esteem: more trust, love and care for self and others.
- Self identity: a greater sense of clarity regarding identity.
- Self control: increased sense of control and hope.
- Self-centredness: finding a better balance between self-centredness and altruism.
- Coping: more relaxed and less of a perfectionist.
- Conflict/entrance: being able to guard her heart more in relation to what comes in.

SPIRITUAL

- A relationship with God which is more real and relevant.

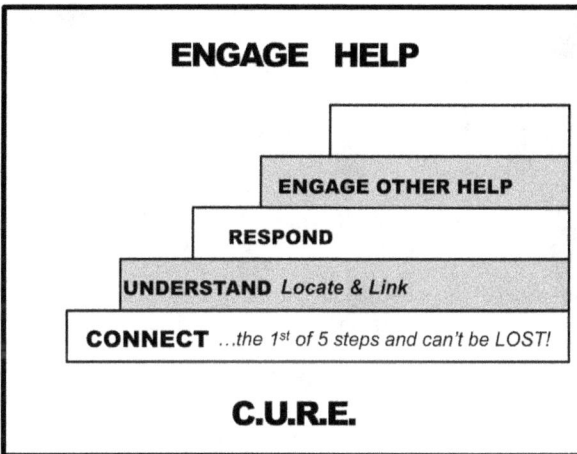

SECTION VI:
ENGAGE HELP AND EVALUATE

ENGAGE HELP

ENGAGE OTHER HELP

RESPOND

UNDERSTAND *Locate & Link*

CONNECT *...the 1st of 5 steps and can't be LOST!*

C.U.R.E.

14: ENGAGING OTHER HELP STEP

*For training purposes, the capacity to stay on this
step is expected at all levels of learning.*

Engaging other help frees us from having to help others on our own. It means we can counsel within our capacity, as we find others who can help in different ways. We do not have to be in competition with each other. We can network together around Mandy, to maximise her capacity for change. Counsellees who are too damaged to be able to engage other help will have a slower course to recovery (prognosis). Thus one of the skills for all counsellors, is not just to connect, understand and respond, but also to facilitate change through helping the counsellee to access other help. In this section we will look at the shape of a Pyramid. This places the range of help available which is around Mandy. We will consider:

- The corners of the Pyramid.
- The benefits of the Pyramid.
- The making of the Pyramid.

Engaging other help: Questions
- What is the role of the church in healing?
- What is the role of the secular health service in healing?
- What is the role of extra therapeutic relationships in healing?

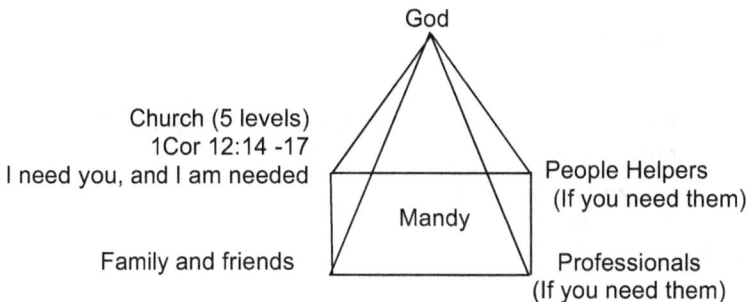

God

Church (5 levels)
1Cor 12:14 -17
I need you, and I am needed

People Helpers
(If you need them)

Mandy

Family and friends

Professionals
(If you need them)

THE CORNERS OF THE PYRAMID

All of these corners need to be places of SAFETY where the CURE steps are walked within the capacity and limitations of each role.

- Family and friends. Their initial role is to Connect and Understand.
- Church, consisting particularly of twos and threes, small groups and the larger church community.
- People Helpers and ministries. These can include:
- Prayer ministry. Examples include:
  - » David Seamonds (Healing of Memories)
  - » Ann White (Victorious Ministries Through Christ)
  - » Leanne Payne
  - » John and Paula Sandford (Elijah House)
  - » Ed Smith (Theophostic ministry)
  - » Healing Rooms (Prayer ministry)

It is considered that these ministries work best in the context of the whole Pyramid. There can be danger in operating in isolation, particularly if the people involved are not aware of their limitations and don't practice in SAFETY

- Other ministries:
  - » Demography specific groups: Youth/senior/singles/separated.
  - » Issue specific groups: Substance/alcohol abuse
  - » Intervention specific groups: Recovery groups using specific approaches
  - » Activity specific groups: Sport/craft.
- Professional.
  - » Professional counsellors/coaches in various areas including financial, psychological, social and medical.
  - » One can include here specialists in areas of ministry ,even though their funding may be different.

THE BENEFITS OF THE PYRAMID

The Pyramid creates a supportive and safe environment where change and healing can occur and are fostered. Mandy will be much better served if she places herself in the context of the Pyramid. In addition, Mandy and her husband may need to be together in another Pyramid for the marriage, where they can be safely positioned as a couple on their journey to healing. A lot of Mandy's move towards Christian wholeness will occur outside the therapy sessions and be facilitated by others in her Pyramid. The Pyramid provides a place of safety not only for Mandy but also for the people in her Pyramid, who will be protected from feeling like they alone must to do everything for her. All participants have a place of significance within the Pyramid and are no less important and no less needed than anyone else. None of us can say, 'I don't need you', or 'I am not needed' (1 Cor 12:14-17).

THE MAKING OF THE PYRAMID

The production of an effective Pyramid is more likely if the people around Mandy are:

- Aware of each other.
- Connected together through the use of a similar language, like the CWF. There can also be greater connection if they are a part of the body of Christ as followers of Jesus.
- Referring to each other, in SAFETY with appropriate Attitudes of Care, Confidentiality and Consent, having empathy for others and enough Time to develop relationships sufficient to allow successful referral to occur. The referral process needs to go towards the professional corner and also in the opposite direction to other people in the Pyramid, where there is greater availability and less cost.
- Serving each other, knowing that everyone is on the same level, but at different points on the line, along the bottom of the pyramid.
- Walking with Mandy, the steps of:
  » Connection
  » Understanding,
  » Response,
  » Engaging other help.

The levels of understanding and response deepen as Mandy moves towards the professional corner of the Pyramid. The amount of connection required will also be increased in order to support the larger amount of understanding and responding that rest on the connection step.

As mentioned, the Pyramid is going to be effective only if Mandy accesses it herself. This can be challenging for people under the water level who often may find accessing and accepting SAFETY to be difficult.

Mandy can also access non-Christian services as part of her Pyramid. It is better if she can have even partial access to Christian services to supplement the secular ones. Secular services include clubs, non-government organisations as well as secular health professionals.

15: EVALUATION STEP

*For training purposes, the capacity to evaluate
is expected at all levels of training*

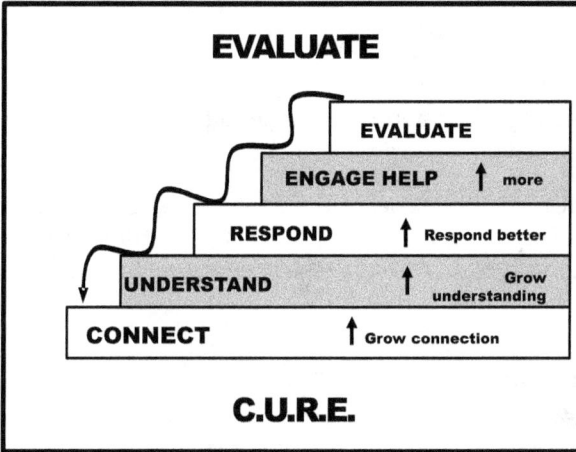

Evaluation ...an ongoing process of all the steps

Evaluating progress needs to occur on all of the steps, not just at the end. It allows for midflight corrections to occur, adjusting the course to be more likely to reach the right destination.

PURPOSE OF EVALUATION

Like a pilot calculating the course of the aeroplane, evaluation involves monitoring deviation from the chosen direction and progress towards the destination. The evaluation is ongoing with assessment and response in a feedback loop to change direction and assist progress. As a result of ongoing evaluation, connection can grow, understanding can be clarified, response can be more effective, and others can become more effectively a part of the Pyramid.

STAGES OF EVALUATION

While walking the CURE steps, an evaluation takes place of how the underlying steps (of connecting, understanding, responding and engaging other help) are holding up.

APPLICATION OF EVALUATION

As an expression of this step, I encourage you to evaluate the usefulness of this book in relation to the development of:

- **A**TTITUDES: This book deals with clarifying the essential knowledge aspect of attitudes. The development of your attitudes will occur in the context of a safe and open experience with colleagues and supervisors.

- **S**KILLS: The book deals with the knowledge aspect of skills. The development of these skills will occur in the context of supervised practice.

- **K**NOWLEDGE: This book is mainly about knowledge development, which can be reinforced in the context of your own counselling practice, in peer group discussion and in further training from others who are more experienced and familiar with the CWF.

The development of the 'ASK' cube:

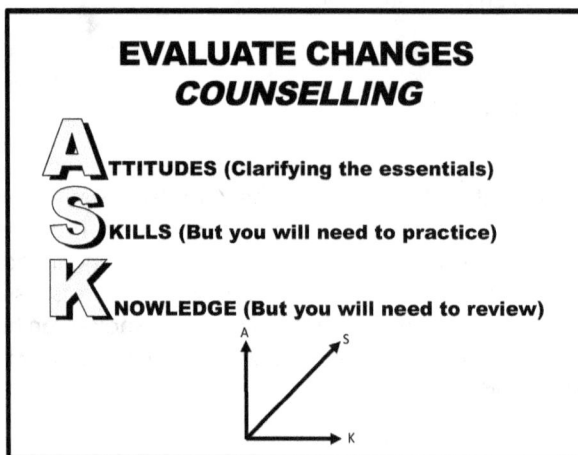

Evaluate your knowledge with regard to...

THE CONTENTS OF THIS BOOK IN RELATION TO: WHAT IS THE CURE?

To what extens has/can this book help you to walk the 5 Steps:

Connection
The essential ways to connect.

Understand–Locate
Locating where the person is at in all the 5 shapes and using the checklist and the Circles. Finding all the jigsaw pieces to make the jigsaw picture.

Understand–Link
Linking the issues: The present, past and future.

Response
The tool bag and the map: to locate where therapy is at and facilitate finding the Social, Physical, Cognitive, Psychodynamic and Spiritual tools. Responding to promote change in all of the 5 shapes.

Engaging other help
The church, health services and others.

Evaluation
An important part of the process to keep on track.

...this is the CURE!

THE PURPOSE OF THIS BOOK

Evaluate the extent the CWF can assist you to:

• Be involved in catalysing the rate of integrated growth in other settings including when two or three get together, small groups, churches, counselling/coaching ministries and professional mental health practice.

- Help others across a range of different ages, genders and culture.
- Counsel and coach by providing a framework for a continuum of care for those who are not going so well to those who are succeeding.
- Facilitate a network of providers including lay people, small group leaders, pastors, prayer/Para-church ministry and professional mental health practitioners.
- Teach a common and uniting language (5 Steps, 5 Shapes) across the Pyramid.
- Have a flexible framework for connecting, understanding and responding so you are released to use your own personality/style of working rather than a restrictive 'cookbook' approach.
- Enable you to become a better counsellor by providing a comprehensive way of seeing and understanding the counsellee's present position. Identifying where they have come from and where they are possibly heading. Improving the accuracy and efficiency of responding to another person. Clarifying your strengths and limitations and reducing burnout. Facilitate engaging together with others.

To what extent could this framework help you to become more:

- **Holistic?**
    - » To have a broader and more integrated spiritual approach to your therapy.
- **Safe?**
    - » To integrate spiritual issues safely, professionally and ethically.
- **Efficient?**
    - » To get to the core issues quicker.
- **Effective?**
    - » To more effectively develop a therapeutic plan and facilitate therapeutic healing and growth.
- **Biblically based and integrated?**
    - » Regarding spiritual, psychological, biological and social approaches to change.
- **Effective at church level?**
    - » Facilitating the presentation of the whole gospel and the great commission of making disciples.

> » ***To live the great commandment: to love God with all of your heart, soul, mind and strength, and love your neighbour as yourselves (Mark 12:30, 31).***

May this book be a part of your personal journey, towards connection and being a whole person in a Christ-centred way. May it inform your professional practice and assist you in your generativity towards others in your Pyramid.

WHAT IS THE CURE?

Connection: The essential way to connect.

Understanding: Locating where the person is at: Using the checklist and the Circles.

Understanding: Linking the issues: The present, past and future.

Response: The Tool bag and the Map; Social, Physical, Cognitive, Psychodynamic, Spiritual Tools.

Engaging other help: The role of the church, health services and others.

evaluation: An important part of the process to keep on track.

...this is the CURE!

SECTION VII:
GOING FURTHER
WITH THE CWF

16: TRAINING AND THE CWF

The CWF can be integrated into any counselling course, at various levels and stages of training. These are presented in relation particularly to the levels on the steps and in the Circles. While people learn in different ways, a preferred process of learning is detailed here. Central to learning is supervision. Key elements to supervision are outlined. What to learn in terms of attitudes, skills and knowledge are defined, with brief reference to content outline for learning. Comments are also made in relation to selection of applicants for training. The 'expectations' are only for those who want to pursue a more formal training in the CWF.

LEVELS OF LEARNING

This text is for counselling professionals who are developing an integrated application of the CWF with a compatible standard of generic counselling capacities (attitudes, skills and knowledge). The term 'professional' is used to describe a person who is developing counselling capacities in the context of their life. 'Counsellor' is a general term for a person providing mental or psychological health care. It is expected that you will be able to apply the CWF up to your current level of generic training and experience.

Professional counsellors may be at various levels:

- Beginning Counsellor – Trainee level
- Counsellor – Counselling at Degree level
- Advanced Counsellor – Mental Health Qualification e.g. Social Work, Psychology, Psychiatry
- Specialist Counsellor – Qualified and Experienced

As described under the capacities to learn, the more advanced the counsellor, the greater the:

- Capacity to apply and integrate the framework into the stages of counselling. Namely connecting, understanding, responding and engaging other help.
- Capacity to retain the SAFETY attitudes in more complex cases.

- Knowledge about more issues and how they may interact with each other in their presentation, causation and management. This requires a greater capacity for pattern recognition within more complex situations.
- Expectation of developing skills to respond to cases with more significant issues.

For example an advanced counsellor should be competent in the processes of maintaining a connection and an understanding with someone who has three simultaneous significant issues. The level of accreditation correlates with the depth and integration of understanding (linking of present, past and future). It also correlates with the capacity to use that understanding (formulation) in assisting change through various responses. The advanced counsellor facilitates change in the context of more challenging situations with a greater capacity for engaging help, networking and referral. The advanced counsellor also has an ongoing capacity for evaluation of the increased complex situations.

Loosely, the more advanced the counsellor, the more knowledge and skills they will have, the greater their capacity to deal with a larger minimum number of problems and their interactions as described below.

Level of Counsellor Accreditation	No. of Issues
BC = Beginning Counsellor	1
C = Counsellor	2
AC = Advanced Counsellor	3
S = Specialist	4+

STAGES OF LEARNING

PERSONAL LEARNING

Personal application of the CWF is foundational to the capacity to apply the framework to others. The counsellor develops the basic knowledge and skills in the CWF by applying them to themselves, their family and friends as well as their church life.

PROFESSIONAL LEARNING

Professional application of the CWF relates to the counsellors' individual practice and his/her relationship with other health professionals.

PROCESSES OF LEARNING

The 3 capacities of **Attitudes**, **Skills** and **Knowledge** (ASK) are developed through 3 processes of learning: academic learning, casework and supervision. While supervision/training of others and knowledge development may occur through such means as this text or online methodologies, these only supplement 'face-to-face' learning. Individual learning is facilitated through linking with one or two others and also in local learning groups exploring the CWF framework and discussing casework. This text is the basis for academic learning and knowledge development, and is to be used in conjunction with casework and supervision.

THE SEVEN PRINCIPLES OF LEARNING:

1. Problem Based Learning (PBL): exploring questions and issues in relation to work-related scenarios through written/videoed or real life exposure to problems that present in counselling practice.
2. Self-Directed Learning (SDL): personal learning through various resources, aided by Cross references and links to videoed or written materials (hard copy or web based).
3. Peer Review Learning (PRL): peer discussion/chat groups, where learning is shared and further developed by useful questions in groups.
4. Tutor Facilitated Learning (TFL): ongoing input from a more advanced counsellor. For beginning trainees, this involves directive/didactic input and for advanced learners greater initiative is taken with specific tailoring of requested information.

And with clients/patients in the context of supervision:

5. **See One** (SO): case (at least one!) by observing another counsellor either direct observation or by video review.

6. **Do Some** (DS): case work, developing and establishing attitudes, skills and knowledge in one's own practice.

7. **Teach Some** (TS): Facilitation of the growth of others hones and develops knowledge and skills of the teacher. Having input into others can occur at any stage of professional development including counsellees, the church and small group settings. Reciprocal input with peers is also an integral part of the training process.

Thus, the three capacities of Attitudes, Skills and Knowledge are developed through the three processes of learning as encapsulated in the Seven principles. So there is:

1. Academic learning (Individual, Peer, Tutorial)
2. Supervision/training of others.
3. Case work (See one, Do some, Teach one)

SUPERVISION

Supervision is central to development of counselling competencies. There are 10 major issues of supervision that fall under five headings. The ten issues include:

THE 'WHO' OF SUPERVISION: SUPERVISOR, SUPERVISEE AND WHAT HAPPENS IN BETWEEN THESE TWO, SUPERVISION

1. **Person fit, differences and roles**
   - » There needs to be a sufficient degree of 'fit' between the supervisor and supervisee in terms of personality and models of working and counselling.
   - » There needs to be sufficient difference between the supervisor and supervisee in terms of maturity of attitudes, skills and knowledge in both supervision and in counselling. Generally speaking a minimum of two years or two levels of training difference is preferable.

» There needs to be clarity of roles as supervisor and supervisee, rather than the supervisor becoming, the supervisee's therapist or counsellor for example.

» There needs to be clarity regarding responsibility for the clients' needs.

2. Initiative

» The less experienced the supervisee, the more directive the supervisor needs to be. This can be expressed on a 0 - 10 scale from directive to non-directive supervision.

3. Atmosphere

The atmosphere of the supervision i.e. the experience between the supervisor and supervisee is defined by the SAFETY attitudes.

» **A**ttitudes of caring, appropriate and clearly defined confidentiality and an invitational posture of consent.

» **F**acing the issues at hand and the issues within the supervisee related to the case, rather than the supervisee 'faking' or presenting what might be pleasing to the supervisor.

» **E**mpathy of the supervisor with the supervisee.

» **T**ime sufficient to achieve the goals of supervision.

» **'Y**ou' questions like 'How are you?' Asked of supervisees in the context of supervision.

THE 'WHY' OF SUPERVISION: WHY ARE WE DOING THIS?

4. Purpose: The general purpose of supervision needs to be defined at the outset.

5. Focus: The specific focus of supervision should be defined as clearly as possible and listed, including competency goals relating to Attitudinal behaviours, Skill and Knowledge.

THE 'WHAT' OF SUPERVISION: WHAT ARE WE GOING TO DO?

6. Plan of time: The parameters of the meeting should be discussed including time, place, cost and boundaries related to the appointment e.g. phone calls, interruptions and urgent supervision meetings.

THE 'HOW' OF SUPERVISION: HOW ARE WE GOING TO DO IT?

7. Process: This should follow the 5 'CUREe' steps on each occasion.

8. **Model:** Generally a *cognitive* behavioural approach to supervision is adopted in terms of assisting the supervisee to think and plan for different strategies and approaches. A *psychodynamic* approach can be used as required, particularly in more advanced settings, emphasising parallel process and transference issues between the supervisor, trainee and the clients/patients. Discussion of *systems* issues in supervision, clarifies matters arising from triangulation scenarios (for example where the supervisee may feel split between two other people or groups of people).

9. **Method:** The more real life the supervision the better. Having the supervisor sitting in or watching a video or role play may be preferable to notes provided by the supervisee.

THE 'SO WHAT' OF SUPERVISION: WHAT ARE THE BENEFITS?

10. **Usefulness.** A subjective rating of the usefulness of supervision is helpful.

These supervision issues should be discussed and agreed on by the trainee and the supervisor at the initial supervision session and at a later progress point (ideally two months) in a *formative* (developing) way. The supervision issues should also be discussed at a later stage like six months or an endpoint of supervision, possibly where a *summative* review can occur if seeking accreditation, noting the different views and ratings of progress by supervisor and trainee. In addition it can be helpful to plan and review a selection of some of these 10 issues at each session as is appropriate. Contemporary notes of supervision by both parties are helpful.

The mutual review of supervision can be facilitated by an evaluation like the one on the following page.

CAPACITIES TO LEARN

Attitudes

The attitudinal behaviour of anyone involved in CWF is based on the capacity to retain Connection with others (including counsellees and colleagues). Accordingly, the counsellor needs to have a capacity to retain connection with increasingly complex cases and more advanced levels of

10 Supervision Processes	1st Session Discussed (Y/N)		Mid Stage Progress 1-5/5		Final Stage Progress 1-5/5	
	T	S	T	S	T	S
Degree of clarity and actioning of:						
The 'who' of supervision:						
Person: fit/difference/role:						
Initiative :% directive:						
Atmosphere: Attitudes:						
The 'why' of supervision:						
Purpose:						
Focus:						
The 'what' of supervision:						
Plan of time:						
The 'how' of supervision:						
Process: CURE:						
Model: Cog/ Behav/ Pdynamic/ System:						
Method: Role/video/notes:						
The 'so what' of supervision:						
Usefulness:						
OVERALL:						

Legend: T: Trainee S: Supervisor 1: not good 2: below goals 3: meets expectations 4: above goals 5: Excellent training. This connection is defined by and promotes a sense of SAFETY. In other words, all levels of training should have the capacity for SAFETY in relation to attitudes, sufficient for the demands of the counselling situation at that particular level. Thus, attitudes are retained longer and deeper, in more challenging cases, for those operating at advanced levels of training.

The particular skills, relate to the above attitudes as well as to the outworking of the knowledge of the CWF. They include the ability to be able to use the 5 Steps and the 5 Shapes, as indicated below.

The skill level is measured by the capacity to retain these skills at the particular level of complexity, increased with greater number and types of issues presenting in the counsellee.

Skills: 5 Steps and 5 Shapes skills at various levels of training

Note that these capacities are **minimum** requirements. Someone at 'counsellor' level may be able to do 'advanced' work (in the context of supervised practice) but should at least meet the minimum requirements for the level they are at as a counsellor.

MINIMUM REQUIREMENTS FOR THE CONNECTION AND UNDERSTANDING STEPS

Beginning counsellor
At trainee level, a counsellor is to have the capacity for:

- **Connection** (using SAFETY) in relation to:
    - » Triangle: the capacity to trialogue
    - » Circles: connecting at all levels
    - » Square: God-centred and positive connection
    - » Cross: to be able to be with the counsellee at the place of unfailing love, Forgiveness and Freedom
    - » Pyramid: be a part of the client's Pyramid.
- **Understanding** and locating the central, peripheral and excluded issues and finding where the person is at in terms of:
    - » Triangle

> » Circles (this jigsaw picture which is the main diagram for
>   professionals)
> » Square
> » Cross
> » Pyramid

Counsellor

At degree level a counsellor is to have the capacity for:

- **Understanding** and linking: the present *diagnosis* with the past
  cause/aetiology and the future *prognosis,* in other words, capacity for
  formulating.

MINIMUM REQUIREMENTS FOR THE RESPONSE STEP

Beginning counsellor

- **Responding**: As for people helpers, asking response questions within
  one's skill level, responding to needs in the 5 Shapes of the Triangle,
  Circles, Square, Cross, Pyramid. In particular, they would have the
  capacity to respond to needs in the Circles:
  - » Social circle: Brief external problem-solving responses. (e.g.,
    weighing up advantages vs disadvantages of particular options,
    to assist decisions.) Note that marriage and family responses are
    expected at advanced levels.
  - » Physical circle: Behavioural and communication responses.

Counsellor

- Mind circle: cognitive and core belief responses.

Advanced counsellor

Mental Health professionals are to having the capacity for:

- Heart/ personality responses (psychodynamic therapies).
- Spirit: and central responses. Note that trialogue and being with
  another at the foot of the Cross should be a thoroughly familiar
  practice, from the most basic knowledge, and which everyone should
  be practising.
- Social: Marriage and family responses.

It is important to note that generalised therapies like Gestalt and experiential, solution focused, narrative and Eye Movement Desensitisation Therapy (EMDR) are relevant across all the circles. Dialectic Behaviour Therapy

(DBT), Inter Personal Therapy (IPT), and Acceptance Committment Therapy (ACT) are associated more with the mind and outer circles.

MINIMUM REQUIREMENTS FOR THE ENGAGING AND EVALUATING STEPS

All counsellors
- **Engaging** other help and knowing individual professional limitations
- **evaluating** self and practice

Knowledge: Contents to learn

PROCESSES OF COUNSELLING

Knowledge of the above attitudes and skills, which are the core of the processes of counselling, should be at the relevant depth for the level of expertise being accredited. This involves the knowledge of the three counselling 'ASK' capacities (Attitudes, Skills, Knowledge), in the five stages of counselling (Connecting, Understanding, Responding, Engaging other help, and evaluating). This allows one to use the framework in the context of the various problems that present for counselling. This is best learnt through the three processes of learning academic and applied knowledge development in the context of reading and cases which are supervised.

PROBLEMS IN COUNSELLING

The range of problems that will cause a client to seek help from a counsellor. These are divided into:

COUNSELLING ISSUES
- Danger issues (e.g. suicide or homicide, abuse or neglect).
- Event related/defined issues (e.g. stress or traumas).
- Demographic influenced issues (e.g. developmental stages: adolescence or midlife).
- Circle defined issues relating to the:
  - » Social, Physical, Mind, Personality, Spirit.

For each issue, the academic knowledge base includes:
- Demographics/epidemiology.

- Presenting symptoms and signs (phenomenology).
- Pattern recognition of symptom clusters (diagnostics).
- Chronological aspects (aetiology and prognosis).
- Responses (therapy and management).
- Referral options.

Miscellaneous counselling matters:

- What causes problems (aetiologies).
- Other issues (ethics, research).

SELECTION OF LEARNERS

The 'ASK' capacities to learn are a helpful tool in selection criteria when engaging candidates in a training program related to the CWF. The most important selection criteria relates to Attitudes, which are largely evidenced by being known by someone over a period of time. As these are critical and in some ways the hardest of the three capacities to change, they are considered a principal aspect for selection. When applicants are unknown to relevant selectors and a high recommendation comes from a trusted person outside this group, these requirements need to be solid and seasoned over time. The attitudes are critical in relating not only to the counsellees the applicant works with but also to colleagues. They are mentioned also above under Capacities to Learn, in the context of the SAFETY attitudinal behaviours.

A helpful selection process includes:

- **Attitudes**: having the capacity for:
  - » Connection and relationship: being a lover of people.
  - » Understanding and respect.
  - » Gentleness: not focused on power or control over others, accountability.
  - » Empathy and servanthood: having a team emphasis as opposed to pushing one's own agenda. Inclusive of others with different approaches and sensitivity to demographic issues of age, culture and gender.
  - » Openness, flexibility and teachability.
  - » Reliability (including with administration).
  - » Motivation and commitment to professional development.

- **Skills and knowledge**, especially in terms of:
  - » Processes of being with others (regardless of particular skill set in counselling) including the abilities to 'CUREe' as described in this text.
  - » Problems of presenting for counselling: current knowledge and skill capacities with various problems of differing complexities.

GOING FURTHER WITH THE CWF

This book has focused on one case scenario, Mandy. There are many other cultures, ages, problems and their causes than are illustrated by Mandy. Males have also not been a feature of this book. To progress further in the knowledge aspects of the CWF, it is hoped that further material illustrating the variety and complexity of these matters (in books and on the web) will become available to you. Supervision is a key to progress further in Attitudes and Skills, relating to the CWF.

APPENDIX: RESOURCES & BIBLIOGRAPHY

Sources which have been referred to and/or influential

Adams J E: *Competent to Counsel.* Grand Rapids. Zondervan, 1970

Advances in Psychiatric Treatment. Royal College of Psychiatrists

Alcoholics Anonymous: 4th Edn, Alcoholics Anonymous, World Services, Inc., 2001.

American Psychiatric Association, *Diagnostic and Statistical Manual of Mental Disorders (4th ED)*, American Psychiatric Press Inc. Washington, 1994

Barker P:*Basic Family Therapy.* Blackwell Scientific Publications, Oxford, 1992.

Beck A, Rush A, Hollon S, Shaw B: *Cognitive Therapy of Depression.* Guidford, New York, 1979

Benner D G: *Christian Counselling and* Psychotherapy. Baker, Grand Rapids, 1987

Benner D: *Psychotherapy and the spiritual quest.* Baker, Grand Rapids, MI, 1988

Berne E: *Games People Play.* Grove Press, New York, *1964.*

Carkhuff R:*The Art of Helping. Human Resource Development Press. 1987*

Chess S Thomas A: *Temperament in Clinical Practice.* Guildford, New York, 1986.

Clinbell H:*Basic Types of Pastoral Counselling.* Abingdon, Nashville, 1966

Cloninger C R, Surakic D M, Pyzbeck T R: *A Psychological model of temperament and character.* Arch Gen Psychiatry 50: 975, 1993

Collins G R: *TheBiblical Basis of Christian Counselling for People Helpers.* NavPress, Colorado Springs, 1993

Collins G R: *How to be a People Helper.* Tyndale, Wheaton, 1996

Collins G R: *Helping People Grow: Practical Approaches to Christian Counselling*. Vision House, Santa Ana, California, 1980

Collins G R: *Christian Counselling. A Comprehensive Guide*. Thomas Nelson Publishers, 2007

Collins G R: *Family Shock. Keeping families strong in the midst of change*. Tyndale House Publishers, Inc. Wheaton, Il, 1995.

Collins G R: *Christian Coaching*. NavPress, Colorado Springs, Col, 2001.

Costa P T Jnr, McCrae R R,: *Personality disorders and the five –factor model of personality*. J Personality Disorders 4: 362, 1990.:

Crabb L: *Basic Principles of Biblical Counselling*. Zodervan, Grand Rapids, 1975

Crabb L: *Inside Out*. NavPress, Colorado Springs Co, 1988.

Ellis A, Greiger R: *RET*. Springer, New York.

Egan G: *The Skilled Helper*. Brooks/Cole, Pacific Grove, 1998

Erikson E: *Identity: Youth and Crisis*. Norton, New York, 1968.

Erikson E: *Childhood and Society*. Norton, New York, 1950.

Fowler J: *Stages of faith*. Harper and Row, San Francisco, 1981.

Frank J: *Therapeutic factors in psychotherapy*. American Journal of Psychotherapy, 25, 350 -361. 1971

Guthrie D: *New Testament Theology*.Inter-Varsity Press, Leicester, UK, 1981.

Hayley J: *Problem-solving Therapy*. Jossey-Bass, San Francisco, 1987

Jones S L, Butman R E: *Modern Psychotherpies. A Comprehensive Christian Appraial*. Inter Varisty Press, Downers Gorve, Il., 1991

Journal of the American Academy of Child & Adolescent Psychiatry, Elsevier

Kaplan H, Saddock B: *Comprehensive textbook of Psychiatry* Baltimore. Williams and Wilkins, 1995

Kendaall P C: *Child & Adolescent Therapy. Cognitive-Behavioural Procedures*. The Guidford Press, New York, 1991.

LaHaye T: *Transformed temperaments*. Tyndale, Wheaton, Ill., 1971

Lewis M: (Ed) Child and Adolescent Psychiatry. *A Comprehensive Text Book.* Baltimore, 1996

Ladd G E: *A New Theology of the New Testament.*Eerdmans, Grand Rapids, MI., 1974.

Lineham M, Armstrong H, Suarez A, Allmon D, Heard H: *Cognitive Behavioral Treament of Chronically Parasuicidal Borderline Patients.* Arch Gen Psychiatry, 48, 1060-1064, 1991

Lewis C S: *The four loves.* Geoffrey Bles. UK, 1960

Marshall I H: *I believe in the historical Jesus.* Hodder and Stoughton, London, 1977.

Marshall T:*Free Indeed: Fullness for the whole man, spirit, soul, body.* Sovereign World Ltd.,Tonbridge, UK., 1975.

Milne A A: *Pooh goes visiting and Pooh and Piglet Nearly catch a Woozle.* Dutton Children's Books.

Minirth F: *Christian Psychiatry.* Revell, Old Tappan NJ., 1977.

McCaulley M H:*MBTI Manual: A guide to the development and Use of teh Myer-Briggs Type Indicator.* CPP, 1998.

McGee R:*The search for significance.* Rapha publishing, Houston, TX.,1990.

Minuchin S *Families and family therapy.* Harvard University Press, Cambridge, MA, 1974.

Meier P D, Minirth F B, Wichern F B, Ratcliff D E:*Introduction to Psychology and Counselling.*Baker Book House, Grand Rapids, MI, 1982

Morris L:*NewTestament Theology.* Academic Books, Zondervan Publishing House, Grand Rapids, MI., 1986.

Olsen D, Sprenkle D, Russell C: *Circumplex model of marital and family sytems I: Cohesion and adaptability dimensions, family types, and clinical applications.* Family Process, 18, 3-28, 1979.

Payne L:*The Healing Presence.*Crossway Books, Westchester, Ill., 1989.

Pavlov I:*Conditioned Reflexes: AN investigation of teh physiological activity of the cerebral cortex.* Dover, New York, 1927

Piaget J:*Psychology and Intelligence.* Routledge and Keagan Paul, Boston, 1950.

Rogers C: *Client-centred therapy.* Houghton-Mifflin, 1951.

Sandler J, Dare C, Holder A: *Basic Psychoanalytic Concepts:I. The extension of clinical concepts outside the Psychoanalytic Situation.* Br.J. Psychiatry, 116, 551-554, 1970.

Sandler J, Dare C, Holder A: *Basic Psychoanalytic Concepts:III. Transference.* Br.J. Psychiatry, 116, 667-72, 1970.

Sandler J, Dare C, Holder A: *Basic Psychoanalytic Concepts:X. Interpretations and Other Interventions.* Br.J. Psychiatry, 116, 551-554, 1970.

Sandford J, Sandford P. *Healing the wounded spirit.* Victory House, Inc. Tulsa, OK., 1985.

Seamonds D: *Healing of the memories.*Victor, Wheaton, Ill., 1983.

Seligman M: *Learned Helplessness and depression in animals and humans.* General Learning. Morristown, NJ, 1975.

Shapiro F:*Eye-movement desensitisation: a new treatment for post-traumatic stress disorder.* Journal of Behaviour Therapy and Experiential Psychiatry. 20, 211-217, 1989.

Skinner B: *About Behaviourism.* Vintage Books, New York, 1976

Smith E:*Beyond Tolerable Recovery.Theophostic Ministry.*Theophostic Ministries. Campbellsville, KY., 1997.

Tan S Y: *Lay Counselling: Equiping Christians for a Helping Ministry.* Zondervan, Grand Rapids, 1991

The American Journal of Psychiatry. American Psychiatric Publishing Inc.

The Holy Bible: New International Version. International Bible Society. 1973.

The Holy Bible: New Living Translation. Tyndale House Publishers, Inc., Wheaton, Ill., 1996.

WInnicott D: *The maturational process and the facilitating environment.* International Universities Press, New York, 1965.

Warlow J & Stebbins P. *Wholly Coping. Overcoming stress and burnout in the Christian Life* Australia. PsyHealth Media 2004

White M: *Systemic Task Setting in Family Therpay.* Australian Journal of Family Therapy, 1:4, 171-182, 1980.

White M: *Practical approaches to longstanding problems.* Australian Journal of Family Therapy, 1:15, 27-43, 1984.

World Health Organization: *The ICD -10 Classification of Mental and Behavioural Disorders: Diagnostic Criteria for Research.* World Health Organization, Geneva, 1992